Voices of Hawai'i

Life Stories from the Generation that Shaped the Aloha State

Voices of Hawai'i

Life Stories from the Generation
that Shaped the Aloha State

Jane Marshall Goodsill

© 2020 Voices of Hawaii, LLC

All rights reserved. No part of this book may be reproduced in any form or by any electronic or mechanical means, including information retrieval systems, without prior written permission from the publisher, except for brief passages quoted in reviews.

ISBN 978-1-948011-49-5

Library of Congress Control Number: 2020950340

Photography from the author except: Nongnuch_L/iStock (front cover), Lauren Elizabeth Arnold (back endflap, p. 227), private collections (pp. 18, 74, 172, 214), Puakea Nogelmeier (p. 29), *Honolulu Star-Bulletin* (p. 36), Hawaiʻi State Archives (pp. 52, 202), Dr. Billy Bergin (p. 90), Luanna McKenney (p. 118), DeSoto Brown (p. 130), Alexander & Baldwin (p. 144), Hawaiʻi Community Foundation (p. 158), Tom Coffman (p. 186)

Design and production
Angela Wu-Ki

Watermark Publishing
1000 Bishop St., Ste. 806
Honolulu, HI 96813
Toll-free 1-866-900-BOOK
sales@bookshawaii.net
www.bookshawaii.net

Printed in Korea

Contents

Preface	2
Introduction	6
1. Voices of My Father's Generation	8

- Why Hawai'i for Marshall Goodsill?
- A Lawyer's Wife: Ruth Caley Goodsilll, Ray Okada, Daniel Lam, Mike O'Malley
- With Regard to Civility: Ronald Moon, David Fairbanks

2. Voices of the Old Days	18

- Pigs, Octopus, and Lobsters: Oswald "Oz" Stender
- Plantation Stories: Kaui St. Sure Goring Philpotts, Kenneth Makuakāne, Carl Carlson, Michael "Corky" Bryan, Bob Liljestrand, Jeff Watanabe, Hermina "Mina" Morita
- 'Ōlelo–Speaking Hawaiian: Moses Haia, Frank Padgett, Jimmy Greenwell, Luanna Farden McKenney, Kenneth Makuakāne, Marvin "Puakea" Nogelmeier, Jeff Watanabe
- Closing the Last Sugar Plantation: Chris Benjamin

3. Voices of World War II	36

- Warriors: Frank Padgett, Fujio Matsuda, Mark Fukunaga, James Case, Dennis Fitzgerald
- Pearl Harbor: James Case, Diane Johnston Beardmore Brokaw Paton, Bill Smith, Duncan MacNaughton, Robin Fern Loomis
- The Internment Camps: Kelvin Taketa, Raymond Okada, Jeff Watanabe
- Pause Your Dreams for the War: Bill Smith, James "Jim" Scott

4. Voices in a Racial Melting Pot	52

- Segregated Neighborhoods: Jane Goodsill, Lois Taylor Clarke, Dean Sakamoto, Jeff Watanabe, Ron Moon, Curtis Tyler, Kenneth Makuakāne, Bob Liljestrand, Stuart Ho
- Integrated Boardrooms: Henry Clark, Mark Fukunaga, Willson Moore, Raymond Tam
- Integrated Social Clubs: Bill Smith, Gerry and Philip Ching, Stuart Ho
- Glass Ceilings: Raymond Tam, Stuart Ho, Ron Lum, Jeff Watanabe

- Unlikely Friendships: Gerrit Judd and King Kamehameha III, King Kalākaua and the Emperor of Japan, James "Kimo" Greenwell and A.W. Carter, Judge Martin Pence and Judge Ronald Moon, Clarence T.C. Ching and Sam Damon, The POW and the Shinto Shrine, Ruth Goodsill and Dr. Patrick Lai, Don Ho and Linda Coble, Arthur Fink and the Men of the 442nd

5. Voices of Changing Land Use — 74
    - ʻAina Then and Now: Moses Haia, Mitch D'Olier, Kelvin Taketa, James Case, Neil Hannahs
    - Around the Dining Room Table: Randy Roth, Moses Haia
    - Taro Talk: John Reppun, William Tam, Oswald Stender

6. Voices of the Ranchers — 90
    - Generations of Ranchers: Whit Hibbard, James Greenwell, Michael "Corky" Bryan, Carl Carlson, Cooper Hibbard
    - Kualoa Ranch: John Morgan
    - Mac Nuts, Plumeria, and Tiny Ranches: Duncan MacNaughton, Mary Moragne Cooke, Kelvin Taketa

7. Voices of Laughter — 104
    - The Last Run of the Oʻahu Railway: Marshall Goodsill
    - Fast Friends: Alice Flanders Guild, Diane Johnston Beardmore Brokaw Paton
    - Three Strikes: Peter McKenney
    - How is Electricity Made? Tom Williams, David Fairbanks, Hermina "Mina" Morita
    - Child's Play: Peggy Dillingham Hannan, Marshall Goodsill

8. Voices of Island Music — 118
    - The Resurgence of Hawaiian Music: Ronald Moon, Jane Marshall Goodsill, Alice Flanders Guild, Kaui St. Sure Goring Philpotts
    - Learning Hula: Luanna Farden McKenney, Betty Solomon Webster, Marvin "Puakea" Nogelmeier
    - *He Mele Aloha* Songbook: Carol Morse Wilcox

9. Voices of Aloha — 130
    - Welcoming Visitors: Diane Johnston Beardmore Brokaw Paton, Kaui St. Sure Goring Philpotts, Stuart Ho
    - Made in Hawaiʻi: Marvin "Puakea" Nogelmeier, Neil Hannahs
    - Agriculture and Tourism: James Case, Randy Moore, William Tam, Kaui St. Sure Goring Philpotts
    - Jets to Hawaiʻi: Willson Moore, Dennis Fitzgerald
    - Enough is Enough: Carol Morse Wilcox

10. Voices of Development   144
    - Stone Houses: Duncan MacNaughton
    - A Realtor Remembers: Jeanne "Frankie" McDonald Anderson
    - Ala Moana Center: Walter Dods, Alice Flanders Guild, Duncan MacNaughton
    - The Groundbreaking Ilikai: Stuart Ho
    - The Rusting of Aloha Stadium: Willson Moore

11. Voices of Philanthropy   158
    - Enriching Hawai'i: Dwayne "Nakila" Steele, M. "Puakea" Nogelmeier
    - Hawai'i's Foundations: Mitch D'Olier, Kelvin Taketa
    - 'Iolani Palace: Willson Moore, Zita Cup Choy, Alice Flanders Guild
    - The Mānoa Heritage Center: Mary Moragne Cooke, Sigrid Boyum Southworth, David Lee

12. Voices of Architecture, Literature, and Art   172
    - Hawai'i's Modern Design Legacy: Dean Sakamoto, Bob Liljestrand
    - Hawaiian Historical Writing: Marvin "Puakea" Nogelmeier, Riànna McCarthy Williams
    - Paintings and Artifacts: James Hustace

13. Voices of Natural Resources   186
    - The Nature Conservancy: Kelvin Taketa, Audrey Newman
    - Let the Rivers Flow: Carol Morse Wilcox
    - Hawaiian Fishpond Heritage: Chris Cramer
    - Endangered Forests: Neil Hannahs, Gary Gill

14. Voices of the Media   202
    - Society Columnists: Lois Taylor Clarke, Kaui St. Sure Goring Philpotts
    - Hawai'i's First TV Anchorwoman: Linda Coble
    - Radio and TV: John Fink
    - The Librarian: Sigrid Boyum Southworth

15. Voices of Inspiration   214
    - Success at a Sears Kiosk: Peter Ehrman
    - A Note of Sympathy: Ron Lum
    - Adjunct Professor: Raymond Tam
    - The Search for the Pū Puhi: Chris Cramer

EPILOGUE   220

INDEX   222

Acknowledgments

Cliff Price figured prominently in the latter part of my father's law career.
All the lives of the Marshall Goodsill family have been enriched in every way
by our contact with the Price family.

Unending gratitude to Marsha Smith, my transcriber
and extra set of eyes on documents.

Special thanks to my Voices of Hawai'i *"Posse"*
Kay, Curt and John Goodsill, my loyal siblings
Meredith Wargo Langley, longtime friend and an author in her own right
Sharon and David Fairbanks, who encouraged and strategized
D.C. Mist Eichelberger, my constant friend
Junie Mist Sullivan, who provided respite in a most significant way
Riley Smith, who opened doors to me
Willie Lum, the guy who knows everyone Riley Smith does not
David Sonoda, who provided deep background
Randall Chung, who introduced me to several Hawai'i Supreme Court Justices
Mark Webb, who encouraged me when this book was just a germ of an idea
Willson Moore, who set me up on Jay Fidell's show, "ThinkTech Hawaii"
Carol Wilcox, who went line-by-line with me through important sections
A.K. Shingle and Steve Siegfried, with whom I renewed important friendships
Alice Guild who, while she was writing and promoting her own book,
always had time to support and encourage me

And all seventy-five of my interviewees and new best friends.

This book is dedicated to my husband, Bruce Kelly,
who has patiently talked me off every emotional precipice
and happily climbed to the heights with me.

Preface

The voices you will hear in this book represent a wide range of backgrounds and life experiences in our Island community. Some of the opinions expressed dovetail with mine; others do not. But everyone who consented so graciously to lend their voices here have one thing in common: a deep and abiding love for Hawai'i.

Please note that this is not a book that needs to be read sequentially. You can pick a chapter or a topic or a character and begin there. Each segment stands on its own. For example, if you want to experience some pure delight right now, go directly to the last chapter!

I was astounded at how willingly these contributors signed my legal release. While I did assure them they'd be able to review and edit the transcripts for accuracy and content, the fact is that most of them had never met me before. My best effort at describing my project was that I was preserving oral histories of people who had participated in the destiny of Hawai'i in the last half of the twentieth century. There seemed unanimous agreement that this was a worthy venture.

For starters, we would usually talk for an hour or more about a particular family's journey to Hawai'i, followed by stories of how their lives had unfolded. It was a remarkable gift that these people trusted me with the details of their lives. I came away from every single interview thinking, *This one was the best one yet*. I remember feeling awe at what I had just heard, and there were several times when I simply had to call my brother or a friend to say, "Oh my gosh, this just keeps getting better and better." And it did.

One fresh morning I was going for my 10:00 interview with a couple I did not know. As I approached their door, out stepped a woman who began chanting a welcome to me in Hawaiian. I stood stock-still in delight as chicken skin rippled over me.

Preface

Another time, I drove to an interview with a man I'd never met, and when he opened the door I felt as if I'd known him forever. A very big hug! We had scheduled two hours to talk, so after an hour and a half I said, "We have thirty minutes left." Then I gave him a fifteen-minute notice. At two hours on the dot his story ended and so did our window of time. He said, "How did you do that?" I had no idea—except that there was magic in this project and these things just happened.

His turned out to be a very personal interview, in which he shared many details of his family history and business. Afterward he said, "Jane, I shared with you as if you were a family member. I'm not sure I want all of it to be public. But I'm glad I said it all. My kids have wanted me to write a book for a long time, but I just didn't want to sit alone in a room to do it."

"Well, now you won't have to," I told him, "because I'll be providing you with a written transcript embedded with your photos."

"Maybe I can bind it into a book to give to my children at Christmas?"

"Yes!" I replied.

"But, how will that help your project?"

"You have just told me the story of how land was left to you by your grandparents' generation," I explained, "and the trials involved in figuring out how to honor the ancestors, remain profitable for your generation, and provide for your heirs. This is a timeless story and I needed to hear the Hawaiian version of it from you. That is your gift to me. My gift to you is to provide your family with a recorded version of your voice and a written transcript of your interview, in order for you to write a memoir for the next generation."

While some interviewees do not appear in this book by their own choice, my experience of being in their presence was no less valuable. They provided me with insight and background. If there are any inaccuracies in these pages, or if I inadvertently misrepresented any person or group or idea, the error is all mine. I have diligently and repeatedly checked with my sources on facts, statements, and intent. But if—in the process of condensing hundreds of hours of talk and thousands of pages of transcripts into vignettes that hold the reader's attention and meet the publisher's requirements—I have made any errors, I take full responsibility.

I began interview number fifty of the seventy-five by sliding my legal release over to my subject, then sitting patiently as he read it. When he reached the part about releasing his legal rights to Voices of Hawaii, LLC, my official entity for the project, I heard him say, "Hmmm." Then as he read, "Interviewee agrees, after approving the written transcript, to donate and convey all rights, title, and interest …" there was another "hmmm." I quietly said, "Problem?"

"Well," he said slowly, "my people have relinquished a lot of their rights over the years. Whereas I'm happy to share my story with you, I am not sure it's necessary for me to sign away the rights to my own story."

I almost laughed out loud. His point of view made so much sense that it made my efforts at being "official" seem ludicrous. Still, I stumbled over how to protect him. What if he wound up mentioning sensitive family information? I wanted assurance that *he* would be responsible for deciding what could be used publicly. I needed his buy-in for the project, and the legal document made it clear it was a joint effort.

Preface

We just sat there looking at each other and smiling. I asked if we could proceed on trust. He agreed, and the form remained unsigned. His interview was one of a kind, in that he described sociological changes that few others had been able to articulate. Once the interview was transcribed and sent to him, he engaged wholeheartedly in correcting names, dates, and sentence structures until he was satisfied that it represented him accurately. Our legal document will remain forever unsigned; we are operating under the guidance of a higher power.

Very shortly after that, my friend Martin Rabbett gifted me with a copy of Nana Veary's book *Change We Must, My Spiritual Journey*.[1] In the opening chapter Nana queries her Hawaiian grandmother about her generosity in feeding a total stranger who appeared at their house. Her grandmother replies, "I was not feeding the man, I was entertaining the spirit of God within him."

Since I first began these oral history interviews, I have tried to figure out exactly what magic was unfolding. The stories people share are truly wonderful, and yet there is more. I think it may be that when people talk, they allow me to entertain the spirit of God within them.

This is why my book is not a research document or a historical treatise and why I do not come to "conclusions." I only have the honor of having my heart touched, and my goal in this book is to share that experience with the reader as much as it is possible.

Love and an open heart to all who have supported me and gone on this journey with me.

---

[1] Nana Veary, *Change We Must: My Spiritual Journey*, © 1989 Institute of Zen Studies, Honolulu, Hawai'i ISBN 1-877982-07-5

Introduction

I often think of my father, Marshall Max Goodsill, as Clark Kent, mild-mannered reporter, with Superman powers of concentration and articulation. With his crew cut, slight stature, blue eyes, and serious demeanor, one might be surprised how often and easily he laughed. Even as a toddler I can remember the twinkle in Papa's eyes as he gazed at his little Jane-Jane.

But as to what this man did at work, I had nary a clue. I visited him at his office often and even worked at his law firm as the weekend receptionist beginning at age fifteen, plus several summers as a messenger, but I never knew what Papa was actually doing at work.

In 2018, after reading the biography of James Case, *Hawaiʻi Lawyer: Lessons in Law and Life from a Six-Decade Career*, I finally began to get a glimpse of what a practicing corporate lawyer in Hawaiʻi did. To learn more, I decided to interview as many of my father's partners, friends, and peers as possible. Each and every person I asked said, "I'd love to talk about your father." In recorded sessions they talked about themselves, their careers, their families, and their passions as well.

Rather than my own professional credentials, I have Papa's Harvard Law School diploma hanging above my desk. It is written in script and completely in Latin. My favorite part is that he is listed as Marshall *Maximum* Goodsill. From what I have learned from friends and colleagues and partners, "Maximum" pretty well describes the man.

I started by interviewing lawyers and then moved on to anyone who had a story to tell about living in Hawaiʻi during the years Papa practiced law in Hawaiʻi—from 1941 to 2004, and in some cases the years before and after. After I took seventy-five interviews I stopped, deciding it was now time to share these "Voices of Hawaiʻi."

The other person with maximum impact on our family was my mother. Ruth Caley Goodsill was a force of nature. Known to her family as Tiny, there was nothing diminutive about her personality. She was smart, articulate, inquisitive, and lived life with gusto. She and Marshall were deeply and truly fascinated with each other. Their

Introduction

Marshall and Jane Goodsill, 2004

marriage lasted sixty-two years, and I can remember hearing a constant flow of murmuring conversation between them. They laughed, fought, problem-solved, parented, practice-built, exercised, traveled, and aged together.

Both my mother and father would be so interested in listening to the stories I've collected. They would be eager for me to connect these tremendously wide-ranging bits of data into one cohesive narrative. So that is what I have attempted to do.

Goodsill home at Puʻu Pānini designed by Vladimir Ossipoff, photographed circa 1957

CHAPTER 1

Voices of My Father's Generation

Why Hawai'i for Marshall Goodsill?
My father, Marshall Max Goodsill, had a long career in Hawai'i as a corporate lawyer. He grew up in the Midwest and went to the University of Minnesota, graduating in three years. In 1937 he went to Harvard Law School. There he met James Barton Phelps, who wrote me a letter describing his friendship with Marshall.

> **Barton Phelps** I am probably your father's oldest friend in every sense. I first met your father in the fall of 1937 when we were first-year students at Harvard Law School. Your dad and I shared many interests: Our fathers were both employed by a railroad, we came from Big Ten schools, we were both Midwesterners to the core and both of us liked to read—not the law but really good literature.
>
> He was an excellent student—way up in our class. After graduation in 1940 I came to San Francisco. Marshall went to New York to work for Cravath Swaine & Moore. Somewhere along the way he fell in with one of the partners in Anderson, Wrenn and Jenks (I think it was Mr. Jenks) and next I knew he was passing through San Francisco on his way to practice law in Honolulu! The last place in the world that I thought he might end up. To me he was a natural Wall Street lawyer bound for the really big time.

It was always, always a mystery to me why Clark Kent (my private nickname for my father) left a New York law firm to go sight unseen to practice law in Honolulu. Around 1999, an unidentified gentleman recorded an oral history of Marshall Goodsill, as follows.

> **Marshall Goodsill** After law school, I worked at Cravath Swaine & Moore in New York. It was a big firm where you rarely met a partner; you worked with other associates. I was there for about a year when a Harvard classmate named Ed Buck sent a telegram saying Anderson, Wrenn and Jenks was looking for somebody. Would I be interested? I was completely flabbergasted. I liked Cravath, and I liked living in New York in 1940-1941. It was a good firm and I guess they liked me all right.

However, we all thought we were going to get into the war and I thought, maybe the job in Hawai'i would be interesting. Anderson Wrenn and Jenks recommended that I talk to two people. One was a very prominent man in New York, head of the City Bar at one point. He was a very nice guy who said, "If I had it to do over again, I wish I had stayed in Hawai'i."

The other was Loftus Becker. He ended up quite high up in the State Department. He'd been with Anderson, Wrenn and Jenks and said he liked it too.

I thought I'd better do a little research, so I went to the New York Public Library and I looked up Hawai'i. All I could find was Kuykendall's book, *The Hawaiian Kingdom*, which was about 100 years out of date (chuckles). I asked a few people about the job opportunity and they said, "You might as well take a chance."

Papa arrived in May of 1941. Fifty years later to the day, he and I were at Punahou School's sesquicentennial (150th year) anniversary and he told me about the day he arrived in Honolulu:

MG I was wearing my wool suit and was it ever hot! I had no idea about the weather, coming from New York City. I sailed to Hawai'i on the *Lurline* and it was a wonderful trip; we sailed right into Honolulu Harbor with the orchestra playing and all the flowers. A couple of young guys met me and took me to the firm's office, which was in the old three-story Bank of Hawai'i building on Bishop Street.

From there we went to Punahou School, which was having its centennial anniversary. There was a parade with *wahine pā'ū* riders in their long colorful skirts on horseback, accompanied by the entire Hawaiian court for each island. Robbie, Junie and D.C. Mist's grandfather, Mr. Austin, was driving the buggy at the head of the parade and their mother, Martha, was on horseback. I had never seen anything like it, all the colors, the pageantry, horses, leis, song and dance. I remember saying, "This is a *high school*?"

Six months later World War II broke out. Papa had applied to get into US Navy intelligence and had been accepted, but the letter had been sent to a wrong address, so he thought he was still a civilian.

MG If I had gotten that letter, I probably would have been down at Pearl Harbor on December 7th. Instead I was mowing the lawn of the Mānoa Valley home where I was living [2329 Beckwith Street]. Being in the valley we could not see the planes and with the sound of the mower I could not hear anything. All of a sudden, a neighbor runs down the street, "The war is starting!" He was the manager for Standard Oil Company in Hawai'i, and they had all the oil supply tanks out at Pearl Harbor. He said, "Don't go anywhere. Stay where you are!" I spent the night at Kūali'i, the Cooke home in Mānoa, with my senior law partner, Heaton Wrenn, and Sam Cooke's father, Charles Montague Cooke, "guarding" the place with a shotgun.

Marshall said it took him about three days to get to Pearl Harbor because everything was such a mess. (However, his signed military papers indicate that he reported for duty on December 8, 1941. Maybe it just seemed like three days.) He was in the Navy from December 1941 to February 1946. The first year he was in Honolulu in the censorship department, working alongside Punahou grad Mickey Griggs with Seymour Shingle as Marshall's secretary. Interestingly, this was the same thing Mr. Phelps, his law school friend, was doing on the mainland. Both said it was a deadly dull job.

His next position was on the Queen Mary, *which had been converted to a troop transport ship. Given his quick admittance into naval intelligence in wartime, he undoubtedly had no officer training. Yet Lt. Goodsill's job was to keep the sailors from gambling, swearing, and fighting. It always struck me as hysterical that my mild-mannered father had this job. I laughingly asked him, "How did you do that, Papa?" And he laughingly replied, "Well, I made a deal. They could gamble and swear but not fight. It seemed to work out okay." As a matter of fact, we have a copy of a written commendation he received from the Navy for his "highly efficient performance in looking after the 2,474 officers and men aboard."*

It has long been family myth that Papa was in both the Navy and the Army. We didn't know quite how this happened until we read his complete military notes, assembled for us by his secretary, Jenifer Weaver, and until we heard him speak of it in that 1999 interview.

MG The Navy didn't have much for me to do, so they loaned me to the Supreme Headquarters Allied Expeditionary Forces (SHAEF). I basically worked with SHAEF at Eisenhower's headquarters. It was a combined headquarters, which started out in Grosvenor Square in London. At that time the US Embassy was in what is now the Canadian Embassy. Was it on Brooks Mews? Soon we moved out to Bushy Park, which is in Richmond, across the park from the famous Hampton Court Palace. In America they would have been called Quonset huts but in England they were long brick buildings.
By the time of the Normandy invasion in June the headquarters moved to Versailles, France.

Every day toward the end of the war, he rode his bike to the Palace of Versailles, where he worked in the horse stables, which had been converted into military offices. (When we were children this image always made us laugh.) I found out as an adult that his job was helping to prepare the terms of surrender for Germany. According to Papa, President

Franklin Roosevelt was undecided on whether to allow Germany to have industrial centers after the war or to make the whole country agrarian. As Roosevelt waffled back and forth on this, the terms of surrender were continually rewritten, which Papa obviously found very tedious in the days before word processors.

>**MG** Eventually we went up to Reims in northern France, where the great cathedral is. That was the new headquarters for SHAEF because Frankfurt was pretty well destroyed.[2] At this point Washington wanted me back. "We want you to go to Japan. We need somebody with your experience." I worked for a man named Charles Kades. He was a bond lawyer in New York and worked in the Treasury Department. He was in charge of [Gen. Douglas] MacArthur's civil affairs.[3]

So Marshall went from Germany, working on the terms of the German surrender, to Japan, where he worked on details related to the drafting of the postwar Japanese constitution.

Undoubtedly, Japan toward the end of the war wasn't an easy place to be. For one thing, housing was in short supply. My younger brother, John, recalls that in 1993, forty-eight years after WW II ended, he and Marshall had dinner at the Imperial Palace Hotel in Tokyo. Marshall told John that the Allies were afraid the Japanese would never surrender if the Emperor were harmed, so the Imperial Palace was the only place in Tokyo they wouldn't bomb. On his first night in Tokyo in 1945, Marshall stayed at the Marunouchi Hotel—located close to the Imperial Palace, it was one of the few hotels still standing. Ironically and completely by accident, when John first went to Japan in 1980 he stayed at the exact same hotel, on the advice of a taxi driver.

Discharged from the Navy on February 27, 1946, Marshall returned home to Minnesota to visit his family and Ruth. (He and Ruth were married the following year.) "At that time," he later recalled, "I decided to return to the job in Hawai'i with the law firm. I'd been in the Navy long enough and thought they could get along without me!" And thus, early 1946 marked phase two of Marshall's tenure at Anderson Wrenn and Jenks—which fifty years later would be known as "the Goodsill firm."

---

[2] Wikipedia: In February 1945 SHAEF moved to Rheims (preferred spelling Reims). On April 26, 1945 SHAEF moved to Frankfurt, Germany.

[3] Britannica.com: Charles Louis Kades (March 12, 1906-June 18, 1996) was a US lawyer who, as a lieutenant colonel under Gen. Douglas MacArthur during World War II, oversaw the drafting of Japan's postwar constitution (adopted May 3, 1947), in which the quasi-divine emperor was replaced with a constitutional monarchy and the nation made a formal renunciation of war. https://www.britannica.com/biography/Charles-Louis-Kades https://www.youtube.com/watch?v=jnzOU4sf3Ms

A Lawyer's Wife

Any discussion of Marshall Goodsill would be incomplete without mention of his wife, my mother, Ruth.

Ruth Caley was born on August 29, 1922 and spent her early life in Minnesota. In 1944 she moved to New York City to follow her passion for fashion. Working at Bonwit Teller, she took to wearing all black all the time. She remembered that one day Eleanor Roosevelt came into the store. The lingerie manager whispered, "We have a secret stash of nylons, Mrs. Roosevelt, would you like a pair?" Eleanor boomed in a voice for all in the crowded store to hear, "Nylons? How wonderful! You have nylons? I must have some." And so did everyone else.

When the woman who ran Bonwit Teller's publicity department went on maternity leave, Ruth was asked to do her job. On her very first day she hired models for a photo shoot, failing to notice that one of them was lame. After the shoot, when her error was revealed, she rushed to the office of Miss Boyer, her supervisor, to apologize. She expected to be fired, but instead Miss Boyer congratulated her: "Caley, it was a stroke of genius to hire that gal! How did you ever think of it?"

Ruth felt sorry for an out-of-work friend and hired him as photographer for the Bonwit photo shoots. He was Richard Avedon, twenty-two years old at the time, who went on to become one of the world's most famous photographers.

Ruth met Marshall while he was on military leave in New York City. His sister, Jane, distracted by her beau, Henry Hibbard, asked Ruth, her roommate and sorority sister, to "take care of Marshall." Marshall went to pick her up at Bonwit Teller, and they both said later that it was love at first sight. They married on February 20, 1947 in Elk River and moved to Honolulu right after that. Again, I draw from the letter from Mr. Phelps, who describes the newlyweds this way:

> **Barton Phelps** Now it is morning and we have taken them to the airport to catch their United plane and we are on the tarmac with them. With her new husband and her new home and her future before her in a place she had never been, she was absolutely incredible. I've never seen any couple as happy or anyone as excited, so much in love, as your mother was that day. That emotional, lovely scene has never left my mind all these years.

During the first few years they lived in an apartment on Waikīkī Beach near the Elks Club. Ruth worked at Gump's on Kalākaua Avenue, but it was a far cry from the New York fashion scene. Mama was not very happy, and she always told us that she made a deal with Papa that if at the end of the first year things were not better, they would move back to the mainland. "Well," she'd say fifty years later, "at the end of that first year I said, 'Marshall, I am ready to go home.' To which he replied, 'Well, you can go but I am staying.'" She swore that this was how it went, but knowing my gentle father I can only doubt it! In any case, she decided she liked him more than she disliked Hawai'i, so they stayed.

It was difficult for her to fit in to a tropical, insular community. However, eventually she found a place for herself and at the end of her life she could not have imagined having lived anywhere else.

There were six of us in the family: Marshall, Ruth, Kay, Curt, Jane, and John. But the house itself was also a family member. We cared for it, celebrated in it, cleaned it, repaired it, honored it, and got married there. There were quirks about that house. It was almost impossible to lock. There was no real front door. There was very little soundproofing, so we could hear each other from one end of the house to the other. With screens open at all times we could also hear our neighbors and vice versa.

During the summers Ruth sat in her living room chair and read out loud to us. She was like the Pied Piper and soon neighborhood children of all ages gathered at her feet to listen to King Arthur and the Knights of the Round Table, The Chronicles of Narnia, Mike Mulligan and His Steam Shovel, *and* The Microbe Hunters.

Ruth was the wind beneath Marshall's wings, a constant supporter, encourager, and adorer. She took care of domestic life so that he could concentrate on work. She always said he was the most interesting man she ever met, and he greatly enriched her life with stimulating people and adventures.

We'd keep a lookout for Papa's car in the driveway after work. Upon spotting it we'd all chime, "Papa's home!" Marshall entered through the kitchen door and Ruth came from the kitchen sink. All activity stopped as they embraced; the kids were invisible for a moment. We all knew it was a good thing. After the kids were greeted, the parents talked in the kitchen while the dinner cooked. The kids could be present or not; it was parent time.

It was my job to set the table for dinner. I liked this job. And I also liked witnessing my parents being interested in each other. I didn't really listen to the content of their conversation—I had my own thoughts—but it was comforting to hear the patter between them. I felt safe. It has always pleased me that my parents liked each other so much.

The conflict that seemed most prominent between my parents had to do with work intruding on family time. Ray Okada, a lawyer at my father's firm, told me a story related to this that I find hilarious.

Raymond Okada When we'd see Ruth at firm events she was like the Queen of England, and you had to be on your best behavior! When your father asked me to help with his estate, I was a bit apprehensive. At our first meeting after Marshall died, Ruth said, "Now that you're my lawyer, I think you ought to know the dirty laundry. Marshall had a mistress! Many of the other partners in the firm had the same mistress. Do you want to know her name?" She says, "The *law*! They were all workaholics because they loved the law so much. They were good at it and they just loved it. It took all of their energy away from everything else." I had to laugh at that because I get that same line at home. The law *is* an unforgiving mistress. She said, "Well, if you laugh at that, I guess we can get along." I thought, *Wow, the Queen of England has a sense of humor!*

One of the joys of the research that led to this book is that I finally learned what Papa did at work. He helped people and corporations, he made things happen, he mentored young lawyers, he was a leader in business and law, he ran the firm, he managed data, and he helped streamline difficult problems. Knowing more about him and his work makes up for the fact that, growing up, I might not have had as much from my dad as I would've liked.

There's an associate at the Goodsill firm named Daniel Lam. Impressed with his insights into how he attempts to balance family life and work, I was sympathizing with how difficult it must be for him to be available for his children and wife and still get his work done. He said, "You have to tell that to my wife."

In fact I'd have a lot to say to the firm's wives and/or partners because I saw my mom when she was one of them. It's not easy to be in full charge of the children and the house and the food and the details of managing everything (sometimes even one's own job) while the partner is "lost" in work. When my father was home my mother expected him to be present, and it was not always easy for him to leave work behind. Even though my mother knew the significance of the work Marshall was doing, she still resented it at times.

I heard good news from both Daniel Lam and Michael O'Malley, the Goodsill firm's current managing partner, about the firm's approach to work and family.

Daniel Lam The Goodsill firm is a good place to be these days. The life/work balance is much more flexible than it used to be. We have a lot of young mothers and fathers that work here. Some have to pick up their kids in the afternoons. We are allowed to do that if we get our work done. I will spend time with my kids and wife in the early evening or go watch a child's sports event, then get on the computer to work later that night.

Michael O'Malley When I was a single dad and my kids were ages five to twelve, I remember looking at the clock and thinking, *I've got to pick them up at soccer practice, and there's PTA tonight* and the pressure was immense. Now my days are longer, but I go work out in between and I don't have anyone to pick up. It's long but it's not stressful. I always tell my associates, "Go, go!" "You sure, Mike?" "Yes, I know what you're feeling. Go. Go pick up your kid. Go to the PTA meeting. I think we've got it covered."

Ruth would approve.

With Regard to Civility
Hawai'i Supreme Court Chief Justice Ronald Moon had a few comments on civility in the behavior of lawyers. David Fairbanks, who is younger than those of my father's generation, also had some thoughts.

Ronald Moon Attorneys have attacked each other and been uncivil in their behavior over the years. When I got into the judiciary, Chief Justice [Herman] Lum assigned me to projects that focused upon the demeanor of attorneys in court. Lawyers are supposed to be peacemakers; they are not supposed to be soldiers who fight to the death. They are supposed to be gentlemen and gentlewomen and try to make peace with each other.

In the 1980s the courts began adopting rules that were based on civility—rules for lawyer organizations and for conduct in court. They were supposed to communicate with one another instead of stonewalling. They could not keep secrets anymore; no such thing as trial by ambush. They had to divulge things and give them over in a reasonable time. Courts throughout the nation have adopted these rules to make things less contentious. Since my retirement, as I talk to trial judges, they tell me that it's back to where it was so many years ago. Attorneys are becoming more contentious and becoming more personal in their attacks.

No lawyer should encourage this kind of behavior. It slows down the courts and creates more costs to the parties involved. When I was a judge, if an attorney came in late for a court hearing, I would say, "You made this other party wait and that other party is paying by the hour. Let's say you are five minutes late. How much would that cost a party? How much does it cost the court to sit and wait for you?"

I had a case in which a state senator was a senior attorney. He was a very good lawyer and he had a good reputation as a senator, but he came into my court late for the first two sessions in a trial. In the third session, when he was late again, I had the jury take their places. I took my place on the bench, all my staff took their places and we just waited for him. He came running down the hallway—you could hear his footsteps. He pushed the doors open, and he was red-faced because the jurors were in place. He came to the bench and I spoke to him confidentially. "I fined you $25 the first time, $50 the second time. This time I don't think I need to fine you, because you have to go some distance now to make it up to the jury who's been sitting here waiting for you." Being late is like saying, "I don't care about your time. It's my time so I'll come whenever I'm ready."

At other times you would have a lawyer from the East Coast whose way of handling things would be very different from our way. So you had to be patient and try to convince him or her that this bull-in-a-china-shop way of doing things is not the way you do it in Hawai'i.

David Fairbanks I don't think Marshall was ever quite comfortable with Aloha Friday attire except on Saturday morning. There was a push for a less formal dress code by some of the younger people in the office because most of the time clients would come into the office wearing aloha shirts. If you are sitting there in a coat and tie, and your client is in an aloha shirt, what are they thinking? Are you talking down to them? Are you better than they are? So we began to dress more casually. But Marshall was always professionally dressed. He was friendly but businesslike.

Jane Goodsill *Do you have any reflections on how the law has changed since the time you started practicing?*

DF The law hasn't changed much but the practice has changed considerably. It is less civil. There is more competition for work. A lawyer is supposed to solve problems, not make things worse. You hear the young lawyers talking about "my case." It isn't *their* case; it's the client's case. You do what is right for your clients. I don't think too many young lawyers today look at it that way; there is a lot of self-aggrandizement.

There is more of what I would call "sharp practice," which you didn't have in Hawai'i back then because this was a small place. If you treated someone shabbily, the next time you worked with them you'd get it back, doubly. Now that code of civility doesn't seem to matter so much, except among the older lawyers.

There seems to be more aggressiveness and less civility, which is not good. I think that the advent of computers, online resources, and e-mail also contributed to that. You see stuff in e-mails that is scathing and acrimonious—almost personal attacks. But people can get away with it because they aren't speaking face-to-face. Many lawyers have lost the give-and-take of talking across the table. In my day there would be adversaries who'd say, "Come over and look at my file." You'd reply, "Come over and look at my file. Here's what I've got." And quite often you could resolve the case. ❖

"Old Hawai'i," John Kelly lithograph

CHAPTER 2

Voices of the Old Days

Pigs, Octopus, and Lobsters
A longtime businessman and community leader, Oswald "Oz" Stender remembers life in his grandfather's world during his small-kid days.

Oz Stender We lived off the land in the Native Hawaiian way. Grandfather John, who died when I was fourteen or fifteen, leased the Hauʻula property we lived on from the Territory of Hawaiʻi. When I was at the university, my sister was living on the property. She wanted to build a house and she needed to find out who owned the land. We never knew who owned it; we just lived there. I researched the property and found that it was owned by the State and we had a lease on it. My grandfather had signed the lease in 1922 and it was for 999 years.[4]

JG *I've never heard of a lease that long. Was that common?*

OS It was common in those days. There are a few left and we are one of them. We had two and a half acres of land and grew all kinds of stuff. We raised pigs; we always had a couple of head of cattle and a couple of horses. We lived right on the ocean, so we also fished.

My grandfather was the park keeper and we had a houseful of people. All the older kids went off to school and I would stay with my grandfather. He taught me how to spearfish. In those days you had to make everything; we made our goggles out of used windowpane glass. We formed the frame for the goggles, cut the glass out of a window, and then put them on. But under water everything was magnified. We had to learn tricks so we didn't get little fish that looked big through our goggles! Every fish had a beak and a gill; you had to know your fish and how far the beak was from the gill. We measured it before we speared it. You only speared the ones that you could use. Our spears

---

[4] This would mean that the lease expires in 2921.

had three prongs and a barb. The barb was always one inch long. *Heʻe* live in a hole, so before we speared the octopus, we tapped around the hole. The first thing to come out is the eye; an octopus is very curious. We put the spear by the eyes and could tell the size by how it measured up to the one-inch barb. Then we knew whether to spear it or leave it alone. Never net a lobster, never spear a lobster; you pick it up and look. If it's a female, you leave it; if it's a male, you can take it.

We didn't even know what a doctor or a dentist was. Everything was home remedy. If you have a bad stomach, you use the sap that comes out when you pick the fruit of the *kukui* tree. You rub the sap on your tongue and it will clean your tongue and it's like a laxative. *ʻInamona* is kukui [nut] that has been cooked in an *imu* (oven) and mashed into a condiment. Noni is a fruit that was awful-tasting, but we had to eat that if we had a bad stomach. Today they make liquid medicine and pills from it.

My grandfather hunted and fished to supplement our diet. We hunted pigs up in the mountains with dogs. When my daughter's cat got sick and had to go to the doctor, by the time we were finished, it cost about $1,000. When our dog got hurt, it cost $1,800! When I was growing up, we had a bunch of pig-hunting dogs. They would go up into the mountains with us. We had no gun or rifle, so my grandfather hunted with a knife. The dogs would corner the pig and my grandfather would go in and kill it. The dogs got badly ripped up from the boar, which would gore them. Our job was to bring the pig home. The dogs would have to be carried home too because they were too weak to walk. When we got home, we put alcohol on the wounds, and my grandfather would take a needle and thread and sew the dogs up. He'd put them in a pen and a week later they would be up and running!

We had our own taro patch—our own *loʻi*. We had three families who shared in this field. Every third week was our family's turn to clean and harvest the taro and make the poi. That was the only time we had milk. You boiled the fresh taro and cut it up into little cubes. It was like a cereal and we put milk with it. Our great-grandson, who is six months old, is eating poi. All our kids grew up eating poi. We love poi when it starts to ferment and it has that tang to it. All our kids love it that way.

Tutu Emily cooked food outside on a wood fire. She did the laundry in the river with a stick, batting the clothes. We had no toys. We walked everywhere. I didn't know what a bicycle was. We made slingshots and used a guava instead of a rock, as a rock could hurt somebody. We made our own toys out of the hau tree. We would skin the bark and make a whip. Zorro was the big thing, right? And he had a whip, so we made whips. We had sugar cane in the backyard. Cane has this tassel with the flower at the top, and it made a great arrow for our bows.

Oz grew up to be an astute businessman who worked for many prominent local companies and is still working for the betterment of the Hawaiian people. Imagine how amazed Grandpa John would be about the life his grandson has lived!

Plantation Stories
Several of my interviewees grew up on Hawai'i's sugar and pineapple plantations. I found these glimpses into plantation life priceless. Kaui St. Sure Goring Philpotts talks about housing, Makuakāne addresses language barriers, Morita describes in detail working in the pineapple fields, Bryan reveals the assets and drawbacks of being a haole boy fluent in pidgin, Liljestrand talks about medical doctors' jobs, and Watanabe shares the impression that plantation life made on him.

> **Kaui Philpotts** Hawaiians didn't want to work on the plantation. You'll read books that will delicately say that the Hawaiians were lazy, or they didn't want to keep those hours. But they really didn't want to live in those places.
>
> Plantation camps had kit homes and different nationalities got different kinds of kits. They differed mostly by size, but the quality was about the same. On Maui I grew up surrounded by Portuguese and Japanese, so those are the cultures I know the best. I ate rice balls with *ume* (Japanese apricot) for lunch. I loved going to my Japanese friend's house because her mother always packed that little *bento* tin. Best food in the world!
>
> Each camp was a village. Upper Pā'ia was where the Japanese lived and some Portuguese as well. There were also a couple of part-Hawaiian families in my neighborhood. There were some Filipinos but not many. There was a sense of community in each camp, and people were grouped together because they spoke the same language and had the same customs. But there was also prejudice and a hierarchy of different races.
>
> In the 1950s the plantations decided to get out of the housing business. They had this really crappy land down in Kahului that I'm sure couldn't be used to grow sugar. It was between the wharf and what is now Pu'unēnē and the airport. It was a flat, sandy, really awful property. A lot of G.I. housing was being built at that time too. Everybody was moving to the housing tracts. The camps dispersed, and people bought their own homes. For a lot of people, this was the only way they would ever own a home. The tracts of homes were usually built of hollow tile but some were made of single-wall redwood construction. After people left the plantations, for the most part the camp homes were destroyed, and more cane was planted.

Kenneth Makuakāne I am three-quarters Hawaiian and one-quarter Chinese. My dad is pure Hawaiian and my mom is half Hawaiian and half Chinese. My Chinese side immigrated here in the late 1800s, to work for the sugar plantation. They were from a poor area of China and needed an opportunity to have a better life for their family.

My grandfather was born here and, as it is for any immigrant, it was a tough life. First there was a language barrier. When they arrived, they were all renamed. His first name was Ah Sam You. In Asia, you say your family name first. So it was Chou Ah Sam You. In America, they thought Ah Sam You was his last name and they couldn't say it, so they changed it to Akamu. Any name that sounds Hawaiian that starts with an "A" was probably originally a Chinese name.

Hermina "Mina" Morita In 1951 my father became the game warden on Lāna'i. Hawai'i was still a territory and game was under the Department of Agriculture, not the Department of Land and Natural Resources as it is now. The bulk of the job was management of animals, birds, and fish. Since my father worked for the Territory and later the State, housing was provided to us by the government. He was one of the few people on the island who was not associated with the Dole plantation. I was born on Lāna'i in 1954 and I consider myself a Lāna'i person, not a Molokai person. They were like different countries to us!

My mother worked in the Dole pineapple fields. It was hard work—hot, bending over, and dusty—but they made the most of it. There were a lot of good friendships that came from working in the fields. She had Japanese, Filipino, Hawaiian, and Puerto Rican friends. Some of my fond memories are of working in the pineapple fields.

It's a rite of passage for every kid growing up on Lāna'i to work in the fields. You were supposed to be sixteen, but if you had a special work permit you could work at fifteen. Usually the grown women got the best fields because they were fast at picking. The boys got the plum jobs such as doing field testing or rain gauge checker or truck driver. The girls had to pick pineapples or *hoe hana*—chopping weeds with a hoe. The ground was hard, dry red dirt with weeds bigger than you were and plenty of dust. Once we chopped out the weeds we'd bend down, pick them up and throw them to the side. This was when the pineapple wasn't quite ripe yet for picking.

Part of this rite of passage was to buy all of your own equipment. We got it at Pine Isle Market or Richard's Shopping Center or the plantation supply shop. You usually wore jeans, and over them you had canvas pants that you slipped on. You usually wore a tee shirt and denim sleeves to cover your arms; they were held back with a piece of elastic or safety-pinned to your tee shirt.

You had leather gloves, which you wore for most of the day. You might start off the morning with rubber gloves because it was damp, and the leather gloves would get wet. Sometimes you wore rubber over-pants, which would stick to you, so you had to kind of soften them up. And then you had a handkerchief around your neck, usually red or blue, to keep the sun off your neck. You could also put it across your face, folded like a triangle, to keep the dust out. And you wore wire goggles with screen mesh to protect your eyes. The screen mesh was a lot cooler than classic eye protection goggles, which would get dusty. And you wore a big hat on your head.

Your *kau kau* (food) tin had two parts; in the bottom part you could put your rice and in the top you put your meat. And there was a handle. There was nothing to keep it cool, but we never got sick. When it is so hot, you aren't that hungry. We usually had breakfast of rice, eggs, and Spam.

There were no irrigation ditches; instead they had huge water trucks with sprayers that would irrigate the fields. I think they tried drip irrigation for a while, but that didn't work. The plant itself gets about two feet high, and on each plant is a pineapple that usually weighs a couple of pounds. It has a crown of spiky leaves, and the plant has spiky leaves. That's why you have to be protected. The fields are planted in rows, and each plot might have thirty rows. You stand behind the boom of a picking machine and break the pineapple off the plant. It takes a technique to break it off the plant. Once the pineapple has been picked, you twist the crown off and put it into the boom, the conveyor belt that takes it up and drops it into the truck. I think the day started at 6:00 a.m. You usually had a morning break around 9:30 and a lunch break around 12:00-ish, and then you would *hoe hana* at around 2:30 p.m. We made $1.60 an hour.

Carl Carlson: Plantation camps were segregated. All the superintendents or senior supervisors were *haole*[5] except for Walter Weight, who I believe was a Kamehameha Schools graduate. The next tier down was the supervisors, and they were all ethnicities. Quite a way down the hill you came to the so-called Plantation Camp and those were segregated. Waikapu [Maui] was a Hawaiian village next to Waikapu Stream. There was a Portuguese camp called Pacific Portuguese camp, the Japanese camp was across the street, and there was a Filipino camp.

At elementary school the population was haole or Japanese. I don't recall any Filipinos. Most of us were children of ranch families or plantation supervisors and superintendents. The Japanese were always good students. Many of their fathers worked their way up to the rank of supervisor, and a lot of

---

[5] Haole, white person, formerly any foreigner

Hawaiians did too, and several Portuguese. There were some Chinese students at the school but not too many Chinese at the plantation. It wasn't their type of labor. I don't recall when the Chinese came compared to the Japanese, but it was several years in advance. I'm guessing that their children had already moved on from the plantations to being merchants.

JG *Do you remember much ethnic tension when you were growing up?*

CC Not in elementary school. When I was in high school, there was more. I graduated from Baldwin in 1963. Very crudely put, I didn't learn that "F'ing haole" was actually two words until I went to college. We were called that but it wasn't necessarily derogatory.

JG *Just a distinction?*

CC Absolutely! Just a distinction.

JG *Did you use any slurs for the others?*

CC I would not admit to such a thing (smiling). We all had slurs, but I don't really recall. But we didn't ever mean anything harmful. When you were around people you haven't met, and you walked by, they might say something to you. We would refer to each other's various ethnicities in whatever the slang of the day was. Nobody cared. There was no such thing as political correctness.

Michael "Corky" Bryan My Caucasian grandmother was born and raised in China and spoke fluent Cantonese. When she got mad at us, she scolded us in Chinese. My grandfather was at Schofield Barracks in the late 1930s. He was assigned to live on Reed's Island in Hilo and became the military governor of the Big Island during World War II. After December 7, 1941, the military took over everything. There are a lot of ugly stories about the days of military rule. They were very prejudiced against the Japanese, but my grandfather was not that way. As I look at it now, hearing those stories, I understand the military point of view—but I'm definitely a local on that.

At one point my father went to ʻEwa Plantation to be the housing director. Plantations provided housing to all the employees and he was the guy who made sure that the houses had water, electricity, and amenities. He eventually became the manager.

I could barely speak English and never spoke it outside the house. I spoke pidgin—I could outdo the best of the brothers! At a ball game I was sitting in the stands with my mother, and several mothers of kids on the other team were sitting behind her. I'm yelling with all the rest of the kids. The women said, "Did you *hear* that white boy talking just like the rest of those kids?" I think that was the final straw for Mom. She sent me to Punahou School.

I can remember going to Rice Hall at Punahou to take the admittance test and praying that I would flunk. I didn't, so I had to go. Beginning in the fifth grade I had to wear shoes for the first time in my life. I caught the bus at 5:30 in the morning from ʻEwa, transferred at Aʻala Park, transferred again on Hotel Street, and finally got to school. I did the same thing in reverse getting home in the afternoon.

Did people behave the same at ʻEwa Plantation as at Punahou? Oooh! It was like night and day. All my small-kid friends and surfing pals were out at ʻEwa. The first day at Punahou I got into a fight because I was from ʻEwa School. You look at me funny and you'd get it. You do something or say something, and my reaction would be, "You like beef?" That's the way I grew up! Punahou was a major culture shock and it took me a good year or more to adjust.

The summer after high school I was working construction at Princeville on Kauaʻi. I spent three straight months speaking *only* pidgin. So when I got to Cal Poly [California State Polytechnic College], switching to "the Queen's English" was *hard* for me! Before I began a sentence, I literally had to translate my pidgin phrases back into proper English. After hearing me talk, my English professor asked where I was from. "You have a different lilt to your speech," he said. "I can't quite place it." It was my pidgin inflection!

Bob Liljestrand Nils P. Larsen was the medical director at Queen's Hospital and was doing a research project on the Honolulu Plantation in ʻAiea. My father was one of his star interns and he was offered a job working on the research project on the plantation. He also became the editor of *Plantation Health* with Mr. Larsen. After he did that for a while, they offered him a job at the plantation hospital, which was called Southshore, then Leeward, and is now Pali Momi.

The plantation ran the hospital. It was one of those U-shaped plantation buildings with deep patios and beautiful grounds. I often sat on a bench along the patio. My dad started as the assistant physician. He was a general practitioner and also a very good surgeon. It was a whole different world back then, more rural. When somebody brought in a German Shepherd that had been hit by a car, the dog was laid out on the table in the emergency room and they sewed him up and sent him home!

ʻAiea was a village with cane fields and reservoirs. We rode our bikes on the dirt roads in the fields. Life today is not like it was then. I grew up in a life of privilege because I was the son of the doctor. We had the big house and the big yard, with the yardman who came with the house that was given to the doctor by the plantation. The staff members were my friends. My dad was very democratic in his appreciation of his staff. He delivered all the kids. When World War II began the chief doctor left—joined the Navy or something—so my dad became head doctor.

Dad talked about joining the Navy. He was ministering to 4,000 to 6,000 people at his hospital. The fuel tanks at Red Hill were being installed, which employed a lot of people, plus there were all the plantation workers. They had to have a doctor. The military would review his situation every six months and he was always given deferred admittance.

Jeff Watanabe I was born on Maui in 1943. My maternal grandfather came to Hawai'i from Japan in the early 1900s as a teenager. My maternal grandmother was born in Hawai'i but was returned by her parents to Japan as a youngster, then came back to Maui. My maternal grandparents met in Pu'unēnē, then the center of sugar cane production in central Maui. In those days, almost everyone in central Maui worked either for Alexander & Baldwin's Hawai'i Commercial and Sugar [HC&S], which ran its sugar operation, or Maui Land & Pineapple Company, which operated a cannery in Kahului.

My paternal grandparents worked for the J.P. Foster family in Kula, on the slopes of Haleakalā. I believe Mr. Foster was a superintendent of a sugar mill in Pā'ia. My grandfather was a gardener, my grandmother a cook and housekeeper on the Foster estate.

Following the onset of the war, Japanese children were encouraged to adopt English names such as Mildred or Robert, often suggested by their teachers.

My parents met through summer jobs at Maui Land & Pineapple Company's cannery. My father visited her in the hospital to apologize after cans he had incorrectly stacked fell on her. Later, my father took a white-collar job with A&B Commercial Company, my mother with a painting contractor.

Much of my time growing up on Maui was spent with my maternal grandparents in Mill Camp, one of the Pu'unēnē plantation camps near its central Maui mill. I attended a Buddhist preschool in Kahului and later Kaunoa School in Spreckelsville before moving to Honolulu, attending Lincoln Elementary, Stevenson Intermediate, and Roosevelt High. Being part of plantation life has made an indelible impression on me.

'Ōlelo—Speaking Hawaiian
Many people discussed their experiences with speaking—and not speaking—Hawaiian as they were growing up. One of these was attorney Moses Haia.

Moses Haia A hundred years ago, court cases were conducted in Hawaiian. Currently English and Hawaiian are the official languages in Hawai'i. Recently there have been protests about observatories on Mauna Kea and Haleakalā, where Hawaiians have been arrested for trespassing while trying to prevent trucks from taking equipment up the mountains to begin construction.

One guy from Maui speaks fluent Hawaiian and wanted to express himself in court in Hawaiian. Traditionally, if you are unable to speak English, the courts provide interpreters. They said to him, "You can speak English, so why are you making us get a translator? You're just making us spend more money."

"Hawaiian is the official language of Hawai'i," he told them. "I am Hawaiian, and I want to be able to explain myself in my language." He got an interpreter [Hawaiian to English]. The day he was to go to court, the interpreter was sick so the defendant pleaded his own case in Hawaiian. Nobody understood what he was saying, so the judge held him in contempt. Then the judge put out a bench warrant for his arrest.

Obviously, as executive director of the Native Hawaiian Legal Corporation, I get calls from the media. I told them, "He was within his rights to ask to speak Hawaiian, and he had an interpreter all set up. In my mind the court should have continued the case until the interpreter could be there." The very next day, I got a call from the Administrator of the Judiciary, who said, "Moses, I want you to know that the judiciary is changing its policy. They will have interpreters for people who want to conduct their cases in Hawaiian."

How about witnessing a will entirely in Hawaiian?

Frank Padgett My friend Tommy Waddoups was not Hawaiian but he spoke fluent Hawaiian. He grew up on a plantation in Lā'ie and spoke Hawaiian as his first language. When he went to Georgetown Law School, he said his accent when he spoke English was so thick that he was hard to understand. [Judge] Sam King's father, Samuel Wilder King, was the delegate to Congress at the time, and Tommy and his friend Corbett got to go to all the diplomatic parties in Washington.

I was with the Garner Anthony law firm for two or three months when Tommy called me: "I want you to witness a will with me." We went out to this house on Pensacola Street, which had once been the home of the president of Castle & Cooke and had been sold to the Chinese family Goo Wan Hoy. When we got to the house there wasn't any furniture on the ground floor. We went upstairs into a bedroom where a little old lady was lying in a four-poster Hawaiian bed. That was Malia Goo Wan Hoy. They conducted the entire proceedings in Hawaiian, and I witnessed the will.

Jimmy Greenwell speaks with great affection of his grandfather, Frank Greenwell.

James "Jimmy" Greenwell My grandfather could understand Portuguese and he spoke Hawaiian well. He had a big roll-top desk with his ledgers on it and he ran the business from there. He smoked White Owl cigars. On the front porch he always had some kind of fruit or produce like mangoes, breadfruit, or taro off the land. People would come up, and in typical Hawaiian style, they would bring him something, such as fish or something from their place. Grandpa always had time to talk.

Since Hawaiian was not her first language, singer Luanna Farden McKenney recalls how she learned the lyrics to songs and her reluctance to pronounce words incorrectly.

Luanna Farden McKenney My grandparents would only speak to each other behind closed doors, because in 1901 the public schools ordered their teachers to punish the children who spoke Hawaiian. You could only speak English. When my grandparents visited our home, they did not speak Hawaiian to my parents.

My father and mother were both born in 1901. Their generation never learned Hawaiian. They all spoke really beautiful English. I'm Hawaiian but I am not going to try to speak Hawaiian, because I'm not going to do it well and it will annoy someone who really does speak Hawaiian. It would be disrespectful to them. It's not being high muck-a-muck; it's just the way I am. My mother was an English teacher. She really wanted to teach me by example, so I have to speak like this.

When I sang professionally, I would look up the words or look at the translations of all the songs I knew and memorize them from little cards.

You know the song "Puamana?" Auntie Irmgard [Aluli], said, "I'm going to write a song about our family." She had the ideas, but she didn't know how to speak Hawaiian. She wrote the melody and my grandfather wrote the Hawaiian words.

My dad died in 1983. He never spoke Hawaiian, but I have all of the three-by-five cards that he used to memorize the Hawaiian lyrics he sang in the same way I did. I've read in books that in the olden days, if you were a chanter and were responsible for learning a chant, if you didn't get *every* word correct, they wouldn't put up with that.

Ken Makuakāne describes the plantation as a non-monochrome world that interwove a multiplicity of cultures.

Kenneth Makuakāne On the plantation everyone spoke everyone else's language. My grandfather was loaned from Ka'ū to 'Ōla'a sugar camp as a chemist to show them how to boil down the sugar syrup. To the haole *luna*, the story goes, the Koreans, Chinese, and Japanese all looked alike. As a result, my Chinese grandfather and his Hawaiian wife were assigned to live in a Japanese camp, and my Chinese-Hawaiian mother was raised in a Japanese camp.

They lived in a duplex next to a Japanese family. Obviously, they became friends and then became *hānai* (adopted) family. My family learned to speak Japanese, and the Japanese learned to speak Hawaiian. My grandfather could speak all languages. Everybody learned everybody else's languages.

With humor and humility Puakea Nogelmeier shares his journey of learning to speak Hawaiian.

Puakea Nogelmeier In the 1970s you couldn't have a car wash without a hula troupe. Every event had Hawaiian activities. At a presentation at McKinley High School, I did a *kepakepa* chant, which is very fast and long. I finished it and had just stepped off the stage when this old gentleman came up and talked to me in Hawaiian. I was floored and said, "I'm sorry, Uncle, I don't speak Hawaiian." He was a little taken aback, and asked, "But how can you know what you are chanting?" I said, "I memorize the English." That sounds a little vapid to me, even now! He said, "How can you know how well you perform?" I don't even know what I said to that because by now I was fumbling. He said, "You did fine, boy" and turned around, walking away and disappearing. I did not know who he was for a long time. Years later I learned it was Luka Kanaka'ole, Auntie's [Edith Kanaka'ole's] husband.

I stood there, befuddled, and thought, *Why don't I know Hawaiian? Why am I learning hula and chanting and not understanding the language?* I talked to my hula cohorts and we went to Auntie Edith McKinzie and said, "We want to learn Hawaiian." She said, "Well, I'm not the best source, but I can teach you what I know." So she started a class every Saturday on her back porch.

Theodore Kelsey

It was only a couple of weeks later that I met June Gutmanis. She was a researcher and a really dynamic woman, a bulldog on Hawaiian topics though she was not Hawaiian. She married Gutmanis, who was a Polish diplomat, I think. She has a number of books out, e.g., *Kahuna La'au Lapa'au* and *Na Pule Kahiko*, which are important reference books.

In the course of her research, she went to visit one of the old gents, Theodore Kelsey, whom she had long relied on. He was eighty-seven years old, and at his house she found him standing with a couple of paper bags beside him by the road. "They said I can't live here anymore." He had been living with his best friend, Henry Kekahuna, and this best friend's wife until Henry passed away. Then he lived with the widow until she died, and their kids said, "Uncle, you're not ours. You have to go be somewhere else." He felt terrible. So June said, "Put your stuff in the car and come live with me." By the time I met them, he'd been living there for about a year.

He was haole, born in Washington State in 1891 and brought to Hawai'i in 1892 or so, when his mother was hired as a teacher for the government schools. First she taught at Hanamā'ulu on Kaua'i and then they settled in Hilo after his father joined them.

In 1896 it became a ruling that English was to be the only language of instruction. They settled in Hilo and he found that if you wanted to have any friends in Hilo, you had to speak Hawaiian. Hawaiian was the common language of that city. He and his friends liked to listen to old folks tell stories. His father set him up in the photography business once he was of age. He worked as a photographer at Queen Lili'uokalani's funeral in 1917 at age twenty-six! At her funeral he felt that what he loved about Hawai'i was being swept away, and he made a promise to himself to dedicate the rest of his life to documenting and salvaging the beauty of Hawai'i, the literature and the language.

I met him when he was eighty-seven. I had just developed this new goal of learning the language, so I asked, "Will you teach me Hawaiian?" "No. I'm not a teacher. There are books on that. I learned it from a book." I lived in Wai'anae, in Mā'ili, and he and June lived up in Wai'anae Valley. So a week later I came back, but this time when I spoke to Mr. Kelsey, I said, "*Pehea 'oe, ē* Mr. Kelsey?"—using my newly learned bits. And he answered back in this wash of Hawaiian. I only knew this much Hawaiian [holds thumb and finger close together]! I only understood four or five words that he said. But I'm not easily intimidated, so I said, "*Ua maika'i au.*" [I'm doing fine.] He was really pleased that anybody was speaking Hawaiian. I explained to him, "*Au li'ili'i wale nō.*" (I only get a little bit.)

June said, "Come up regularly and try to work with him." Then she gave me an article from the newspaper and said, "Ask him if he'll explain this to you." So I sat with Mr. Kelsey and he explained the whole thing to me. It turns out that he'd been translating everything that she gave him, but he would not translate anything that was sexual, anything that was deeply political, or anything that was not appropriate for a lady. He was very Victorian—very old-fashioned. Ladies, in his mind, were a special breed; he was always protecting her ladyhood.

He was actually quite deaf. My voice cut through that, so he and I would always have a very good time. He lived to be ninety-six. I saw him three days a week for the next six years and always on Sundays for the rest of his life. He's the foundation of everything that I do in language. He always said he was not a native speaker. And he wasn't. His pronunciation was his own. And because he was from an English-speaking household the flavor of his language was interesting. But he spent much of his life with Hawaiian speakers. He's the one who recorded Kuluwaimaka, the chanter for King Kalākaua. He stayed with Kuluwaimaka in the late 1930s, early 1940s. Because of him I went to school and got degrees, one being in the Hawaiian language, and I became a teacher of Hawaiian language. I ended up working with lots of native-speaking Hawaiians. It was to them that I turned for pronunciation and flavor. Mr. Kelsey was for understanding. In my PhD dissertation there is a major piece about that.

Closing the Last Sugar Plantation
Chris Benjamin heads Alexander & Baldwin, a company with 175 years in the sugar industry. He discussed the conditions that led to the closing of HC&S, Hawai'i's last sugar plantation.

Chris Benjamin When I came to Alexander and Baldwin (A&B), the company had recently shut down the McBryde Sugar Plantation on Kaua'i. We still had the Hawaiian Commercial & Sugar Company, commonly known as HC&S, on Maui, but in 2000, the year prior to my arrival, HC&S had consolidated from two sugar mills into one. The company shut down its Pā'ia Mill and kept the Pu'unēnē Mill open. The plantation contained fields that were very different in terms of weather, with the fields around Pā'ia often wet and muddy and the fields that were processed at the Pu'unēnē Mill drier and often sandy. Dealing with the mud from the fields near Pā'ia at the Pu'unēnē Mill caused us to lose productivity, and I think it contributed to our eventual shutdown.

Maui has many microclimates and different soil types. I'm *not* saying that the decision to shut down the Pā'ia Mill caused the shutdown of HC&S. In some ways, had we not shut down the Pā'ia Mill, we might have had to shut the whole business down earlier because the costs would have been just too great.

In 2009, Stan Kuriyama, the president of A&B, asked me to run HC&S. Business had been bad; we were in the process of losing almost $30 million that year, but I believed that we could turn it around. For the next two years I commuted to Maui. I returned to Honolulu most evenings because I had two daughters in high school, and I wanted to be home for dinner. It was a labor of love and I enjoyed working with the HC&S team immensely.

A key to the success we achieved over the next two years was a change in irrigation practices. As context for this, I should explain how sugar in Hawai'i was grown. Sugar crops in Hawai'i, unlike anywhere else in the world, grew for two years. Other places grow sugar cane for a little less than one year. And they cut it like you would cut grass. New stalks, the ratoons, regrow from the roots. Typically, you will ratoon a crop—cut it and let it regrow—about three times. After three or four years, you plow it under and you replant, because yields eventually decline.

In Hawai'i, they did it very differently because they figured out that if you let the plant grow for one year, you get decent yields. But in the second year, the cane stalks get very heavy and lay down on the ground and send out new shoots. You get this tangled mat of cane, but the growth you get during that second year is disproportionately higher than the first year of growth. You get much higher yields by growing it for two years instead of one. Sugar becomes concentrated in the stalk and the total biomass growth is greater over time. Not only are the stalks thicker, there are more of them. But because of that, you can't harvest it the way the rest of the world does. Think about cutting grass in the first example versus trying to cut what would be a tangled web of thick grass in the second example. In Hawai'i, rather than cutting it, you bulldoze the sugar cane into piles, pick it up, and bring it to the mill.

The milling operations in Hawai'i are very different as well. In other parts of the world, they bring in very clean stalks without mud or rocks. In Hawai'i, unlike any other mill in the world, there are cane cleaners at the front of our sugar mills. Hawai'i was creative in developing technology relating to irrigation practices, harvesting practices, and cane varietals. The Hawai'i Sugar Planters Association (HSPA)[6] was a leader in cultivating specific varieties of cane that grew best on a two-year cycle as opposed to a one-year cycle.

This brings us to the changes we made in irrigation practices. In the years prior to 2009, the amount of water pumped to the crop was reduced in order to meet obligations to sell power. HC&S had a power purchase agreement with Maui Electric Company (MECO). We produced power by burning bagasse—sugar cane fiber—in the power plant. We could do one of two things

---

[6] HSPA has evolved into the Hawai'i Agricultural Research Center. They have transitioned out of sugar cane research into researching cacao, coffee, sorghum, stevia and various other crops.

with that power: sell it to MECO and get a certain amount of money now, or use that power to pump water to the crop and get a return in a year or two when we harvested the crop. When the business started going downhill, there was pressure to generate more power revenue, so the plantation pumped less water to the crop and sold more electricity. The problem was that yields went down. When I refer to yields, I mean the amount of sugar produced per acre. When yields went down, they had to harvest more acres to get the same amount of sugar, and more rapid harvesting meant the crop grew for a shorter period of time. Rather than the cane having twenty-four months of age before it was harvested, it had about eighteen months. We were sacrificing some of the best growing months in order to hit our production quota.

We made the decision to stop selling power to MECO. We declared force majeure, which we were allowed to do in the summertime if we didn't have enough water for the crop. Force majeure means if there are forces outside your control that keep you from honoring a contract, such as summer weather or drought, and you can't deliver the power, then you don't have to sell it. That meant we did not have to deliver as much power to MECO.

Our production the next year went up nearly 40 percent, mostly due to higher yields, but also due to improvements in the milling process. The decision to pump more water to the crop had a positive impact on our farming operation, but even more important than the increase in yields was the signal this decision sent to the organization. It instilled confidence in our employees, who had most likely assumed that I was there to shut the business down. To stop selling electricity and start pumping water told everybody on the plantation that we were focused on the long term, not the short term.

The other action we took in 2009-2010 was to shut down for an extended maintenance period. We stopped the annual harvest early in 2009 and started up late in 2010. That gave us five full months to do maintenance. The mill was in need of a lot of deferred maintenance. There were steel plates underneath our mill line with holes in them. When we squeezed the sugar cane to get the juice out, the juice dripped though the holes into the sewer! In that five months of downtime, we were able to replace all of that sheet metal, reduce leaks, and improve the performance of the mill. Not only did we "get age back on the crop" through this extended shutdown, we improved some of our harvesting practices, increased the efficiency of the mill, and reduced losses in the milling process. All these things factored into our production increase of 40 percent.

The other fortunate thing that happened, and this was just pure luck, is that sugar prices went up. We had a $50 million swing in profitability between 2009 and 2011. We went from a $28 million loss in 2009 to a $22 million profit in 2011.

We did an analysis that showed that almost exactly half of that benefit was production-related, and half was price-related. If you go to the halfway point between those two numbers, you are still at a loss of $3 million. If we had not had the price improvement, we still would have been losing money, but it would have been only $3 million a year instead of $28 million a year. This turnaround was a new lease on life for the plantation!

But the rest of the story was that eventually sugar prices went back down a couple years later. We then faced opposition to some of our farming practices, including field burning, which limited our ability to burn the cane. In most places in the world, sugar cane is burned in the field before it is harvested. The reason for that is that nearly half of all the biomass or fiber that is in the sugar cane plant is leaves, which have no sugar in them. By burning, you get rid of all that biomass so that in the mill, you are only grinding stalks that have sugar in them.

JG *Isn't there something about the heat condensing the sugar into the stalk? Or is that a myth?*

CB I have to confess that I have heard both sides of that story, that the heat somehow releases the sugar and makes it easier to extract. I believe there is truth to that because ultimately you are trying to break the cells in the stalk that hold the sugar. When you bring in a piece of burnt sugar cane, it looks just like an unburnt piece. It will be a little darker and have some char on it, but none of the sugar is coming out of it. It's only when you crush it that you release the sugar.

If left in the field, cane will start fermenting and losing sugar content. There will be times when you may burn a field and then it starts raining. If it gets too muddy you can't get the bulldozers in to harvest it. You might have to wait three to seven days and every day that you wait, the sugar content goes down a little bit. That's why you try to burn small areas every day that you can manage right away. Burning is a common practice, and there are other crops around the world that are burned before harvest, including rice.

In 2011, I was promoted to president and chief operating officer of the company. Rick Volner took my place as general manager of the sugar plantation and did a great job under increasingly challenging circumstances. For the next five years, I was overseeing, not running, the plantation. On January 1, 2016, I became CEO of the company and my first act as CEO was to announce that we were shutting down HC&S. This wasn't by design or desire, but it was necessary. That was the day that I had to announce not only the end of Alexander & Baldwin's 145 years in the sugar industry in Hawai'i, but the end of roughly 175 years of commercial sugar cultivation here. Truly the end of a very important era.

I made the point that there were a number of factors that influenced the decision: the price of sugar, the price of fuel, labor costs, and the challenge of harvesting without cane burning. We went from being able to burn the sugar cane 95 percent of the days we harvested to being able to burn only 75 to 80 percent of the days. On the days when you can't burn, you have to grind twice as much fiber to get the same amount of sugar, which slows your production down. That was just one factor.

JG *It was an air quality issue?*

CB Air quality on Maui, in general, is excellent, but the effects of cane burning could be significant locally. If people have asthma or other issues, it can be a problem. We did a lot to provide advance notification of where we would be burning on any given day so people could prepare. We also tried to work around populated areas, didn't burn near schools, etc. We were also very careful to make sure the wind was blowing in the right direction to take the smoke out to sea. But you have days where the wind shifts, and the effects can be felt where you didn't anticipate. It was challenging and it led to tremendous backlash from small but vocal segments of the population. But I would never blame the anti-cane-burning people for shutting down HC&S. I would never blame any single group. Water opposition didn't help us much either, but our demise was a result of many, many factors.

It was very difficult for me to be the one to shut down the plantation—and the industry—because I had worked there, and I knew all the employees. On the other hand, I was the perfect person to make that decision because I wasn't some bean counter from Honolulu coming in to say in a heartless way, "We're going to shut this thing down." I knew all those people. I cared about them tremendously and they knew that if I was making this decision, it was unavoidable. They knew how much I loved the plantation. It was a sad day. ❁

Elementary School gas mask drill, World War II

CHAPTER 3

Voices of World War II

Warriors

I had the honor of speaking to a few military veterans or family members of veterans who told me stories of their time in service. Judge Padgett recalled his final days in a Japanese prison camp at the end of World War II.

Frank Padgett[7] When the Japanese Imperial Army Rescript came into our prison camp in Indochina on the 15th of August 1945, there were 4,500 Frenchmen and five American prisoners. We would have to count off in Japanese—*ichi, ni, san, shi, go*. After the five Americans counted off, the Japanese guard stood in front of the Frenchmen and said, "*Bango!*" (Count off!) The French POWs said, "*Un, deux, trois, quatre, cinq, six...*" The guard said, "*Mate, mate* (stop) *bango.*" The guy in the front row said, "*La guerre c'est fini.*" (The war is over.) That ended the count-off.

During my nine months recovering from being a Japanese prisoner of war, I fell in love with my nurse. We married after the war and we've been married all this time.

Follow Mr. Matsuda's journey from being a high-schooler on Pearl Harbor Day to the final days of World War II in Europe.

Fujio Matsuda[8] I was a senior in high school on the morning of December 7, 1941. I was at Mother Waldron Park in Kaka'ako, shooting baskets with my friends. We didn't see any airplanes, but we could see the smoke. My sister was

---

[7] Judge Padgett gave me this interview in November 2019. He has been interviewed extensively during his life and with his son, A.J., has written *The 13th Mission*. Also see Leslie Wilcox's interview of Padgett on *Long Story Short* https://www.pbs.org/video/long-story-short-leslie-wilcox-frank-padgett/.

[8] The late Mr. Matsuda kindly gave me this interview in November 2018. He was interviewed extensively in his life, as any search of the internet will reveal. Please see his concise yet thorough essay on his life in *The Journey from Within: Lessons from Leaders on Finding Your Philosophical Core,* edited by Glenn K. Miyataki.

working at the *Honolulu Advertiser*. She came to tell me to come home because Hawai'i was being attacked by the Japanese. Mr. Know-it-all said to her, "That can't be right! There are Japanese envoys in Washington right now negotiating to lift the embargo." My sister said that a bomb fell across the street from the *Advertiser*. It turned out it wasn't a Japanese bomb but a US anti-aircraft shell.

I was an American citizen, but my parents were in potential danger because they were still Japanese citizens. I experienced no feelings of discrimination or hostility from my high school friends, who were Chinese, Korean, or Filipino, whereas the Japanese on the mainland were discriminated against immediately.

In Hawai'i martial law was declared right away and everything was shut down. School was cancelled for a couple of months. During that time, I volunteered to do labor—dig dirt, trenches, or whatever needed doing. Some of it was in town and some up in the mountains, to get soil to build bunkers.

I thought my parents might be arrested, but the local authorities were very discriminating in whom they wanted to put away. Leaders of Japanese language schools and some Japanese businesses, and Japanese fishermen who could go out long distances with radio equipment, were rounded up. In some cases, they were confined on the mainland. But my parents were okay. Their customers were not fearful of warm-hearted *mamasan*. Hawai'i had been their home for nearly forty years by that time. My father used to say, "Lucky come Hawai'i." They didn't suffer any personal insults or harassment

When the 442nd Regimental Combat Team was formed, I was eighteen years old, just old enough to join. I didn't consult my parents and when I told them I had signed up, my father, who was not too communicative—which was typical of Japanese fathers—said, in Japanese, "Do your best." And my mother said, in Japanese, "Take care of health."

A call went out to Japanese Americans in Hawai'i and on the mainland to join the military. In Hawai'i, they were oversubscribed, but on the mainland they couldn't raise as many people. By then many Japanese were in the relocation camps and being treated as enemies. Many of them said, "Why should we join? They have violated our civil rights." But some of them wanted to prove their loyalty and did join.

I joined the 442nd and went to Camp Shelby for basic training. I was assigned to the all-Japanese-American 232nd Combat Engineers Company. Toward the end of basic training, I was ordered to go to an Army specialized training program. I assumed that as a member of the 232nd I would be taught some additional skills and then come back to the 232nd. But it turned out that it was a program to train engineering officers in a compressed three-year program. When that program was discontinued, I said, "I want to go back to the 232nd." They said I could not because while I was gone, they had been through live ammunition maneuvers without which you couldn't go overseas. So, I was assigned to the 291st First Field Artillery Observation Battalion. It was a pick-up team, basically young soldiers from all over the country. I was the only Asian.

JG *(laughing) How did that work out?*

FM Just fine. We would swap stories, of course, and I was a curiosity to them. They had never met anyone like me. Because I'm from Hawai'i, they thought I was Hawaiian. (Laughter.)

The 442nd and the 100th Battalion went first to North Africa, then to Italy and France. In the 291st we went north instead of south. The combat route was through Monschau, Lammersdorf, Aachen, Sittard, and over the Elbe River to Stendal [confirmed on a map dated January 1, 1945 to May 9, 1945].

We landed at Normandy six months after D-Day. The beach was secure and safe to land on but littered with the wreckage of vehicles and armament. I think we were one of the first units deployed to Belgium. We were an observation battalion directing the corps artillery's big guns where to aim. They would tell us what the target was on the map and we would tell them where they needed to aim and the distance. They figured out the actual settings calculating for wind or whatever corrections they needed to make. It was safe when the guns went off because the corps artillery was not at the front lines. But then we had to go up to the front to see where the shot had actually landed. We guided the guns where to shoot and then reported back to them if they were short or on target. So during post-op observation, we were subject to enemy fire on the front line—and not safe.

Toward the end, we were on the Elbe River, the line of demarcation, waiting for the Russians to join us. To the east was Russian territory and to the west was British-American territory. Germans soldiers were trying to escape from the Russians to surrender to us. Some of them were just young boys. We were not allowed to help them, and they were desperate. They made makeshift rafts to cross the river, but the river was flowing too fast and none of them made it. That was difficult to watch. Our unit ended the war there. As we were calibrating some of the big guns, getting ready to ship them to the Asian theater, the war ended when the second A-bomb was dropped.

My buddies in the 291st became friends for life. One of them, my very good friend, was an accountant with Peat Marwick in Boston. There was another guy from Moscow, Idaho, one from Philadelphia, and a couple of rednecks from down South [chuckles]. We all got along. In fact, I ended up as a squad leader with about fifteen guys under my command. And I was the youngest!

JG *That's pretty amazing. The Japanese guy gets to be the squad leader. (Both laugh.)*

The following stories are drawn from military experiences in both World War II and the Korean War.

Mark Fukunaga My father, George, was born in 1924 in Waialua. He attended Waialua Intermediate and High School. Then the family moved to Honolulu and he went to ʻIolani School, graduating in 1942, just after World War II had started.

He joined the US Army and was slated to go into Military Intelligence as an interpreter. I think he went to language school at Fort Ord, then Minnesota.[9] He knew some Japanese because my grandmother Ruth was a language teacher at a Japanese school in Waialua. He got really good in Japanese in the US Army language school.

He was sent to Korea as a lieutenant in charge of a POW camp in Korea, which was reprocessing all of the Japanese POWs who had been stuck in Manchuria and Southeast Asia, and were returning to Japan through Korea.

Apparently, the job of US Military Intelligence was to debrief the Japanese soldiers coming back from China, as a way to prepare for what the US saw as China potentially going Communist under Mao Tse Tung. They wanted to get as much intelligence as they could about the Chinese countryside. I also assume they were evaluating which soldiers were potential security risks for the Occupation Forces. My father said it was pretty interesting work. On R&R he was sent back to Japan, which was when he explored the Fukunaga village. But most of his time was spent in Korea.

After World War II he went to the University of Hawaiʻi on the GI bill. That's where he met my mother, Alice Tagawa. A month after they got married in 1950, he was called up for the Korean War because he was still in the Army Reserves. He was still in Military Intelligence and helped interrogate Korean prisoners. He did not speak Korean, but a lot of them spoke Japanese because Korea had been a Japanese territory.

Dennis Fitzgerald I was born on May 28, 1934. When I was a student at Bradley University in Peoria, Illinois, I was about to be drafted into the

---

[9] *Nisei* originally went to Fort Ord in California for language school and when the US started interning Japanese in California, the school was relocated to Camp Savage in Minnesota.

Korean War. The Navy was on campus recruiting for flight school, and I certainly didn't want to get drafted if I could avoid it, so I joined the Navy as a flight student. The Marine Corps is a division of the Navy.

As a fighter pilot, my permanent duty station was the Marine Corps Air Station at Kaneʻohe Bay. I arrived one evening at midnight in November of 1955. A staff car picked me up and took me to the Kaneʻohe Officers Club. I got up the next morning, walked out, and it was the most fantastic sight I had ever seen. The Koʻolau mountains stretched out over there, Kaneʻohe Bay from the Officers Club was over there and the ocean was behind me. It was just absolutely beautiful. There couldn't have been a better greeting in Hawaiʻi. The other side of the story is that was probably the last time I ever saw the Koʻolau range totally clear in Kaneʻohe.

It was one of the best times of my life! Flying fighter planes was very challenging. It was a busy job with a lot to learn—just like driving the best sports car ever, all the time. And the things you get to do in the air! It's an amazing adrenaline flow; I loved everything about it.

A Missouri farm boy who finds himself in Hawaiʻi knows enough not to go home. And I didn't! The Koreans heard that I'd graduated from flight school and was coming, and they gave up. Actually, the war ended just as I got out of flight school, so I didn't have to go.

And from a Hawaiʻi broadcast executive and proud son, a tribute to the Greatest Generation:

John Fink After Tom Brokaw wrote *The Greatest Generation*, Disney or National Geographic was going to do a show on the first mini sub to go into the submerged *USS Arizona*. Brokaw was going to narrate the opening and closing statements at the Arizona Memorial. He flew all the way out from New York for one day to participate.

As the general manager of the local NBC affiliate, I went to Pearl Harbor with my anchor, Howard Dashefsky. We got to talk to Tom Brokaw, and I told him, "My father was part of that generation and, like your father, he never talks about it. I asked my dad about going to see the movie *Saving Private Ryan*. He had no interest. He said, 'John, I was there.'" I asked Brokaw if he would autograph my copy of his book. Tom said, "What's your father's name?" I said, "Arthur or Art." So he writes in the front of the book, *To Art, one of the greatest. Tom Brokaw.*

I drove to Kailua and held up the book as I walked into my father's house. The inscription was in script and hard for him to read. "Dad, it says, *To Art, one of the greatest. Tom Brokaw.*" He started crying.

I saw Tom Brokaw at the NBC Convention at Rockefeller Center six months later when he was retiring. This is a guy who was from very humble beginnings in South Dakota and became one of the top news guys in America. I went over to him and reminded him who I was. I told him my dad's reaction to his dedication because I wanted him to know what he did for my father.

Pearl Harbor

Attorney Jim Case, one of my first interviewees for this project, wrote a book about his World War II experiences called From Hawaii to the Carolinas: One Sailor's War (1941-46). *In his interview with me, he described the efforts undertaken on O'ahu before the bombing of Pearl Harbor.*

James Case In September 1941 I applied for work as a civilian at the Materials Testing Laboratory section of the Army Corps of Engineers. The office was located in the basement of the Alexander Young Hotel in downtown Honolulu.

We were preparing for a Japanese attack, which the military expected at any time. We were building airstrips. You will be surprised when you learn how much we were doing in preparation for an attack:

- Ala Wai Golf Course: We replanted trees so that there was a grass emergency landing strip. We kept it secret. After all, the managers of the golf course were always changing the holes.
- Bellows Field, Waimānalo: a full air base
- Kualoa Ranch: a fighter strip on the grass
- Hale'iwa: a small fighter strip on the grass
- Dillingham Field: a full air base
- Helemano: a fighter strip adjacent to Wheeler Field, the main air base at Schofield Barracks
- Kīpapa Air Base: a full-time air base in central O'ahu
- Hickam Air Force Base at Honolulu Airport

Another interviewee was eight years old when Pearl Harbor was bombed. I asked him if he remembered that day.

Of course! We were in Blessed Sacrament Church up in Nu'uanu. The statues were swaying and falling over. We didn't know what it was. We used to go to the corner store and buy pastries on Sunday. In there, the Clorox bottles were all exploding. Bombs hit at Punchbowl and Pacific Heights.

Four hours later they took my father and we didn't see him for about four months. The men were taken to be defense workers. He was putting up telephone poles that had been knocked down and similar repair work. We had no food because the ships weren't coming in. The women were there for the family, and right away we started planting gardens and building bomb shelters. We always had chickens. My mom somehow got a cow and a pig and we started raising animals.

We had no school for about one year. When we did go back to school, we had to go in a morning shift and an afternoon shift.

One woman told me about her trauma following Pearl Harbor.

On December 7th each year, I go into a sad hibernation. Many Hawai'i families left for the mainland; many stayed. Mother convinced a friend of hers to take me on her lap on a transport plane to California. Once there I was delivered to Mother's older sister. Mother and Daddy stayed in Hawai'i. I'm not sure where my siblings went but we were eventually reunited. In three years we lived with five different families. I remember being on a streetcar in San Francisco and yelling, "Mommy!" when I saw a woman who looked like her. This was very hard on me and had to be very hard on Mommy, but she never talked about it. She had to choose between us and Daddy.

The next two stories relate family experiences of evacuation from Hawai'i during World War II.

Diane Johnston Beardmore Brokaw Paton Having breakfast on our *lānai* on December 7, 1941, my dad, an Army Reserve Officer, heard on the morning news of the Japanese attack on Pearl Harbor. He leapt to his feet, raced off to active duty and we barely saw him again until the war was over. We could see the planes in the distance and quickly learned that the air raid siren meant that we must dive for cover beneath a bed, and remain there until we heard the all-clear signal. Huge coils of barbed wire separated our lawn from the beach as the military feared Japanese mini subs coming ashore. I remember nightly blackouts and censored mail.

My mother, two brothers, and I were evacuated on a giant seaplane from which all of the seats had been removed in order to cram in as many women and children as possible. One of the engines burst into flame just before reaching the point of no return, and we were required to turn back, wait many hours for repairs, then reboard the exhausted mothers, their wailing children and a few fragile old men for the sixteen-hour flight to San Francisco. We continued on to Lexington, Kentucky, where we spent World War II with my mother's loving family.

Duncan MacNaughton My father predicted the war and sent my mother to the mainland about a year before the Japanese bombed Pearl Harbor. I'm not exactly sure how he predicted that, but there was a bunch of speculation at the time. The military secured Oʻahu against invasion with concertina wire on all the beaches and coastline. You can see the remnants of it at the old Fort Ruger near Diamond Head. Those concrete embankments that we hike up to today were gun emplacements to fire on enemy ships. They thought the Japanese would arrive by sea and invade. My father decided there was no point in all of us being here, so he stayed to work at Dole while my mother and the kids went back to Oregon and stayed for five years.

After the war my mother determined it was time for her to come back to Honolulu. When I was six weeks old my mother took the train, with my three older siblings and me, from Portland to San Francisco, where we got on a ship. There were still Japanese submarines threatening ships. No one knew what a maverick captain of a submarine might do in anger over the Japanese having had to surrender.

My mother was on the ship, ready to sail from San Francisco to Honolulu, when my father's brother, Malcolm, who was working in San Francisco for Castle & Cooke, arrived with a case of oranges. He delivered them to the room where Mother was taking care of four kids. The ship finally sailed, and twenty-four hours out on an eight-day trip, my sister Trudie came down with chicken pox, which was highly infectious. The captain of the ship quarantined my mother and four kids in one room and wouldn't let us come out. She said the only reason we survived was because we had that case of oranges!

When we arrived at the dock in Honolulu, my father was there to greet us. We piled into a car and were driving home to Kāhala. My father began telling my mother how he had survived without her: "A lot of Japanese nationals had come over to work for the sugar industry before the bombing. They were unable to get work afterward, so I hired one of these guys, very inexpensively." He told my mother that this guy acted as his butler and would lay out his clothes every morning and make him feel important. My mother said, "I've lived with three kids and now four kids for five years in Portland, struggling to survive, and I've just gotten off a ship after eight days where we were locked in quarantine, and you're telling me you have a *butler*? He's out of there!" (Laughter.)

Here's a description of how education was disrupted during the war years. (And we complain about having to wear masks during the 2020 pandemic!)

Robin Fern Loomis The night of December 7th, most of the men went down to Pearl Harbor to help. Daddy had an air rifle and he patrolled the area.

The whole elementary school at Punahou was taken over by the military for the first few months. The engineers rolled in and took over the campus on December 8th. Our classes were relocated to the University of Hawai'i campus. I think some classes were held in people's homes. Across the street were open fields where we would tend to our Victory Garden.

We carried gas masks for the whole time of the war. We carried them in a bag along with our schoolbooks. I hated that! When I went away to college they took posture pictures. One of my shoulders was cocked because I'd been carrying a gas mask for four years. Before we got the gas masks, we had to have kerchiefs that you would wet in a baking soda water mixture, and you were supposed to put the kerchief around your nose.

The Internment Camps

The following stories speak for themselves. All of them were shared by descendants of people who live in Japanese-American internment camps during World War II.

Kelvin Taketa My paternal grandparents came from the Hiroshima region of Japan. My grandfather, Kazuto Taketa, was from an upper middle-class family, some of whom were Buddhist priests who had cared for a Hiroshima shrine for centuries. Grandfather Kazuto was not a first son, and if you were the second or third son, you had to make your own way, because there was nothing left to you by the family.

He and my grandmother moved to Waimea, Kaua'i, where some of the big sugar companies were located. He worked as a bookkeeper for an emerging group of Japanese merchants. Right before World War II a number of plantation workers were able to save up enough money to start their own stores, giving workers an alternative to shopping at the plantation stores. My grandfather was an independent bookkeeper for these storekeepers.

My grandfather was one of the few people interned during World War II from the island of Kaua'i. He was a Japanese citizen, not an American citizen, and he was a civic leader in Waimea, having started a Japanese language school and a tennis club. He was taken in 1942, and it was the winter of 1945 before he came home. He was sent to Lordsburg, New Mexico, which was where a lot of Japanese community leaders were taken. The Americans had a great deal of intelligence about the Japanese community and they understood the Japanese in Hawai'i weren't really a threat. However, the Japanese culture was very hierarchical, and leaders had the authority to speak on behalf of the community. My grandfather was one of those people, and that's why he was singled out to be interned. In Hawai'i the leaders were removed, and their families remained at home, whereas on the mainland whole families were moved to camps.

He refused to talk about the camps even though I asked him a number of times. My dad's thirteenth birthday was on December 7, 1941. There were six kids in the family. The two oldest girls had to quit school to help my grandmother because all their bank accounts were frozen. My grandfather was lucky because he was well known in the community and had commercial relationships with many merchants, who helped his family while he was gone.

Everyone in the family had a Japanese name, but after the war all except my dad changed to English names. Everyone felt they had to assimilate more. I remember when the US government sent reparations checks to those who had been interned during the war. I asked my grandfather what he was going to do with the money. He said, "You mean my all-expense paid vacation courtesy of the US government?" He was pretty bitter about it.

When my grandfather died, I flew back from Europe to Kaua'i, and my dad said, "You're a public speaker, so you have to do the eulogy." He handed me notes about my grandfather's life that he and his siblings had put together, most of which none of the grandchildren knew! The Kaua'i Historical Society has done a lot of research on those who left Kaua'i during the internment. Many years later they gave me copies of pictures and documents, which I shared with my cousins. I feel regret that there was so much to his story that was not shared with us.

When I was in law school in San Francisco, learning about affirmative action cases such as the Bakke decision in California, I intersected with the mainland Asian-American community. It was interesting to me how different the Japanese on the mainland were from the Japanese here. The Japanese in Hawai'i, for all of the infighting that may go on, are still a pretty homogeneous group of people, through my generation anyway. But on the mainland there were two groups that traced back to the internment experience. There was a group of Japanese leaders like Fred Korematsu, who were suing the US government, refusing to join the military or the 442nd military unit because they felt their constitutional rights had been abridged. And they were right! Then there were the others who said, "We just have to do more to prove we are Americans." But Hawai'i was really different. Everybody enlisted. We all had parents, uncles and cousins who served in the US military.

Raymond Okada Both my parents were born in America. My father's name is Shigeo Okada. My mother is Masaye Teraoka Okada. My grandparents did not speak English and I did not speak Japanese, so it was very difficult to communicate. They originally came to California from Japan because there were too many kids in the family and they couldn't support them all. They were very poor peasant farmers from the countryside.

They moved to Fresno, California, and it was pretty brutal. It's 105 to 108 degrees when you're out in the sun, stooping over tomatoes and cucumbers. We all worked on the farm. We took our cucumbers, tomatoes, lettuce, onions, and squash to a produce house, and they would ship it in big lots to a dealer, mostly in Los Angeles. All of us kids were thinking, "We are *not* going to be farmers!"

We were certainly affected by World War II. Both my grandparents and my parents went to relocation camps in Jerome, Arkansas. The only time my mother talked about it was when her friend came to visit and they started talking about the camp days. There were two camps in Arkansas, believe it or not. If you lived on one side of the highway in Fresno you went to one camp, and if you were on the other side you went to a different camp. If you were in southern California you went to Manzanar, a camp that got a lot of press. Some of these outlying places, like Jerome, you never heard about.

My grandparents were some of the older ones in the camp. It was bittersweet for my parents, who were teenagers. For the first time in their lives they were with people of similar background and culture. None of them were quite American and yet not quite Japanese. In the camps they were judged by how they performed, not how they looked. The first time in their lives! A lot of people came out of their shells and they made lifelong friends. And their kids became our friends.

We always wondered why our parents were so clannish. It is because the outside world might not accept them, so they hung out in clusters and rarely ventured outside of them. Those who didn't speak English locked onto other Japanese people, naturally. I think those kinds of insular clusters are dissipating now. Everybody is kind of getting assimilated. It would have been accelerated but for the camps. Other cultures have assimilated much faster than the camp-based Japanese nationals.

In the internment camps during the later years of the war, the kids were told, "You can go out of the camp to work, but it can't be on the West Coast." So Dad went to Chicago and worked in a Swedish orphanage. They hired him to be a gardener, bus driver, and maintenance guy. He loved sports. The orphans wanted to form a team and he was asked to coach them. I think he was twenty or twenty-one years old and the oldest kids were sixteen. He hit fly balls to them and had batting practice. He had more fun than they did, I think. Some of the kids kept in contact with him until he was in his nineties. In fact, he outlived all of them. He'll be ninety-seven next month. I remember one time somebody called saying, "I used to be in the orphanage, and he was my coach. Tell him Merry Christmas." Some of those kids came by to visit too, after all those years.

Back at the camp the young men were asked if they wanted to volunteer for the US military. They needed interpreters in occupied Japan. So Dad went.

He spent time at the Imperial Palace. When we went to Japan years later and stood with our backs to the palace looking at the skyline, he said, "This is *very* different than I remember. It was all bombed out and burned." There wasn't an atomic bomb in Tokyo, but the city had been fire bombed. He described what he remembered.

He was working for the US government, questioning citizens and Japanese military officers. While there he went to visit a relative who was in the Japanese Army. In the military, in occupied Japan, you had to wear a uniform, so my father was wearing an American military uniform. It was very awkward, I'm sure.

When they came out of the internment camps after the war, there was this big push to be Americanized. That's why the children in my generation have English middle names. Mine is Kirk, probably from Kirk Douglas. When we took my parents to Japan about ten years ago, they realized that they are not Japanese. The culture is totally different. They didn't realize how Americanized they had become. And part of it was that they are holding onto the 1890 and early 1900 Japanese culture in the 1990s. It's like us trying to hold on to cowboy days. Things change over time when you are not living in a country.

After the war the whole family moved back to Fresno, California, because they couldn't get jobs anywhere else. Before the war they were renting their farms because Asians couldn't own land. If you were not European [heritage], you could not own land. When their children were born, they put the land into the names of their children who were citizens, having been born in the US. Most property was put in the name of the oldest son, who continued farming. This practice, of course, resulted in a lot of family disputes about the fairness of their inheritances.

JG *Given your exposure to those issues when you were growing up, Ray, it comes as no surprise that you ended up an estate and trust lawyer!*

Jeff Watanabe Maui was the only island, other than Oʻahu and Niʻihau, that was directly affected by the Japanese attack. An offshore submarine shelled Kahului. Other than that, not much happened. Ordinary Japanese and Japanese Americans, except for community leaders, were not immediately affected by the war. About 1,000 to 2,000 Japanese community leaders—teachers, clergy, and so forth—were interned at the Honouliuli, Oʻahu, relocation camp. Many were later transferred to mainland camps. This was very different than the Japanese and Japanese-American experience on the West Coast of the United States, where involuntary removal to interior relocation camps was universal. Hawaiʻi author Tom Coffman has written extensively about this seeming contradiction. I suspect that part of it was economics. Hawaiʻi's

Japanese population made up 20 to 25 percent of the total and was a significant labor force, especially on our plantations.

Tom Coffman recently wrote *The First Battle*, a story of local non-Japanese community leaders who helped protect Hawaiʻi's Japanese from what was done on the mainland. Until 1960, Hawaiʻi's governors were appointed by the president of the United States. A group of men, largely associated with the YMCA, gathered to influence important elements of Hawaiʻi's community, urging Hawaiʻi's appointed governor and military leaders to avoid universal internment of Japanese citizens.

As an example, Judge Alva Steadman, an influential judicial and business leader of the day, wrote a letter to Hawaiʻi's governor after Pearl Harbor, imploring him to avoid universal internment, based largely on his personal knowledge of the loyalty of Hawaiʻi's Japanese community and the potential economic impact. Coffman found the letter during his research at the Hawaiʻi State Archives and sent me a copy, knowing I was a close friend of Judge Steadman's son, Richard, who lives in New York. Richard said he was totally unaware of his father's efforts. These efforts were effective and they worked.

My sense is that prior to the attack on Pearl Harbor and the onset of World War II, there had been sufficient time and opportunity for the economic integration, albeit not necessarily social integration, to take place between the Japanese and Hawaiʻi's ruling class. Of course, the heroic efforts and sacrifices of *Nisei* volunteers making up the 100th and 442nd infantry units had a dramatic impact on how Japanese Americans were viewed during and after the war. And it continues to this day.

My generation was culturally handicapped by the outbreak of World War II. The Nisei generation went to Japanese language school, so they spoke Japanese. Once the war started, Japanese teachers were targets for internment, so their schools closed. This resulted in a greater cultural distance between generations, especially with the *Sansei*, to which I belong, whose Japanese language skills were lacking. It became difficult for my generation to find out what really happened from the often more close-mouthed Nisei and *Issei*.

Pause Your Dreams for the War

Many islanders saw promising careers and other aspirations put on hold or even curtailed by the war. One of these was Bill Smith, a standout swimmer who trained with the celebrated Maui coach Soichi Sakamoto. Bill started swimming competitively in 1939 in the Waikīkī Natatorium and went on to Ohio State University on a swimming scholarship. In 1943 he set his college and swimming careers aside to join the Navy. In 1946 he returned to college and swimming and in 1948 won two Olympic gold medals in London!

"When America entered the war on December 7, 1941," wrote Kelli Y. Nakamura in The Hawaiian Journal of History, "prompted by a Japanese attack on Pearl Harbor, Sakamoto could only watch as hundreds of the young men he had trained and mentored—former students, track and field athletes, basketball and baseball players, members of his Boy Scout troop, and of course his swimmers—went off to war, some never to return. In lieu of training, Sakamoto wrote them long, inspiring letters, 'just like a doting father.' Although his Olympic dreams were temporarily shelved, Sakamoto never forgot about them or the hundreds of young men he had taught over the years."

Bill's son, Riley, provided me with Bill's notes handwritten on yellow lined paper.

> **Bill Smith**
>
> At the time I started training I did not have any goals. It was just to have fun and to develop good fellowship with my friends. However as time went on I began to realize that improvement was forthcoming so in 1940 I made the cut offs for the Nationals. At these Nationals I got second in the one mile swim. At this point I began to realize that besides self improvement swimming teaches pride commitment discipline perseverance and it keeps one focused on what one wants to achieve.
>
> One of the good things that came out of this trip was that the coach of the Hawaii team was a man from Maui named Coach Sakamoto — He was a master motivator. He was always positive and exciting.

Bill Smith Swimming has been one of the most exciting happenings in my life. It is an activity that is very healthy and one that a person can participate in for the rest of his life. If you are willing to train hard and listen to your coaches, the rewards are unlimited. From swimming I learned the values of responsibility, integrity, cooperation, sharing, setting goals, and providing a reason for participation in sports. It helped to develop a positive philosophy and personality to carry over into my adult life.

In 1938 when I first decided to train for swimming competition, it was at the Waikīkī Natatorium, a 100-meter saltwater pool. In 1940 at the Nationals I got second in the one-mile swim. One of the good things that came out of this trip was that the coach of the Hawai'i team was a man from Maui named Coach Sakamoto. He was a master motivator. He was always positive and exciting.

I decided to go to Maui to swim with Coach Sakamoto in the Three-Year Swim Club. It was formed in 1937 and its goal was to make the 1940 Olympics. The motto of the club was "Olympics First and Always." In 1940, if the games had not been cancelled, he would have had at least four swimmers on the Olympic team. The 1944 Olympics were cancelled as well.

We practiced at least three hours every day with two-a-day workouts on weekends, holidays, and during vacation. When the pool was closed, we practiced in the irrigation ditch in the cane field. We swam with the current for a certain distance, took a short rest, and swam back against the current. I believe that this training in the ditch was responsible for our success.

After graduation from high school in 1942, I was offered a number of scholarships and I chose Ohio State University, one of the three top swim schools in the country. One of my teammates from Maui, Keo Nakama, was enrolled there as well.

At the completion of my first year of college in 1943, I was drafted into the service. Because of my swimming ability, I decided to join the Navy. After three years in the Navy, I returned to Ohio in 1946 and resumed my swimming career. The climax of my athletic career came in 1948 with the revival of the Olympic games. I realized that if I stayed in school with all of my commitments, that would not be possible, so I dropped out of school, came home, and trained with my old coach.

I participated in the games held in London, England. I won the gold medal, beating my teammate who was the favored swimmer, and I set a new Olympic record. I also anchored the 800-meter freestyle to a new world record. For me, the highlight of my performance was the presence of my coach, who in 1937 had set the goal of "Olympics First and Always." We embraced each other and cried like babies.

James "Jim" Scott, the president of Punahou School from 1994 to 2019, talked to me about how the war interrupted high school careers, including his mother's.

Jim Scott When people ask my mother about her high school years, she says, "I went to Roosevelt High School when it was an English Standard School." Roosevelt was a selective public school and you had to gain entrance to it through a test. And that's why the Punahou-Roosevelt connection was so close for a couple of decades. One was public and one was private but they had same type of academic rigor. In the late 1950s, they did away with it, claiming it was not democratic to have some public schools be so exclusive.

The US Corps of Engineers took over Punahou School after Pearl Harbor. The class of 1942 never finished high school. It was my dad's junior year and he finished in an area near the University of Hawaiʻi, I think, but it was still Punahou Class of 1943.

A lot of haole kids went to the mainland because there was a fear of invasion. Many of the people in those war-year classes had not been together until they came back for their 50th Punahou School reunion. A fourth to a half of them never graduated from Punahou, but we still claim them. ❖

Fort and Hotel Streets, downtown Honolulu, circa 1950

CHAPTER 4

Voices in a Racial Melting Pot

Segregated Neighborhoods
I grew up in an ethnically segregated neighborhood and didn't even know it! I never heard anyone talk about it, no one explained who could live there and who couldn't, and I never noticed that our neighborhood was different from any other.

Many of the men had just returned from war in the Pacific, and they resisted living next door to those who were ethnically related to people who'd been sworn enemies only a few years earlier. To sell houselots, real estate brokers assured buyers that their neighbors would be like them.

> **Lois Taylor Clarke** "Newspapers are much more racially inclusive nowadays. When I started working at (the *Honolulu Star-Bulletin*) as a society columnist, we covered the Hawaiians, the Chinese, and the haole populations but avoided mention of the Japanese. When my husband and I were married, we had to go down to the Bishop Estate to change the names on the ownership of the land. They said [sotto voce], "We'll have to meet Mrs. Taylor." By that they meant they had to *see* that I was haole!"

Were such intentionally exclusive neighborhoods just an anomaly? To find out, I dug deeper in my interviews and learned that it was an open secret that such pockets of ethnic concentrations were commonplace. Exclusionary clauses in deeds and other documents weren't allowed, of course, but there were plenty of other explanations.

When a block of property was offered for sale in fee simple, for instance, advance word would get out in certain circles, and when sales closed, nearly every buyer in the neighborhood was Chinese. One Honolulu hillside, carpeted by carnation farms, was populated mostly by Japanese. Through a valley ran a stream lined by the homes of Native Hawaiians, whose forebears had been there for generations.

Dean Sakamoto told me about living in Moanalua Valley when it was first developed. In this case, it seems the neighborhood was established more through occupation than ethnicity.

> **Dean Sakamoto** Moanalua [the old Damon Tract] was pretty ethnically diverse because it is situated between four military bases. I would lose a friend after two years when our military neighbors or classmates transferred.

Initially the neighborhood—the people who bought there—were Japanese, Chinese, American, a few Filipino families, but mainly Japanese and Chinese. At the time it was a middle-class neighborhood. Almost everyone's dad was an engineer. They all knew each other. They either met at school studying engineering or they worked at Pearl Harbor. My dad worked for the federal government at Housing and Urban Development.

Someone who lived in an all-haole neighborhood told me how it was set up. The "rules" were rather complicated. The war had just finished, so it was the mid-1950s and Hawai'i's form of segregation was alive and well. The Japanese were the big offenders because they had tried to conquer the world with Hitler. There was not a lot of forgiveness going on.

Segregation wasn't illegal but it was close to it. The lots were sold under a contract of sale, and a lien was set against the property in the form of a ground lease, which was designed to last twenty years, after which the land would be the owners' with a fee-simple title. During those twenty years, control could be exacted over those who moved into that neighborhood.

Those who lived on plantations talk openly about the segregation in the workers' camps. In Hawai'i, which is land-restricted by nature, that meant that mixed races lived side by side.

Blending Japanese and Chinese cultures…

Jeff Watanabe During the early part of the 1950s, my mother's elder sister married a Chinese schoolteacher. The roof on my grandfather's house went up about three inches! (Laughter.) There weren't too many intermarriages by the Nisei in that era.

Marriage between Hawaiians and Chinese…

Kaui Philpotts The Chinese came in the 1840s and almost immediately there was intermarrying between the Chinese and the Hawaiians. It was Hawaiian-Chinese marrying Hawaiian-Chinese and for generations the bloodline was not watered down.

Korean intermarriage…

Ron Moon I'm Korean, right? So I have somewhat of an attachment to the Koreans in Korea. The children of my friends in Korea have adopted Western ways to a large extent: K-pop music, Korean soap operas on TV, and so on. Korean children want to be American whereas the Koreans living in Hawai'i are becoming interested in their ancestry. My oldest son is married to a Caucasian girl, and my daughter is married to a Caucasian guy.

This story features a young seaman from Washington state who fell in love with and married a Hawaiian, beginning a blended lineage.

Curtis Tyler My father, Joseph Curtis Tyler, Jr., was born May 11, 1916, in Spokane, Washington, and graduated from high school at age fifteen. In 1931 he signed up with the Grace Line and for a number of years sailed between the Port of New York and the west coast of Central and South America. He was probably one of the youngest steersmen who ever guided such a ship through the Panama Canal.

Afterward, he attended the University of California at Berkeley. In 1936 his ROTC program took a cruise on the battleship *USS New York*, part of Admiral Dewey's Great White Fleet. They steamed to Hawai'i and did gunnery practice in Hilo Bay. In Honolulu they docked at Pier 2 and went for a tour of the Dole pineapple cannery. My mother, Thelma Weeks, was a guide; they didn't call them docents back then. She was born in Kona on June 26, 1919. She was the youngest of five children and attended Punahou School, known as O'ahu College at the time, and graduated in 1936. She was part Hawaiian. They fell in love and married in 1938. On December 7, 1941, they lived at Pearl Harbor and survived the attack.

This story touched my heart. It speaks to the bonds of community being broken by a young boy going to boarding school.

Kenneth Makuakāne Our whole community lived like one village. For instance, I would play with my "cousins" at their house. When we got hungry, we went into the icebox and ate whatever food was there. If it was evening: "I think I'll stay at Auntie's house." So Auntie called Mom, who would say, "Okay, tell him to come home at seven o'clock in the morning before school."

The first time I was truly shaken in life was when I got to Kamehameha Schools at age twelve. At Kamehameha they started researching our lineages. I found out for the first time in my life that most of the people who were my "cousins and aunties and uncles," weren't even related to me! *What?* We were as close as can be. It was a terrible shock!

What about adopting? Interviewee Bob Liljestrand's family adopted three children.

Bob Liljestrand My dad's attitude was pretty much, "There are lots of babies who need to be taken care of, so why should we make any more?" When they decided to adopt a third, they couldn't find any children in Hawai'i, so they began a search on the mainland. My dad said the reason they couldn't find any more babies locally was because the war was over and the sailors were gone.

JG *Were all these adopted children Caucasian?*

BL Yes. I think adopting outside your race simply wasn't done back then. But this does illustrate an interesting contradiction. My parents may not have adopted outside their race, but at the same time they were totally open to Asians, Asian culture, and a mixed society. In fact, they intended to live in China, the country that my dad felt was "home."

How going to school together helped break down social barriers...

Stuart Ho Everyone recognized early on that there needed to be some interface between the races without necessarily welcoming them as neighbors. How was this to be accomplished? They left it to the wives to figure it out. They used carpools. Finally, after the kids mixed for a while, "This Asian kid seems to be okay. Let's have him over."

    We moved into a home on Diamond Head Road. It is currently the residence of Roy Disney's widow. She was very gracious. She invited us to visit the home and was curious to know what had survived. They had torn the whole thing down. I said the only thing that had survived were the plumeria trees near the garbage area. We were right between the Allen Renton and Harold Dillingham families. They didn't say anything, but I'm sure there was a lot of sniffing. (Laughter.)

With so many ethnicities living and working in close proximity, it's no surprise what happened next. A generation or two down the line, the haole men who lived in those segregated neighborhoods now had sons and daughters married to non-haole partners. It happened in both the Goodsill and the Watanabe households.

Jeff Watanabe It's really grandchildren who drive social attitudinal change. Look at my family. One set is Italian-Japanese-English-Irish-Chinese-Hawaiian-Welsh-Korean. Another set is English-Irish-Italian-Japanese-Columbian-Panamanian-Basque-French! Even more important, I married an extraordinary partner fifty years ago, Lynn Manildi, who is Italian-English-Irish and was raised in Pasadena, California. Can't "talk stink" about anyone anymore!

    We were standing on the shoulders of many who came before us. Demographics can be deceptive. I was speaking with Dr. Dennis Ogawa, a professor at the University of Hawai'i, about ethnic change. He opined that Japanese Americans will no longer exist as an identifiable ethnic group in a few generations: "It's simple. We marry later, have fewer children and don't marry each other!"

Integrated Boardrooms
There was a time in Hawai'i when the big companies were comprised of all-haole boards of directors. An excerpt from an interview taken from Henry Clark by his son, Sefton "Bee" Clark, on September 5, 2002, is apropos.

Henry Clark When Dr. Putnam decided to retire from the Honolulu Gas Company, he asked me if I wanted to be on the board and I said that would be fine, I appreciated it. The next thing I knew I was on the board of the gas company.

I noted that racially the board of the gas company was all haole. When I asked how come, they said that was the way it has always been and that's the way it probably would be for a long time. I said, "That doesn't make sense at all. Look at our stockholders. At least half of them are of Oriental extraction, maybe more than that. Look at your employees, more than half of them are of Oriental extraction. Why don't you have someone of Oriental extraction on the board?" They said, "All right, why don't you look into it?"

So I did and found there were two very fine candidates, and I brought them to the board and the board said fine. One of them was a Japanese man [George Fukunaga] who ran his own successful business. The other was a Chinese man named Zane, who was involved with Liberty Bank. By bringing them on the board it broke the barriers and all the other companies began to do the same thing.

Peter Fukunaga was born in Hiroshima, Japan, left his family and immigrated to the Big Island. There he worked as a demolition man blasting flumes out of lava rock to transport water from the mountains to the flats. This had to be difficult and harrowing work! Eventually he made enough money to move to O'ahu and put himself through 'Iolani School, after which he started his primary business and about ten others as well

His son, George, was born in Waialua, O'ahu in 1924. During WW II he worked for U.S. Army Intelligence, debriefing Japanese soldiers coming back from China and later he was a Japanese language interpreter in POW camps during the Korean War.

His grandson, Mark, was born on O'ahu in 1964. He ultimately chose to continue to run his grandfather's company, which celebrated its 100th anniversary in 2019.

Mark has his own personal remembrances of Henry Clark.

Mark Fukunaga Henry Clark was a great storyteller and had a big heart. I think he was a key guy in the integration of Honolulu. Thurston Twigg-Smith also did marvelous things when he took over the *Star-Bulletin*. I was told that the *Star-Bulletin* was somewhat racist in its view and its stories. When Twigg took it over, against many obstacles, he provided completely different, more serious news and unbiased views. Twigg was really important in that respect.

The following stories highlight how power structures were interwoven in the Honolulu business world.

Frank Padgett In Hawai'i the business community paid absolutely no attention to the idea that you should diversify. For instance, Atherton Richards was a trustee of the Bishop Estate and his brother-in-law, Frank Midkiff, was a trustee of the Bishop Estate. This was very prevalent in Hawai'i. You couldn't turn around but you saw interlocking relationships.

Retired First Hawaiian Bank chairman Walter Dods seemed to turn up in about every ninth interview I took, and yet I had never met him. A mutual friend introduced us, and he very kindly agreed to be interviewed. Walter and I talked about many things, but the following two stories seem pertinent to the subject of Hawai'i's racial melting pot.

Walter Dods While [our company was producing] *On Bishop Street: Avenue of Hawai'i Pioneers*, written by Kenneth Ames, we asked all the companies on Bishop Street to allow us into their corporate minutes, so that we could write a historically accurate book. Example after example of interlocking directorates appeared. Here's a typical conversation at a board meeting. The president of the bank says, "I would like to build a new headquarters on Bishop Street." The CEO of another firm says, "I'll go along with it if you buy the safes and the insurance from us." The other CEO says, "I'll go along with it, but we have to have this and this and this." It's right in the minutes! Everybody was in each other's pockets. Several companies owned Matson Navigation together at that point. They could decide what the shipping rates were going to be and everything else.

When Bert Kobayashi[10] became attorney general of Hawai'i [in 1962], the business community was frightened to death. Bert met privately with the

---

[10] Bert Takaaki Kobayashi, Sr. (1916–2005), a lawyer, was attorney general of Hawai'i during the 1960s and subsequently served as justice of the Hawai'i Supreme Court. In 1940 Kobayashi went on to Harvard Law School, graduating in 1943. During this time, World War II broke out. After his long absence on the mainland, Kobayashi returned to Hawai'i in late 1945. In 1948 he entered private practice, and soon built a law firm. In 1952 Kobayashi became an O'ahu district magistrate, in which position he served six years. In 1959 Kobayashi was elected president of the Hawai'i Bar Association. In 1962 Kobayashi was named attorney general of Hawai'i. Densho Enyclopedia encyclopedia.densho.org

CEOs of the Big Five and the other large companies, and basically said, "Look, I'm giving you six months—or some amount of time—to get rid of all these interlocking directorates. If you do that, you'll never hear from me again. There will be no lawsuits, no front-page newspaper articles. I'm not going to attack you. Just clean it all up." And they did. The way he did it was admirable. Everybody expected it to be the opposite, with front-page exposés, because here was a chance to get back. After fifty years of being "hands" on the plantations they had the power to change things and it could have gotten nasty.

Word in the downtown business community about [Hawai'i governor] Jack Burns was, "He's a Communist. He's going to wipe out society!" Burns, knowing the business community was concerned about him and the ILWU [International Longshore and Warehouse Union], asked to meet Lowell Dillingham, who was the CEO of Dillingham Corporation. He was given the runaround. They wouldn't schedule a meeting. So he drove down there and asked Lowell's secretary, Anita Rodiek, to meet with him. She said, "Well, he's tied up in meetings." He said, "That's fine. I'll just wait until his meetings are over." Finally they realized he wasn't going to leave. Eventually he and Lowell met and started talking. Who knows what they said, but that was the beginning of an incredible bond and friendship. Burns talked him into meeting with [ILWU vice president] Jack Hall, and Lowell Dillingham turned a very-much struggling Community Chest into what is today's Aloha United Way.

Favors are often done in the business world, of course, but I like the ones that reveal a willingness for cultures and races to commingle. One interviewee told me that Castle & Cooke's Boyd MacNaughton paved the way for former governor George Ariyoshi to be on the board of the Hawaiian Insurance and Guaranty Company, and George Ariyoshi invited Boyd to be the first haole member on the board of the Japanese Club. Now that had to be a climb for all involved! It is stories like these that inspire and encourage me.

Integrated Social Clubs
All-haole social clubs were the norm well into the 1960s. Riley Smith, the son of 1948 Olympic gold medalist Bill Smith, told me this story:

Riley Smith When my dad returned from the London Olympics, having won two gold medals in swimming, he was honored with a complimentary membership at the Outrigger Canoe Club. Because my dad was fairly well known at the time and a lot of other watermen were members, he considered it an honor. One day, he invited Keo Nakama to lunch at his new club. The two were very close friends, having swum under Coach Sakamoto in the

Puʻunēnē irrigation ditches in the Three-Year Swim Club, as well as at Ohio State University. Keo was also the first person to swim the Molokai Channel, in 1961. I was pretty young, but I remember his swimming into Hanauma Bay at night, with a lot of people watching.

When they sat down in the Outrigger dining room, the manager refused to serve Keo, since he was Japanese. My dad was very upset. He walked out of the club and never went back, ever. He also rescinded his membership. There was an article in the *Star-Bulletin* on this incident.

As a follow-up in 2012, a friend of mine, who sits on the board of the Outrigger Duke Kahanamoku Foundation, having learned of my dad's accomplishments, asked if he would want to be considered as an inductee to the foundation's Hall of Fame. I thought it best to check with my dad to see if he was okay with that nomination. My dad's response was that the manager at the time they had been refused service didn't know any better, and that he had no ill feelings toward the Outrigger or its members, many of whom were his friends. Based on that position, my dad was nominated and selected for induction into the second Outrigger Duke Kahanamoku Foundation Hall of Fame class in 2013. The interpretation of my friend on the foundation board was that the notoriety of this incident opened the door at the Outrigger for non-Caucasians to be considered for membership.

Jeff Watanabe had many interesting anecdotes related to fused economic and political power in Hawaiʻi.

Jeff Watanabe The person who had the greatest political impact on the immediate postwar Hawaiʻi was, of all things, a Honolulu police captain from Connecticut, Jack Burns, of whom much has been written. He believed there needed to be a "redistribution" of Hawaiʻi's political and economic pie and was instrumental in convincing many Nisei to run for political office. This "political revolution" started taking shape in the mid-1950s. By statehood in 1959, the Democratic Party was starting to dominate local politics, particularly the state legislature. Large-scale unionism began taking hold, generating another synergistic and concurrent political force. Much has been written about this period in Hawaiʻi's history, yet ironically, the first elected governor of Hawaiʻi was William Quinn, a Republican and Big Five executive. Change in Hawaiʻi always takes longer than one might anticipate.

Prior to the mid-1960s, economic and political power were fused and held by the same forces that controlled Hawaiʻi's oligopolistic economy, largely a Republican ruling class with both economic and political power. The Democratic Party revolution began sending economic and political power in different directions. Before this phenomenon, partners of law firms needed to practice good law while looking like their clients—people who belonged to the Republican Party, the Pacific Club, Oʻahu Country Club, Punahou School, etc.

Philip and Gerry Ching recount the story of being among the first people of Asian ancestry to become members of the Pacific Club. The tale is prefaced here by two entries from the historical timeline on the club's website.

> **1954** Art Committee recommends relaxing racial policy. Denied by membership.
> **1968** Racial policy scrapped. Philip Ching and Asa Akinaka join Club.

Philip Ching One day Henry Clark and Frank Damon came to me in my office at First Hawaiian Bank. They said, "Philip, you know about Masaji Marumoto getting turned down for membership at the Pacific Club, right?" "Of course, it was in the newspapers." "Well, we want you to put in an application for membership." "You've got to be crazy. If I made an application and the word got out, my name would be mud in the entire Asian community. 'What! The *pake* thinks he's too smart, he wants to go join the haoles?' I'd be a laughingstock."

But one of my friends said, "It is time, and someone has got to do it." I said, "But why me? I don't care about being a member there." I was told it was for the principle of the thing, breaking racial segregation, so I gave in and submitted an application. They had some closed meetings where the discussions were quite heated. But Henry Clark led the charge; he was a very persuasive guy. So in 1968 Asa Akinaka and I were voted in as members and that changed things forever.

Gerry Ching I was also asked to be a member of the Junior League.

JG *Do you think they specifically chose you to be the one to break the racial barrier?*

GC I don't know.

PC The front page of the *Los Angeles Times* read, "Asian, Gerry Ching, becomes a member of the Junior League." I'm not sure, but I bet at that time she was the first Asian in the Junior League of America.

Henry Clark had an impact upon Stuart Ho as well.

Stuart Ho I had the most respect for Henry Clark. As soon as I understood what he stood for, I thought Henry Clark walked on water. He was fair. There wasn't an ounce of prejudice in his judgment. He was practical. He knew how to handle people. He was easy to like and was a very generous person too.

When the Pacific Club was first considering admitting Asians, the story goes that one of the haole members approached Henry and made his objections known. Henry looked at him and said, "Then you should quit." That was Henry's operating style.

Glass Ceilings

Many people talked openly and engagingly with me about hitting the glass ceiling of racial discrimination that existed in Hawai'i not so long ago. I was dining with Sally and Willson Moore when Willie saw Raymond Tam across the room. "You should interview that guy. He was a great lawyer. He has a lot of my money in his pocket from all the cases I lost to him." Raymond has written a book about his own life[11] and another about the accomplishments of his Saint Louis School classmates, and he also helped with a biography of his uncle, the developer and philanthropist Clarence Ching.[12] But I am so glad he spoke with me too. I was intrigued with his passion for learning his craft at Notre Dame Law School and his stories about the struggle for racial equality in his profession.

Raymond Tam At Notre Dame I was one of two winners of our Law School Moot Court Competition. We competed against teams from law schools in Indiana, Michigan, and Illinois, and stood victorious. The final match, against the University of Illinois, was held at the Illinois Supreme Court in front of its five justices. The courtroom was packed. There were many top lawyers from Chicago and outlying areas in attendance. After grueling arguments, we were adjudged the winners.

After the decision, many of the lawyers in attendance crowded around my partner, Bill Ragan, and the two members of the losing University of Illinois team. I could hear talk of possible jobs and placements. I was left standing alone. I was a winner, but not one person talked to me. Right then and there, I came to the conclusion that there was no opportunity for an Asian like me in the Midwest. Hawai'i, here I come!

---

[11] *A Saint Louis Man: The Story of Hawai'i's Ray Tam* by Lance Tominaga
[12] *A Prophecy Fulfilled: The Story of Clarence T.C. Ching* by Lance Tominaga

In Hawaiʻi in the summer of 1957 before my final year of law school, I was selected for a summer job as a claims adjustor at Fireman's Fund. I loved it. It was my first experience in an adversarial setting. Nothing big, just property damage cases, but it involved investigation of claims, negotiating with claimants, and denying some and approving others where appropriate. Tom Hoperoft was my supervisor, and we had a very good working relationship.

Apparently I had been "scouted" for hire by James Thropp, Sr., a vice president at Amfac [American Factors, Ltd]. I must have made a good impression because one day Mr. Thropp stopped by my desk. He told me that he'd been observing me at work, that he was very impressed with my work ethic, and that after law school I should come to work at Amfac. He said "You have a great future at Amfac. We could use someone like you."

I graduated from Notre Dame Law School in June 1958. My parents attended the graduation ceremony and witnessed my receiving my law school diploma. It was a proud moment; they had made great sacrifices to allow me to study law at Notre Dame. I repaid their confidence by passing the bar exam on my first attempt in 1958. I received my law license from the Supreme Court, Territory of Hawaiʻi.

For the next two years, I fulfilled my military obligation as a second lieutenant at Edwards Air Force Base in the Mojave Desert in California. I was assigned to the legal office as a judge advocate, and I tried many court-martial cases. As the lowest ranking officer in the legal office, I was assigned to prosecute, or to defend, just about every court-martial case tried on the base, which allowed me to hone my trial skills.

In June 1960, having completed my tour of duty, I arranged to have a meeting with claims manager Tom Hoperoft at Fireman's Fund. I was dressed in a coat and tie, and Tom and I hugged each other and shook hands. It was such a happy moment to renew my acquaintance with an old friend. After some small talk, I told Tom that I was now back home for good, that I had acquired a lot of trial experience as a US Air Force judge advocate, and that I was ready to try cases for Fireman's Fund. "Let me try some cases for Fireman's Fund," I said. "Anything, the worst cases that you have, the kind that nobody wants, the $50 subrogation case. Let me show you what I can do."

Tom replied, "Ray, I really like you. You worked well and did a great job for us. But I'm really sorry — we have a policy at Amfac that we only hire lawyers from Robertson Castle or Anthony Smith Wild Beebe and Cades or Anderson Wrenn and Jenks. I'd love to use your services, but policy is policy."

I was shocked. Stunned. Blindsided. Crushed. The firms he mentioned were all haole firms. All Caucasians. No Asians. No Hawaiians or

Polynesians. No blacks or Hispanics. Only whites. I left, angry and very disillusioned. I applied at four other insurance companies. Same answer. Same result. At that time, Hawaiʻi was being touted by the Hawaiʻi Tourist Bureau as the "Melting Pot of the Pacific" and "The Land of Aloha." Yet here I was, a local boy who could not get a job because of professional racial discrimination.

I made a silent resolution. If they won't have me, I'll go to the other side. I was ready to shake down the thunder from the sky. It was the best thing that ever happened to me. Today, when I reminisce about my career, I thank the good Lord that I was rejected by Fireman's Fund and the other four insurance companies. I wound up spending my entire career representing injured plaintiffs against insurance companies—and loving it!

Ron Lum was the first Asian hired at the Anderson Wrenn and Jenks law firm. Here is his story.

Ronald Lum Even at Harvard Law School I knew I wasn't going into litigation. I focused on tax law because of my background in accounting at Marquette University. I specialized in tax and wrote my senior paper on the question of whether a gift was a capital contribution or not.

I came home to Hawaiʻi in August of 1967 to interview at law firms. When I went to Anderson Wrenn and Jenks, your father and Marty Anderson interviewed me. Neither Livingston Jenks nor Heaton Wrenn was there at the time; I think that's what allowed me to get in. I was the first Asian in the law firm and the nineteenth person hired at what is now Goodsill Anderson Quinn & Stifel.

Because of my interest in tax, I was assigned to your father. We represented the electric company and another utility. Hawaiian Electric wanted to run a power line over the Koʻolau Mountains into Kaneʻohe town. That would mean building a tower at the top of the peaks to carry the high voltage line. There was strong opposition from the naturalists. I worked with Marshall doing the research.

During my fourth year with the firm I got a call from Livingston Jenks saying, "Ron, I'm working with C. Brewer and we are going to form a farmer's co-op of the sugar cane planters on the Big Island. If we form a farmer's co-op under the co-operative laws, they can get a bank loan from Berkeley Bank of Co-ops at a very low percentage rate and we want to take advantage of this. We are going to assemble all the growers of sugar cane on the Hāmākua Coast and put them in a co-op. They are going to sell their output to C. Brewer & Company. Your job is to learn as much about co-op law as you can to help me through this process." For a full year I worked on that. I learned everything I could about co-op law and how to form a co-op and keep it going, and how to govern it. I did the bylaws and the articles for both C. Brewer and the farmers' company.

JG What was it like, working for Mr. Jenks?

RL It was fascinating. He was such a taskmaster! And he was very stubborn! At one time, towards the end, we had a disagreement and I said, "No, I think the answer should be this because of these various factors." He said, "Come into my office, Mr. Lum." His secretary, Dorothy Evans, had a typewriter on a tiny stand across from his desk and she would take live notes; as he spoke, she would type. He said, "Dorothy, take a memo to Mr. Lum. He's either too dumb to think, too deaf to hear, or too blind to read." He dictated that memo to her to be given to me! I'm sitting right there! (Laughter.) At the end of the year, he recommended me for partnership! But, boy, were my ears red! *Too dumb to think.* That's how tough he was!

Jeff Watanabe discusses the pressure on law firms in Hawai'i to include non-haole ethnicities.

Jeff Watanabe The established law firms, Goodsill included, found themselves in an awkward position. On one hand, they needed to stay loyal to their current client base, but they also recognized the changes circling them. The larger firms—Goodsill, Cades, Carlsmith—wisely made a concerted effort to hire more culturally and ethnically diverse, locally-raised young lawyers. Several other established firms of that time, which were unable or unwilling to alter direction, failed.

Discrimination was not aimed solely at a person's ethnicity. Being a mainland haole instead of a kama'āina had its drawbacks too.

Stuart Ho Fred Merrill was a man with ambitions. He set a goal of one day being head of a Big Five company. He had heard stories that you could not be the head of a Big Five company unless you were kama'āina. And this guy was pure mainland haole. When he was in his seventies he told me his story as we were fishing in Australia off the Great Barrier Reef.

His superiors at Hawaiian Trust came to him and said, "Hey, Fred. We know that you're fronting for this guy, Chinn Ho. That's against the rules." Fred was a hard-headed guy. He lived up on Hibiscus Drive beneath Diamond Head. One day he attended a meeting and happened to overhear, "This guy can't be promoted because the next guy has got to be the CEO and he's got to be kamaʻāina." Fred picked up and took off for San Francisco, where eventually he became the CEO and chairman of Fireman's Fund Insurance Company. Hawaiʻi missed out there.[13]

Unlikely Friendships

I came across a number of very charming stories about unlikely friendships. The result of these friendships made important imprints upon Hawaiʻi and are worth telling. The first story is told by Kualoa Ranch manager John Morgan.

Gerrit P. Judd and King Kamehameha III

John Morgan Dr. Gerrit P. Judd was our first ancestor to come to Hawaiʻi. He was a devout Christian and he wanted to be a missionary, but the American Board of Commissioners for Foreign Missions did not accept him. However, he was a doctor and the mission needed doctors, so he came as a doctor. He and his wife Laura arrived in Hawaiʻi in 1828.

He practiced medicine for many years before he became a confidant and advisor to King Kamehameha III. At different times during his service to the king, he was the Minister of Finance, the Minister of Foreign Affairs and the Minister of the Interior. He also was the second Western person to renounce his American citizenship and pledge his allegiance to the king and the Kingdom of Hawaiʻi. He was devoted to the people of Hawaiʻi.

One of his duties as the Minister of Foreign Affairs was to try to negotiate treaties with world powers, so they would honor the independence and sovereignty of Hawaiʻi. In that capacity he went to the United States, England, and France. He took Prince Lot and Prince Alexander Liholiho with him, to expose them to the world beyond Hawaiʻi and educate them about the art of diplomacy.

When the Great Mahele happened in 1848[14], Kualoa was part of the King's personal property. The king sold the 622-acre *ahupuaʻa* of Kualoa to Dr. Judd on November 20, 1850, and so began our family's stewardship of the land in this area.

---

[13] Fred Merrill's name is engraved on a plaque at Honolulu Police Department headquarters as one of the reserve officers who served on December 7, 1941. The Diamond Head home he once lived in on Hibiscus Drive was demolished by fire in 2020.

[14] The Great Mahele marked the beginning of private land ownership in Hawaiʻi.

King Kalākaua and the Emperor of Japan
Fujio Matsuda My parents came separately from Yamaguchi Prefecture, Japan. They met in Hawai'i after they had put in their mandatory three years of work.

The story of these work contracts goes back to King Kalākaua. A representative of the sugar industry recruited the Japanese to come to work in Hawai'i in 1868 when the Meiji was installed as the Emperor. This was the year the Tokugawa samurai rule ended and modern Japan began. Roughly 150 people came and were called *gannenmono*[15]. The gannenmono experience in Hawai'i was not good. Out of the 150 who came, one third went back to Japan, one third went on to the mainland, and one third remained in Hawai'i.

Because they had such a bad experience in Hawai'i, no other Japanese immigrants came to Hawai'i until King Kalākaua went to Japan on his round-the-world trip in 1881. During his stay he was the guest of the new emperor. Apparently they hit it off. There is the famous story about Kalākaua suggesting that the son of the emperor marry his niece, the Hawaiian princess Ka'iulani. He had in mind forming an alliance with Japan.

Kalākaua and the emperor discussed Hawai'i's need for sugar workers. Sadly, Native Hawaiians had been exposed to Western diseases and their number went from over 500,000 to a few tens of thousands, so Kalākaua wanted to repopulate his country. He said that the Hawaiians and the Japanese had the same values and philosophy about the importance of the land: "We don't just want workers. We want workers who will become citizens of Hawai'i and help build Hawai'i."

The Emperor liked what he heard. They reached a formal agreement called *kanyaku*, which means agreement between a king and an emperor. Whereas the first effort brought 150 Japanese to Hawai'i, this agreement brought 94,000. Eventually the number ballooned to 500,000, if I recall correctly. This program was terminated when the federal government passed the Asian Exclusion Law prohibiting any immigrants from Asia to come to the US.[16]

---

[15] Literally, "first year people"

[16] Plainshumanities.unl.edu: As a result of restrictive immigration legislation, the Chinese population in the Great Plains declined after 1890, while Japanese migration to the region increased, especially to Colorado and Nebraska in the United States. Both nations, however, soon extended the exclusion laws to effectively bar emigration from Japan and persons of Asian ancestry from *any* nation.

My parents came under the kanyaku agreement. They didn't come just to work, make some money, and go back home. They came with the idea that they would settle in Hawai'i, their children would be born in Hawai'i and be US citizens, which they were.

James "Kimo" Greenwell and A.W. Carter
Jimmy Greenwell In those days Parker Ranch, on Hawai'i Island, was about 130,000 acres. It was excellent cattle country, very well managed by its sole trustee, Mr. A.W. Carter. An opportunity to work for Parker Ranch was really prized.

My dad, Kimo, and A.W. met on a steamship voyage when my dad was enroute to the West Coast to go to boarding school in the Bay Area. It was quite common for high school-aged young men from Hawai'i to be sent off to a mainland prep school, not necessarily to graduate but to take the rough edges off these country boys. Picture this high school boy and this ranch owner sitting in the deck chairs, talking at length. I guess they both made an impression on each other. My dad spent his senior year at Punahou School and after graduation went back to Kona for the summer to work cattle on the mountain. One Friday afternoon my grandfather came up the mountain with a letter for my dad from A.W. Carter. The gist of the letter was, "If you'd like the job, be in Waimea on Monday and bring your saddle." So he did.

You can tell from my tone of voice that recalling this stirs deep emotion, which comes out of respect for my dad, respect for A.W. Carter, and appreciating what they did for each other. Dad went to Waimea and initially lived at Mr. Carter's manager's house while he worked on the ranch. He was very much under A.W. Carter's wing and learned so much from him. Dad later became the foreman of Parker Ranch's Pu'uhue Section before being sent to O'ahu to manage Hawai'i Meat Company, which was majority owned by Parker Ranch.

Judge Martin Pence and Judge Ronald Moon
Ronald Moon After law school I came back to Hawai'i. This was in 1965 and the Big Five were still in power. None of the big law firms would allow a non-white to join. I was going from little law firm to little law firm because the big law firms wouldn't talk to me. I finally got to Judge Pence, Chief Judge of the United States District Court in Hawai'i. I explained to him that I had just graduated from the University of Iowa College of Law. He was from Kansas. He and I took to each other right away. He was a fantastic litigator in private practice on the Big Island as well as an avid hunter. He said, "Ron, why do you want to work for me?" I said, "I need a job. I got married in law school and I have two little kids. I'm living with my parents. I need money to get a home of

my own." He said, "You're hired!" It was primarily because I had gone to Iowa. (Laughter.) I was his law clerk for one year, which was the length of each of his clerkships.

He was an amazing guy. He came to Hawai'i in the 1930s as an insurance adjustor. He was an avid hunter and after working for a few years on O'ahu, he was told, "If you want to hunt, the Big Island is the place to go." So he went to the Big Island. I remember him telling me that he ran for office and he was the only Democrat to be elected that year. All the Republicans got voted into office. He was a thin, diminutive haole from the mainland, about 5' 5" or 5' 6" tall, but he was a very tough guy.

He said when he ran for the prosecutor's office, he had to learn pidgin English because all the voters were immigrants, from the Philippines, Japan, or Korea. He said the majority of the voters were plantation workers and he would have to go out there and speak to them. He said learning pidgin was very difficult, but he mastered it. When I clerked in his courtroom there would be people who would speak only in pidgin and he could converse with them. They were shocked! Here was this haole guy speaking their language. And that's how he got voted into office. His reputation in the community was fantastic as a judge as well, because he could relate to people and communicate with them. He settled most of his cases with compromises by each party. That was unexpected from a judge.

JG *Did you have to brush up on your pidgin or was your pidgin good already?*

RM It was just natural for me. (Laughter.) English was my second language! After my one-year clerkship, I worked in the prosecutor's office and loved it! In those days, prosecutors would go with the police on gambling raids in Chinatown. We got involved in the prosecution of the cockfight raids in Wai'anae as a result of being on the scene. That didn't cause any conflict of interest.

Born in Waipahu in 1940, I was proud to serve as Chief Justice of the Hawai'i State Supreme Court from 1993 to 2003.

Clarence T.C. Ching and Sam Damon
Raymond Tam During World War II everything was rationed and Hawai'i was under martial law. You couldn't buy all the gasoline you wanted; you were given a coupon and you could buy ten gallons per month or some figure like that. You couldn't buy all the sugar, butter, rice, or all the liquor that you wanted. Sam Damon, head of the Damon Estate, loved his booze, so my uncle Clarence made sure he got all the whiskey he wanted by using everybody else's ration coupons. They became the very best of friends.

World War II ended in 1945 and rationing ended in 1947. Uncle Clarence was going to San Francisco, and it just so happened that Sam Damon was going to San Francisco. They met at the airport. In those days they didn't have reserved seating, so Clarence and Sam Damon sat together and enjoyed the trip. On the plane over the Pacific, Sam Damon said, "Clarence, you want to buy the ahupua'a[17] of Moanalua?" My uncle said, "Sure. How much?" And Sam Damon said, "Eight million dollars." Now in those days eight million sounded like eight trillion zillion dollars. My uncle laughed and said, "I don't even have eight thousand! I cannot pay you." And Sam Damon said, "Clarence, I trust you. As you develop, you will pay me." And on a handshake, high over the Pacific, with no lawyers involved, no CPAs or real estate agents, they made one of the biggest private land deals in Hawai'i.

The POW and the Shinto Shrine

Frank Padgett After law school graduation, I missed the deadline for taking the bar in Hawai'i, so I had to wait a year. I took the exam in 1948 and passed. That day my senior law partner, Garner Anthony, came to me and said, "Tomorrow I've got this case in federal court, where the Alien Property Custodian is confiscating a Shinto shrine, Kotohira Jinsha."[18] I was a Japanese prisoner of war for nine months in Japan during World War II and here I was representing a Shinto shrine against the American government. It was a hell of way to start your law practice, the first day after you pass the bar! (Laughter.)

A newspaper journalist thought this was the best story she had ever heard and made an article out of it for the American press. My mother got a call from the Indianapolis newspaper asking if she had heard about Frank. She said, "Yes. He sent me a letter and said he had passed the bar." They said, "No, that isn't the story. He beat up on the government attorneys!"

---

[17] Literally, "from the mountain to the sea." The Damon Tract went from Tripler Army Hospital all the way to what was first called John Rodgers Airport, then Honolulu International Airport, and now is Daniel K. Inouye International Airport.

[18] His first case was representing a Shinto shrine in Kalihi Valley on the island of O'ahu. The case involved the seizure of the Kotohira Jinsha temple by the federal government's Alien Property Custodian in June 1948 and the subsequent attempt to sell the property in 1949, on the grounds that the Shinto religion was enemy-tainted and associated with emperor worship.

Ruth Goodsill and Dr. Patrick Lai
Ruth Goodsill There came a point in my life when all my physicians were retiring. It was rather unusual for a Caucasian woman to select a Chinese doctor, but that is what I did when I chose Patrick Theodore Lai, MD[19] to be my physician. I got an excellent doctor and a great friend. He and I were devoted to each other and he remained my primary care physician until he retired!

Don Ho and Linda Coble
Linda Coble When I first got to Hawai'i I worked taking pictures in Waikīkī restaurants. I would walk up and down Kalākaua, taking pictures and selling them to the people. With so many couples here on R&R, it was a great business. I had a big Nikon camera in one hand and a wad of cash in the other. Nobody ever hurt me, kicked me, or stole from me.

After that I would go see Don Ho at the International Market Place. We'd sit in the front row where all the broads sat and every once in a while he would call me up to do "Hey La Di La Di Lo." At Christmas time I would sing, "Don is like Santa Claus I hear, Hey La Di La Di Lo. He only comes but once a year, Hey La Di La Di Lo." The grandmas would just die laughing. "Uncle Don" and I were so close. I had relationships with local people on both sides of the law. I would be friends with "the Family," as it was called, and at the same time the police trusted me.

Arthur Fink and the Men of the 442nd
John Fink One of my dad's customers in the jewelry business in Hawai'i was Tommy Kakesako whose store, Kakesako Brothers Jewelers, was in the heart of downtown. Tommy was a gentleman and a member of the 442nd, the most decorated troop in World War II. My father had lost 85 percent of his hearing in World War II, and they both fought in Italy, so there was a natural bond between them.

Tommy said to my father, "You should join us at the DAV [Disabled American Veterans] down at Ke'ehi Lagoon." So, my father goes down there, and they take to him! They made him an honorary member of the 442nd. They called him Kazuo, which I believe means "first son" in Japanese. My mother, Alice, became Kazuka because they had to give her a Japanese name, too. Here are all these wonderful, incredible heroes and Arthur Fink, the Jewish kid from New York.

---

[19] Dr. Lai was born in 1927 and died in 2006.

I got to meet these guys when I was a sports announcer on television. We covered University of Hawai'i sports at KHNL-TV. When they would have a function at Ke'ehi Lagoon, my father would say, "You've got to come down." I said, "Dad, it's your thing. I don't want to intrude." He said, "No, these guys love you. You *are* UH sports to them and these guys live and die with UH sports." So I would go down there and they would say, "Hey, John. How are the Wahine [UH women's volleyball] going to do this year?" I loved talking to them.

I get choked up thinking about it. These guys were heroes. They were discriminated against, their families were sent to camps in California, which was a crime, and yet they helped save this country. All of them were injured in the war and they were now in their seventies and eighties and still passionate. I have a lot of compassion for them. These guys never complained. They did what they had to do for the country they loved.

I'll never forget one time when I said, "Dad, I can't come this time. I'm the emcee at a big event." He said, "These guys will go until 10:00 p.m. Just come afterwards." They were putting on a scholarship/fundraiser where Tommy Kakesako would donate jewelry, the plant guy would donate flowers and plants, and another guy would donate stuff from GEM Stores. I came in while they were raffling things off, this frickin' TV guy, and one of the guys—it might have been Tommy, it might have been Jake Jichako or Alan Nakamura—said, "Hey! John Fink is here! Come on up and say a few words." I said, "Why are you calling *me* up when *you* guys are the heroes?" I still get emotional. (Chokes up.) I love them. ✤

Voices in a Racial Melting Pot

"Halekulani," Huc-Mazelet Luquiens etching

CHAPTER 5

Voices of Changing Land Use

ʻĀina Then and Now

I feel humbled by the honesty and passion with which people addressed difficult topics with me. One of these topics was land reform then and now. Far be it from me to know which answers were right and which were wrong, I leave that for others to determine. However, I am honored to share opinions from interviewees who were on different sides of the issues.

> **Moses Haia** The Great Mahele[20] happened as an attempt to prevent any further attacks on the Hawaiian Kingdom's sovereignty. One third of the property went to the Kingdom; one third went to the *aliʻi*, and one third to the *makaʻaina*, the commoners. Commoners could make legal claims of ownership for their *kuleana,* but ownership was such a foreign concept that not many Hawaiians did it. Hawaiians may have made a *kuleana* claim in the past, and then been excluded from their land by fences and gates, or perhaps they had to move off the land for a job. Or they did not know how to protect their rights. Out of all the lands that were available to Hawaiian commoners, only 23,000 acres actually got into the hands of Hawaiian people. Thousands of acres ended up in the hands of the Big Five and the king's family and the chiefs.

---

[20] HawaiiHistory.org: The Mahele: Under the reign of Kamehameha III, Hawaiʻi's traditional system of land use underwent drastic change. Guided by foreign advisors, the king divided lands that had formerly been held in common and administered by chiefs and their *konohiki*, or overseers. The Mahele allocated 23 percent of land in the Islands to the king (called crown lands); 40 percent comprised konohiki lands to be divided among 245 chiefs; and 37 percent was declared government lands, to be awarded to commoners who worked the land as active tenants. An appointed Land Commission and Court of Claims administered the land division. The Mahele was followed in 1850 by the Kuleana Act, which established fee simple ownership of land. Historical land tenants were required to document their claims to specific parcels in order to gain permanent title. Once granted, a kuleana plot was entirely independent of the traditional ahupuaʻa in which it was situated and it could also be sold to parties with no historical ties to the area.

In 2017 [Facebook CEO] Mark Zuckerberg purchased 600 acres of land on Kauaʻi and immediately filed Quiet Title Actions in an attempt to acquire title to the land. Within those 600 acres were a number of kuleana lands that were originally in the hands of Hawaiians. Zuckerberg's lawyers said, "Nobody lives there or has used it for at least twenty years, so we claim adverse possession." If they had won the case, any rights of Hawaiians or descendants would have gone away. "Since Hawaiian descendants didn't even know they have an interest in that land, what is the big deal?" That *is* the big deal—that people don't know their ancestors worked that land or made a claim for it, so their heirs can't inherit it.

When Zuckerberg filed his suit, I, as executive director of the Native Hawaiian Legal Corporation, was asked to write an editorial. A few days after the editorial, Zuckerberg pulled all his lawsuits saying, "We are sorry; we did not understand the history and want to find a more *pono* way to go forward." Zuckerberg bringing this issue to light in his suit has made people more aware of this issue.[21]

As an example of a mismanaged kuleana land claim, the Haia family had land in Lahaina on Maui. My dad, Moses Kalei Nahonapiʻilani Haia, Jr., was a full-blooded Hawaiian with twenty-four siblings. Dad was named as a defendant in the Lahaina suit because his great-great-grandfather had a claim. This was before I started working in this field. We were disappointed that the court on Maui decided in this specific case that Pioneer Mill owned my dad's interest in the parcel by adverse possession. It was not right.

After the Great Mahele, the Republic of Hawaiʻi became the Territory of Hawaiʻi, and the Kingdom's land was ceded to the government. Ceded lands are public land and there are a lot of laws that impact what you do on that property. Mauna Kea and Haleakalā are conservation district lands, which must be kept in their natural state. If you wish to do any sort of development on such land, you must file an application with the Department of Land and Natural Resources to prove your impact on the land will be negligible.

Hawaiʻi is unique in the respect that you don't necessarily have the right to exclude people from your property. If a person can establish that he or she has a right to go on your "less than fully developed" property to engage in traditional and customary Native Hawaiian practices—religious, spiritual, or cultural—and it does not unreasonably impact the landowner's rights, the landlord has to let them engage in these practices on their land. For example,

---

[21] https://www.usatoday.com/story/tech/news/2017/01/27/zuckerberg-drops-Kauaʻi-land-suits-hawaii-quiet-title/97152332/

if you have ancestors buried in an area and you can establish that you are a direct descendent or that you are culturally related to them, then you can go to that property and engage in traditional Hawaiian burial practices. Hula *hālau* can go on land to gather *maile* or other plants for their dances.

In the mid-1990s a case about this went to the Supreme Court. Some huge landowners lobbied the legislators to come up with a bill that would require any person who claimed the right to go on someone else's land to engage in practices to register the right to do so or lose that right. For three days and three nights a group of Hawaiians camped out in the Capitol and demanded the legislators kill the bill. It did not take long for a couple of legislators to rip up the bill right in front of them. Today people can go on someone else's land to engage in traditional practices.

There is an argument that some Hawaiians are making that I totally disagree with. There are a number of Hawaiians who are arguing that land in Hawai'i remains held by Hawaiians and that anyone claiming interest in the land does not have any interest in the land unless they can show that they are a direct descendant of the original owner. The language these people rely on actually says that the awardee and his heirs and assignees hold title forever. People are trying to argue that an assignee can only mean family, but that is not the definition of assignee. An assignee can mean anyone. If you die without a will or transfer your property during your lifetime to get your land to your descendants, then you may have a claim to the property. But if you sell your property to someone or quitclaim your interest in the property to someone else, that person is an assignee. In this case, I come from a legal frame of reference and they come from emotion.

JG *It must be hard to walk that line.*

MH Yeah, it is.

Mitch D'Olier has worn many hats in his career: lawyer, president and CEO of Victoria Ward Limited, president and COO of Hawaiian Airlines, director of the Harold K. L. Castle Foundation, and president and CEO of the Castle Foundation and Kane'ohe Ranch Company. Here he shares a few insights into changes in Hawai'i land use over time.

Mitch D'Olier For many years there was very little fee simple land available to single-family homeowners in Hawai'i. One goal of the Hawai'i Democratic Revolution of 1954 was to change that. There was resentment toward big landowners, bad feelings on all sides, and fights about the prices. It went back to the hard feelings about the way workers had been treated on the plantations for so many years. Japanese Americans largely led the Democratic Revolution, and they wanted to own their own land; part of being a first-class citizen is owning your own land.

There was a legal question as to whether Kaneʻohe Ranch and other landowners could sell huge numbers of parcels of land to lessees and pay tax at capital gains rates. There was a provision in the tax laws to allow farmers to subdivide their fields and sell them off and get 90 percent capital gains. This ruling was to encourage urbanization of rural properties. There were some rules: You couldn't build the houses, you couldn't build the roads, but if all you did was subdivide and sell, you could get favorable capital gains tax treatment. Kaneʻohe Ranch and a lot of the other owners didn't build the roads and didn't build the houses; they had third parties do that. A ruling from the Internal Revenue Service allowed a for-profit for the first time to sell huge amounts of property and get a favorable capital gains rate. This freed a lot of land for fee simple purchase by Hawaiʻi's citizens. It was a socially significant event.

Kelvin Taketa told me that he was lucky to work at the Nature Conservancy at a time of hyper-growth. "It went from being a small part of the conservation world to becoming the largest conservation organization in the world and one of the ten largest non-profits in the United States."

Kelvin Taketa In my opinion, the 1978 Hawaiʻi Constitutional Convention's codification of sovereign rights had an unintended consequence: the demise of the Big Five local corporations. Third generations of some family landholders were coming of age and did not want to sit on their land; thus began the fracture and dissipation of a lot of family land-holding groups.

Jim Case was a corporate attorney in Hawaiʻi for 63 years. He reflects upon events in the late 1990s when many long-standing Bishop Estate residential leases were expiring.

James Case The most impact I had on Hawaiian land ownership in my law career was the fee conversion work I did. Fee conversion broke up the system so people could own their own land and not be subservient to some rich landowner. It was the second major revolution in Hawaiʻi land ownership after the Great Mahele.

I got into the fee conversion work when it was time to renegotiate rents with the Bishop Estate for the leasehold land in Kāhala. My thought was, "Rather than negotiating the rent, there is a law that has been passed that allows a group of landowners to force the landowner to sell the fee to the lessee for a fair price. Why don't we do that?" So we formed the Kāhala Community Association and forced the State to condemn the land. This involved buying the land from Kamehameha Schools and selling it to the landowners. On Oʻahu we went up the coast to every town between Diamond Head and Hawaiʻi Kai, one by one, negotiating the conversions.

Before that, large landowners held ownership of the land, Bishop Estate being the most important. But the Castle Ranch owned the entire windward side of Oʻahu and there were a whole bunch of landowners out toward Pearl Harbor and ʻAiea.

JG *Were there people who opposed this, and what was their point of view?*

JC There weren't any lessees who opposed it. Kamehameha Schools opposed it but eventually made a fortune in the conversion. They weren't making a fortune renting to the landowners. With the money from the sale, Bishop Estate was able to build campuses for Kamehameha Schools on all the islands.

When we got to one of the ahupuaʻa on the coast near Hawaiʻi Kai, the association went to the landowner and said, "You are earning one percent on the value of your land. We recommend that you form a community association, help it get started, and we will negotiate with it." They did that and got an eight percent return on their land. In that transaction we were still representing the community association but we advised the landowner that they would be better off selling their land.

The Bishop Estate took us all the way to the Supreme Court. I hired a law professor at Harvard Law School who did nothing but handle cases before the Supreme Court. He said, "This is a rent control case. The Supreme Court has already decided that rent controls are a matter of local jurisdiction, either the city or the state. I believe that we're going to win this case and I believe we may win it unanimously." The Supreme Court said, "We are not going to handle condemnation cases and decide what should or should not be done. City, state, and federal governments can do condemnations for a proper public purpose, but each local jurisdiction must decide what is a proper public purpose." We won that opinion 8-0.

Many years later, when my daughter-in-law was in law school, they studied condemnation. The law professor said, "The law on this case is completely settled. Read *Midkiff v. Kamehameha*." [*Kamaʻāina businessman Robert Midkiff was a major player in the Bishop Estate story.*] So she did, and *my* name is on the decision! She called me up and I told her all about it. *Midkiff v. Kamehameha* is the law on condemnation. It was a feudal system.

Neil Hannahs worked for Kamehameha Schools in the same time frame described by Jim Case above. Neil tells the story from a different point of view.

Neil Hannahs In the 1970s, land reform was a major issue. I accompanied [Bishop Estate trustee] Pinky and Laura Thompson to the United States Supreme Court to witness Bishop Estate's attorney get his hat handed to him. He was contesting the findings of fact that precipitated Hawaiʻi's use of eminent domain to condemn land of one private party [the lessors] to transfer its ownership to another private party [the lessees].

The state legislature had rationalized this controversial use of government power by claiming that Kamehameha Schools, or Bishop Estate as we were known back then, was part of an oligopoly of landownership in Hawaiʻi and this oligopoly unfairly controlled the market to the harm of citizen homeowners. They further argued that the use of the government's condemnation powers was necessary to break the oligopoly and liberate the market.

We were prepared to attack the validity of the legislature's findings of fact and the logic of expecting that lower prices would result from expanded fee simple land ownership. But the Supreme Court said, "We're not going to sit here in Washington and question what the Hawaiʻi legislature has done. What your legislature has done is well-nigh conclusive." We replied, "But it's lies! It's the tyranny of the majority abusing the rights of a minority of landowners. It upsets the equity of mutually accepted contracts that assured landowners the opportunity to recalibrate rent to current land values after giving the lessees the benefit of thirty years of fixed rent. We didn't tear up the contract when it favored the lessees; how can it be fair for government to help lessees escape their obligations when terms favor the landowner?"

Admittedly, these rent increases were very steep, because land values had increased remarkably in Hawaiʻi over the 1950s, '60s and '70s. It was an imperfect system: the lessee was hurt, the lessor was hurt, and it was a mess. To this day I think that a better designed residential leasehold system would temper the spiraling cost of housing that is causing locals to leave our state and is contributing to homelessness and a host of other social and economic problems. But back then there wasn't a lot of interest in repairing a system that had proven to be so polarizing. At the end of the day we were outnumbered, the legislature went the way of the votes, and the US Supreme Court deferred to the legislature.

Proponents of this use of condemnation, as well as the courts, said, "What is the problem? You'll receive fair financial compensation." But that did not take into account the cultural connection we had to these lands of the Kamehameha royal family. Bernice Pauahi Bishop, like other aliʻi, did not look upon land as a fungible economic asset that could be replaced by something else of equal or greater value. They realized that our very identity as a unique people on this planet was born in the adaptations we made to this particular set of islands and the practices that forged a worldview that differentiates us from the rest of mankind.

To assure this ongoing relationship, the aliʻi placed their lands into perpetual charitable trusts that were designed to provide services that would foster the well-being of their people. Not wanting to tie the hands of her future fiduciaries, Pauahi gave her trustees the power to sell lands with the caveat that such sales should not be the normal course and only executed if it serves the best interests of her trust. Leasing lands for residential use was a way to derive income from the land while also meeting Hawaiʻi's growing need for housing. At the end of the prescribed lease term, the lands were to be returned to the trust. It wasn't the most lucrative type of investment but it balanced our complex interests.

To collectively address issues such as land reform or processes for regulating development, landowners created the Land Use Research Foundation (LURF) and I served a stint as its president. I saw my role as bridging disparate constituencies and trying to get people to understand each other's perspective. As you might imagine, the landowners were very protective of their rights, sought efficiency and lower cost at every stage of the development approval process, and wanted government to make the infrastructure investments to support growth. That put landowners and developers at odds with those concerned about the environment or cultural practices or Hawaiʻi's historic sense of place and scale. Many of the landowners' antagonists were people I had come to know during my years of working in rural Hawaiian communities. I thought I might be able to de-villainize the view that each of the parties held of the other.

Since LURF's positions were dictated by the majority of its members, at times I found myself associated with testimony or policy changes that were land-rights oriented, and often not very favorable for cultural rights and practices. That really gnawed at me. I was determined to increase mutual understanding, but I realized that there was a risk that I might be judged as selling out my culture. I'll let others determine whether I succeeded or failed, but I definitely developed a better understanding of what divides the parties.

Some of Kamehameha Schools' efforts to navigate in the space between our development desires and cultural identity were not very authentic. One of the more outlandish positions came from attorneys we retained for the Waiāhole Ditch water controversy. We were among the leeward landowners who wanted to continue to use waters diverted from windward streams for various agricultural and miscellaneous activities. We proposed to use our allocation for construction dust control and golf course irrigation under a big urban development plan for our Waiawa lands. Our position was disputed by the Hawaiian community as failing to meet the constitutional standards of beneficial use, so we found ourselves aligned with other development interests in conflict with our own beneficiaries.

In an ill-conceived effort to be both developer and Hawaiian, we asserted that our ali'i lineage gave us a superior claim to other applicants. It was an elitist argument that not only lacked cultural precedent, but more importantly reflected values that contradicted a Hawaiian worldview which holds that royal status comes with a profound responsibility to serve and benefit the people. Instead, we were attempting to leverage our ali'i status for more privilege. Our beneficiaries called BS and condemned this position as a fraudulent abuse of our culture. Once again I found myself between a rock and hard place. These kinds of experiences were rough at the time but were beneficial because they provided a crucible for forging my own beliefs.

Fortunately, to help me navigate such moments, I had the blessing of what we would call *hōkūpa'a*, or guiding stars. Some very extraordinary people took me under their wings—Papa Lyman, Pinky Thompson, Winona Beamer, Auntie Gladys Brandt, Jack Darvill, and Fred Cachola, the man who hired me. They served as wonderful examples of leaders with the courage to stand up and fight for our culture and our people. They were older than I was, so in many ways it was so much harder for them. I count my blessings for having these brilliant, amazing leaders to serve as my navigational guides.

Around the Dining Room Table

Every evening the Goodsill family ate together at the round table in our formal dining room. When my brother John was very young and sitting on telephone books, Mama spread newspaper beneath his chair to catch spills, especially rice! We went around the table and took turns reporting on our days. We were taught to bring with us some information to share—something about our academic day, athletics, a new idea, a story about a friend. The overriding rule was that we spoke one at a time so that everyone was heard, even our parents. We often had guests to dinner, and the rules for talking applied to them as well.

Mama was a good cook, and the food was always delicious and plentiful. When she served special dishes such as mushrooms, artichokes, or asparagus—delicacies in Hawai'i at that time—or a soufflé she had made, she would tell us that we could try it, but that she and Papa preferred that we didn't eat too much. (In fact, they didn't care if we didn't like it at all, as that would leave more for them.) As a result, exotic and specialty items became our particular favorites.

As Papa was building his law practice, my parents often did business entertaining at home. I suspect they chose dinner parties at home for various reasons; it wasn't as loud or distracting, or as expensive as a restaurant. They were raising a large family, had kids in expensive schools, and were paying off a house and saving for great vacations.

Here's one story that took place around our dining room table.

Randy Roth My wife, Susie, and I attended a dinner party at the Goodsill home in May of 1997. Herb and Jean Cornuelle were there, as were Bud and Dee Smyser and Dwayne and Marti Steele. Herb and Dwayne were both confidants of Oz Stender, one of five Bishop Estate trustees.

Two years earlier, the *Wall Street Journal* had described the Bishop Estate as the nation's wealthiest charitable trust and added that the five trustees enjoyed "so much clout no one stops them." It was true. Local media in those days rarely questioned the trustees, and the local officials responsible for trustee oversight—state attorneys general, court-appointed masters, and probate judges—consistently chose not to scrutinize conduct of Bishop Estate trustees despite indications of serious misconduct.

I had become convinced it was just a matter of time before the IRS would revoke Bishop Estate's tax exemption because of trustee misconduct. I also believed the selection of Bishop Estate trustees by the state's Supreme Court justices was corrupting judicial selection.

The guests at the Goodsill dinner party discussed these concerns and also the potential impact of a dramatic protest by the Kamehameha School's 'ohana (family) just five days earlier. More than a thousand marchers had proceeded solemnly from Princess Bernice Pauahi Bishop's final resting place at Mauna 'Ala to the trustees' downtown headquarters to present a list of grievances. These same people had previously defended the trustees from any and all criticism, but now they were the ones protesting! It suggested that they and the rest of the public would be open to a hard-hitting legal analysis by a law professor like me.

Toward the end of the dinner conversation, Herb suggested that Oz might be willing to share with me his specific concerns about the other trustees. When I called Oz the next day, it was clear that Herb had already told him about the dinner conversation and had encouraged him to meet with me.

The involvement of your father and the others at the dinner was probably also important to Oz. It was as though I enjoyed a halo effect by having gained their trust.

At the first two of what would eventually be eight meetings with Oz, I explained that he had significant legal exposure by virtue of having been a Bishop Estate trustee during many years of apparent trustee misconduct without effectively blowing the whistle on the others, and perhaps also for sharing information with me. I told him I wasn't there as his lawyer and that he should probably hire a lawyer to watch out for his personal interests. Without a moment's hesitation, he said, "Don't worry about me. What happens to me isn't important compared to what happens to the trust."

I eventually gathered additional information from dozens of other insiders, such as senior staff members at Bishop Estate, retired Supreme Court justices, past and current lawyers for the trust, deputy attorneys general, former court-appointed masters, judges familiar with the role that trustee selection had been playing in the selection of Supreme Court justices, current and former members of the Judicial Selection Commission, key legislators, county prosecutors, and senior members of a former governor's cabinet—but none of them provided the quantity and quality of information provided by Oz.

After putting everything together in the form of a long essay, I asked Federal District Court Judge Sam King if he would be willing to comment on my latest draft. He had been one of my many sources so he already knew of the project. After reading the draft essay slowly, Sam said, "What you've written is good, but it's not going to accomplish anything because it's coming from a haole from Kansas." This was his characteristically direct way of saying the messenger would be as important as the message.

I thought the chances of a sitting federal judge getting personally involved were not good, but I asked if he'd be willing to co-author the essay. He immediately responded, "I will if it's okay with my wife." The next day he called me to say Anne had given it her blessing, but that we needed to recruit several more co-authors. Within twenty-four hours, Gladys Brandt, Monsignor Charles Kekumano, and Walter Heen had joined us. And within days of that, the five of us had taken apart and rewritten the essay, which the *Honolulu Star-Bulletin* ended up publishing under the title, "Broken Trust."[22] As Judge King and I would later detail in a book of the same name, the justices quickly got out of the trustee-selection business, all five Bishop Estate trustees were ousted, and the IRS agreed not to revoke the trust's tax exemption.

Oz's help had been a lynchpin of sorts, and his willingness to help can probably be traced directly to the dinner conversation at your parents' round dining room table.

Another story, affecting me very personally, came from around our table. We grew up as close friends of the Carl Mason family. Michael, Lynnie, and Jeanie were similar in age to the Goodsill kids, and Jean, their mother, was one of my mother's closest friends. Lynnie married Moses Haia, who is handsome, charming, and likeable. One evening early in their marriage, he and Lynnie came to dinner. The conversation turned to Hawaiian legal

---

[22] *Broken Trust: Greed, Mismanagement & Political Manipulation at America's Largest Charitable Trust* by Samuel P. King and Randall W. Roth. Available in free online format at https://www.hawaii.edu/news/2017/10/03/broken-trust-free-online-format/.

issues. Moses expressed some controversial views. I remember the temperature at my father's end of the room getting cooler—and hotter at my mother's end. I could tell, even though I didn't understand the issues, that my parents did not agree with some of Moses's assessments. After this I wasted a lot of years not talking to Moses about his work or his views.

In 2018 I finally got over myself, and we talked openly. I asked him if he was in touch with his Hawaiian identity as a young man, and whether being Hawaiian was important to his father and family members.

> **Moses Haia** My family was superior at lūʻau preparations. They were untouchable at that. But no one spoke Hawaiian or practiced other customs. There was a time in Hawaiian history [1898] when the Hawaiian language was outlawed, and our traditions and customs were being lost. Our family assimilated into American life. I ignored my Hawaiian heritage growing up and, in fact, grew up apologetic for being Hawaiian.
>
> Then I became pretty extreme about Hawaiian rights. I have no doubt that at the time I came to dinner at your parents' house, I wanted to impress your father with how much I knew. And in doing so, I probably stepped on his toes.

He and I both laughed at the thought. What I hadn't known but learned from our conversation was that he and Lynnie had many conversations with my parents about these issues after that first one, and over time they educated each other and came to a consensus. Moses has warm feelings about his relationship with both my parents.

> **MH** I don't think you give your dad enough credit. He had his clients' best interests at heart, and at the same time he welcomed me into his house. Your parents invited us to participate in their life events. They let me sit at their dinner table a number of times. I respect your father and mother. I actually boast about having known them.

I am very proud of Moses and the work he has done as executive director of the Native Hawaiian Legal Corporation. He bravely walks the line between parties with differing opinions. He has engaged and educated many local corporate leaders just as he did my parents.

Our dining table was the setting for many of my interviews for these oral histories. Even though Mama and Papa are gone now, the table still occupies a place in our family memories, as well as in the memories of others in the greater Island community.

Taro Talk

The root vegetable taro thrives in Hawai'i's soil and climate but needs plenty of water. It was once the staple of the Hawaiian diet and held an important spiritual place in the center of Hawaiian agricultural society. It still remains sacred to many.

In the 1970s, John Reppun and his brothers were farming taro in the Waiāhole and Waikāne valleys. They relied on natural watersheds for irrigation. The brothers occasionally struggled to find enough water to grow their crops. Over the years, water from the watersheds had been diverted to irrigate agricultural lands, golf courses, and housing developments. The lawsuit Reppun v. Board of Water Supply challenged the removal of water from the watershed, based on the common-use laws established by ancient Hawaiian custom.

One simple but profound story helps introduces us to the lo'i.

John Reppun In the midst of our fight for the return of water to the streams to restore the taro lands, Marian Kelly and a professor from Japan showed up at an event we held at our taro patches. We were lamenting the fact that because of the gap created when taro farming stopped around here, we could find no experts in Hawaiian taro cultivation. Marian suggested we talk to the Okinawan community in Hawai'i, because Okinawa was one of the only other places where taro was grown in wetland fashion. Okinawan, Hawaiian, and Chinese families have intermarried over the years and as a group they have preserved quite a bit of lo'i knowledge.

Dr. Don Mitchell was a haole historian of Hawaiian culture who wrote a lot of the early curriculum for Kamehameha Schools. He lived up in 'Āhuimanu Valley and was close friends with my mom and dad. He grew beautiful bananas and we'd sell them at market for him. I knew Bob Nakata because we were both involved in the lawsuit against the Board of Water Supply about diverting water from taro streams. One day I asked Dr. Mitchell if he knew the taro farmer Old Man Nakata, Bob's father. "No, but I'd like to."

So we march out to Nakata's lo'i and find him there with his shovel. His shovel handle is always wet; he uses it like a fulcrum to pry out taro, so the handle has a beautiful bend to it because he is always leaning on it, you see? Dr. Mitchell pulls up his pants legs, goes into the lo'i, shakes hands with Nakata and starts speaking to him in Hawaiian. Here is this haole historian talking to an Okinawan farmer in Hawaiian! I literally saw the lo'i become a place where cultures could intersect.

Oz mused upon the ways he saw local customs and even the economic system change following WWII.

Oz Stender I was born in Honolulu in 1931 and grew up in Hauʻula in a very traditional Hawaiian family in the middle of the Depression. My sister always said she didn't know we were poor until somebody told us we were poor. We thought we had a great life. We had two and a half acres of land and grew all kinds of stuff and we raised animals. We lived right on the ocean, so fishing was a way of life. And we were right next to a river.

When World War II came, things changed. Before that people could live off the land. After the war money became the medium and people started working for money and let the taro patches go to ruin. The beaches were all closed off with concertina wire, so fishing was not easy. We stopped hunting in the mountains. My grandfather's hours as park keeper at Hauʻula Park were reduced, and someone had to watch him to make sure he did not "collaborate with the enemy." All our Japanese friends disappeared. The war changed everything.

Lawyer William Tam is a former deputy attorney general for the State of Hawaiʻi, who represented the state in water matters for more than twenty years. He was instrumental in drafting the Hawaiʻi Water Code[23] and later served as the Department of Land and Natural Resources' deputy director of the State Water Commission. Here he shares a legal perspective on ancient and modern taro farming practices.

William Tam Ancient Hawaiian practices diverted surface water from streams to the taro patches, which held the water, releasing it later into the ocean where it nourished the reefs and fed the fish. Hawaiians shared water based upon: 1) need and 2) did you do your share of the labor? The job of the konohiki[24] was to sort out sharing arrangements: "Maybe *you* get some in the morning and *you* get some in the afternoon. *You* didn't do your labor so you're going to get a little bit less today. This area has a lot of trees and is cool, so *you* don't need as much water to keep the taro patch cool. (To grow taro, you have to keep water below seventy-six degrees; otherwise you get taro rot.) This area is in the midday sun, so *you* need more water to keep it cool."

When stream water was diverted out of the watersheds to sugar plantations on the leeward sides of the islands, the previous ecological balance was

---

[23] Hawaiʻi Revised Statutes Chapter 174C (1987)
[24] Konohiki are the heads of ahupuaʻa land divisions under the chief of a particular district. They managed land use, fishing rights, and the people who resided in the ahupuaʻa.

upset and the taro patches suffered. Many dried up. Downstream uses were undermined when water was diverted away from the stream and the ahupuaʻa.

In 1973 the Hawaiʻi Supreme Court decided a six-decade long water fight over the Hanapēpē river water on Kauaʻi.[25] The Territory of Hawaiʻi owned public land between the upstream and *mauka* landowner, Robinson [Gay & Robinson sugar plantation], and the downstream and *makai* landowner, McBryde [Plantation]. McBryde sued the upstream Robinson to leave more water in the stream. The Hawaiʻi Supreme Court reaffirmed historic taro water (appurtenant) rights and re-established the ancient Hawaiian custom of sharing surface water under the Western legal doctrine of riparianism.

One of the essential characteristics of a riparian, or shared use, surface water system is that water cannot be removed or diverted out of a watershed without depriving downstream landowners with riparian rights of their shared uses. As a result, sugar plantations on the leeward and central portions of the main Hawaiian Islands, which had developed elaborate "out of watershed" diversions and transfer systems, were no longer in compliance with the law, although the Court did not enjoin the conduct.

In the United States, there are two basic approaches to managing surface water. Riparianism is a shared-use doctrine where every property owner adjacent to a river shares in a non-quantified shared-use right to the stream water, When there is not enough water, every landowner shares in the cutbacks.[26] Prior appropriation is a first-in, last-out inventory model. In a drought, the first landowner that took or "appropriated" water may continue to use the water until all other later or junior appropriators give up all their water use. Water is not shared.

In 1982 the Hawaiʻi Supreme Court decided *Reppun v. Board of Water Supply*, reaffirming taro (appurtenant) rights in an eloquent description of ancient Hawaiian water practices. Appurtenant rights are quantifiable (unlike riparian rights) and are determined by the amount of water needed to grow taro on a particular parcel of land in the same manner as the land was used at the time of the Mahele in 1848. Appurtenant rights have priority over other water rights and are constitutionally protected. They do not lapse due to periodic non-use.

---

[25] *McBryde v. Robinson,* 54 Hawaiʻi 174 (1973).
[26] In all systems, water may only be put to a "beneficial use." Water may never be wasted. [Groundwater is governed by the shared "correlative" rights doctrine which in many ways mirrors the riparian surface rights doctrine. *City Mill v. Honolulu,* 30 Hawaiʻi 912 (1929).]

In 1987, after nine years of public negotiations, two advisory commissions, multiple court proceedings, and a water roundtable that fashioned a working draft, the Hawai'i legislature adopted the Hawai'i Water Code, which provides a comprehensive, forward-looking system for addressing water in Hawai'i.[27] In many ways, the decision to finally adopt a water code was a tribute to the widely shared view that people in Hawai'i want the most important decisions about water and natural resources to be made in Hawai'i, not in a boardroom on the mainland or in some foreign country.

In 1997, the State Water Commission decided the Waiāhole (O'ahu) Contested Case Hearing water rights case. In 2000, the Hawai'i Supreme Court issued a landmark decision adopting a broad public trust view of Hawai'i's water law.[28]

Since the Waiāhole decision, water disputes have moved to Maui where conflicts over the 'Iao aquifer and the Waihe'e and East Maui streams continue, after more than thirty years of proceedings and multiple appeals to the Hawai'i Supreme Court. Community struggles over Molokai ground water and Kaua'i surface waters continue as well.

It has taken fifty years of legal and community effort to wrest some measure of public control over Hawai'i's land and water resources. The framework created by the pioneering and landmark legal battles of the 1970s, 1980s, and 1990s toward a public, not private, decision-making process and the public trust values in Hawai'i's water and natural resources has changed the course of Hawai'i's future. There are no guarantees, but the tools and methods are now established. It is up to Hawai'i's people to use them. ❦

---

[27] Hawai'i Revised Statutes Chapter 174C (1987).
[28] *Waiāhole Contested Case,* 94 Hawaii 97 (2000)—public trust doctrine applied to Windward stream water.

Parker Ranch paniolo Fred ""Nesso" "Nepia" Maertens

CHAPTER 6

Voices of the Ranchers

Generations of Ranchers
I have an affinity for ranchers. This is because my father's sister, Jane Goodsill Hibbard, married a rancher and my cousins and their families are all ranchers. My siblings and I have spent a lot of time with these cousins and learned a great deal about ranching as a business and a passion.

Whit Hibbard is a fourth-generation Montana rancher and a protégé of the legendary livestock expert Bud Williams. Whit is an expert on low-stress stockmanship, is the publisher/editor of Stockmanship Journal, *and has written dozens of articles for* Drovers Magazine, On Pasture, Progressive Cattleman, *and others. He is also a Doctor of Human Science and when we get together you can imagine the depth of our conversations.*

An article by Tamara Choat for the Tri-State Livestock News *on October 20, 2016 offers this description:*

> "The term 'low stress livestock handling' was coined by stockman Allan Nation in 1990 to describe the unique livestock handling of Bud Williams. It is defined as a livestock-centered, behaviorally correct, psychologically oriented, ethical and humane method of working livestock which is based on mutual communication and understanding.
>
> "The romantic image of the dashing American cowboy—rope in hand racing after stampeding longhorns under the stars—is deeply embedded alongside the ranching industry. Despite the bravado, most ranchers realize that fast and wild is not necessarily the best way to handle livestock. However, good stockmanship is more than just calm and slow—it's a series of doctrines, principles, and methods of working with cattle in non-conventional ways."

James Case I grew up on Kauaʻi on a sugar cane plantation. Sugar was king, pineapple was number two and ranching was number three. Each island was separate from the other. The steamer only went twice a week from Kauaʻi to Honolulu. If it arrived on Kauaʻi on, say, Monday and Friday in the early mornings, business executives would go to the post office and bring the mail back to their offices. They would spend all day answering mail and getting it on the boat that night.

As noted in my acknowledgments, Willie Lum and Riley Smith were members in good standing of what I call my "Voices Posse." Willie expanded the ethnic coverage of my project with many introductions, while Riley paved the way for the interviews with the ranchers on Hawai'i Island.

When speaking to these ranchers, I asked about livestock management practices, and they all gave thoughtful responses. But a broader theme developed, which included the evolution of age-old ranching and land management practices. It became apparent to me that "low-stress cowboy management" was just as important as livestock treatment. I was also impressed by the respect with which these aging ranchers regard the younger generation.

JG *How well do you remember Frank Greenwell, your grandfather?*

Jimmy Greenwell Very well. He was a classic gentleman—tall, lanky, wise, and humble. He was my idol. I remember, as a kid, going up and staying with him. Many days we went into the *makai* country, and what they called the *kula* country—the lowlands—where they had cattle down in the rocks and the sticks and the lava. Grandpa would be on his horse and I would be behind him on a horse or sometimes a mule.

In contrast to kids today who have to have a bottle of water before they go down the street, we didn't take water on these long, hot rides. We would get on our horses up at Grandpa's house and my grandmother would come out with two tall glasses of water. You drank your glass of water and off you went. That was your water for the day. Nana would make these white-bread-and-cheese sandwiches. When you are thirsty that is hard to swallow! Coming home from the real low country there would be mountain apples or a mango tree. Oftentimes from his horse Granddad would pick a mango. He'd get his pocketknife out and peel the mango. "Here, son, have one of these." That got us by.

The business is more expensive to run now. Expenses are going up and it's a question of whether your revenues can keep pace. With some good, young, energetic, fresh eyes looking at the challenges, important operational changes have been implemented. Over the past five years we have gone from many small herds, say eighty head, rotating between two or three paddocks, to 300 head rotating through ten or twelve paddocks. In essence, fewer larger herds rotate more frequently and the paddocks rest for longer.

It's more challenging when you brand cattle or wean the calves or have to move a lot of cattle with a really small crew. Our crews have shrunk from eight and a half cowboys to four. Out of necessity, we are trying to do more with less and trying to take better care of the land. It is a more progressive way to do it, but has some real risks as well as real rewards. I think we are all satisfied that it is a better model. In the process we had to go back and rework a lot of infrastructure; we had water troughs that were designed to water eighty head and now they are watering 300. Our equipment has to be more mobile. We have more ATVs.

But most of all, we have an incredible cowboy crew that makes it happen! It's hard to get good cowboys. There was a lot of transition around the time I retired, and the new guys came in and literally took the bull by the horns and made some really significant and exciting changes. I give this next generation, as well as the guys who work for them, a ton of credit. It is tough work.

Carl Carlson Growing up (on Maui), my choices for career were either plantation life or cowboy life. When I was in the fifth grade, Eddie Rogers had a ranch and his son and I were good friends. Eddie had a string of racehorses. Horse racing was big and the racetracks were at the old Kahului Fairgrounds. Eddie's son often invited me to go riding. After we were hooked on riding, Mr. Rogers said, "Here's the deal. You fella wanna ride horse? You have to feed the cows first." He always referred to us as "you fella." Pretty soon, "You fella wanna ride horse? You have to feed the cows and clean the pigpen." Our chores just kept expanding and the amount of time that we could ride horses decreased. (Laughter.)

All of the plantations back in the old days had ranches, and Wailuku Sugar had a ranch and a dairy. You have land that you own or control that won't grow sugar cane, you don't leave it fallow. You produce something on it. So they ranched it, but in the end that didn't work because of the cost of labor. Then they leased it out to other ranchers. For a period of time my dad was the manager of what was called Waiheʻe Ranch.

JG *Low-stress livestock management is popular these days. Did you know anything about that back then?*

CC No. Back then the ranches all had breaking pens for the horses. You break the horses in a round pen to train them. Now they talk about horse whispering. You no longer break a horse; you train a horse. When you train a horse, you ask him permission. It took me a few years to learn how to do that. When I tried to put my horse in my horse trailer the first time and he didn't want to go, it wasn't his choice, it was mine. We weren't real gentle on helping him get in the trailer in the old days. Eventually we learned that the easiest way to get them into the trailer was to bother them. So in essence what you do is you stand behind them and have a little switch with something on the end and you just keep shaking it. They don't like that and eventually they learn that if they step forward, they get further away from the switch and eventually they walk into the trailer. Takes a little bit of time, and it's different than trying to whack them with a whip or a rope.

The thing with cattle is they are just like people. It's hard to make them go where they don't want to go. They are creatures of routine. We are creatures of routine. If you want to take them someplace, design the timing based on when they want to go and it becomes easier. Design your facilities with this in mind. Cowboys like to drive them in the morning and get the job done. A cow likes to go to water late in the afternoon. So if you try to drive them in the morning, you are forcing them to do something they don't want to do. If you go late in the afternoon, they'll just run down to the water.

I learned a lot from Freddy Rice, who was the son of Oskie Rice. Freddy was at Kahuku Ranch and then he came to Maui. He designed a system that he learned about in New Zealand. Basically it was one water trough and a pen with four or five pastures around it. He moved the cattle once a week after they had grazed their pasture down. The pasture that had been grazed would then grow and the livestock moved to a different pasture. I learned that particular design from Freddy, and how easily it worked. It's only one water trough. Think about it, would you rather have fresh food or leftovers? Cows are the same way. You go up to the gate of the fresh pasture and they are all waiting.

Michael "Corky" Bryan I started working in the slaughter plant and knocked (killed) my first animal when I was twelve years old. From then on, I was hooked on the whole thing. I loved the guys and I got a hell of an education from all of them—in many, many ways! I was the guy who was there during summers, Christmas vacation, Easter vacation. I was always down there, working. Alex Napier became the manager and he took me under his wing. I was thirteen or fourteen and he said, "I can't pay you, but I'll give you a quarter of a beef for this amount of work." Eventually I had a regular job, which was to be the knocker and scale the beef and wash it. In the summertime when guys took their vacations, I did whatever their job was plus the knocking.

I learned my station in the hierarchy by starting on the bottom. The foreman was a Japanese fellow, Masaru Sugai, and he really took care of me. He would pick me up at the house at 5:00 or 5:30 in the morning, knocking the first calf or steer at 6:00 a.m.

How did things change over time? At one ranch, we started out with about 1,500 cows and twelve people, and when I left there were 2,000 cows and four people. At the ranch I work at now, two of us work 650 cows. When I got there they had fourteen different bunches of cattle and now they have two.

JG *How about low-stress livestock management? Do you believe in that?*

MB Oh yes. It's just intrinsic to me. Treat the livestock as you would like to be treated. I can ride through the cattle and get this close to a cow and she won't even move. The calves are the same way. When I move them, I just call them to where I want them to go. Now they know where they are supposed to go, so when they see the ATV they are already moving, even if it isn't time! You open the gate and get out of the way.

I worked at Parker Ranch for eighteen years, until I retired in January 2010. It was an honor. I built the herd up to almost 20,000 cows one year—in the second year of a four-year drought, by the way.

Intensive grazing means a lot of cattle in a small area for a short period of time. Then we move them to the next pasture, letting the old one regenerate. You have to make sure the land where you have been grazing has enough time to rest.

At one point, the changes required to make a large ranch sustainable meant reducing overhead by one-third. This involved reducing office and shop staff and retraining the cowboys. Corky talks about what was required to change the organizational chart of the cowhands from hierarchical to horizontal, basically meaning that nobody was the "boss of them." Each cowboy was responsible for his own area.

MB I think the crowning thing for me was the *hoʻoponopono*[29] that we did with Kauila Clark. He was from Wahiʻawā. He had a magical touch on how to instill Hawaiian values.

JG *Kind of like a people whisperer?*

---

[29] *Hoʻoponopono* means to make right. Essentially, it means to make it right with the ancestors, or to make right with the people with whom you have relationships. We believe that the original purpose of hoʻoponopono was to correct the wrongs that had occurred in someone's life. www.ancienthuna.com

The word comes from hoʻo ("to make") and pono ("right"). The repetition of the word pono means "doubly right" or being right with both self and others. In a nutshell, hoʻoponopono is a process by which we can forgive others to whom we are connected. www.psychologytoday.com

MB Yes, he was like that. It changed the whole attitude at the ranch. These cowboys were now in charge of 2,000 to 3,000 cows. Most of the cowboys ran kuleana (areas of the ranch) that were bigger than most ranches in the country, which meant they'd better work cooperatively and not anger this guy or that guy, because if they did, they would be stuck with no help if they needed it.

It was wonderful just to see these guys "get it"—the whole hoʻoponopono concept. We're all in this together; everyone is the same and you can't get along without him and he can't get along without you. The whole thing empowered the cowboys.

Kauila passed a couple of years ago. (Long emotional silence.) He gave me a *raku* ceramic piece called Pōhaku Pele *ipu*. It is made to look like lava. He created over a thousand raku-style ceramic pieces; the sister to this one is in the Smithsonian. The kukui nut lei on it was given to me by a Hawaiian group; it is the old style, not all polished up.

And in terms of the younger generation, I'm proud to say that the Sieben Livestock Company in Adel, Montana is now being managed by a fifth generation Hibbard descendant, Cooper Hibbard.

From TomKatRanch.org by Kevin Alexander Watt: The Hibbards have a strong commitment to land stewardship and economic sustainability and have carefully tested and thoughtfully implemented a variety of regenerative practices. Including adaptive planned grazing and no-till hay farming to improve the health of their soil, increase forage quantity and quality, and reduce animal feed and healthcare costs. With nearly 1,600 cow/calf pairs, 1,300 yearlings, and sixty ewes, the effects of these changes have scaled quickly and had a significant positive impact on the ranch and the company's bottom line.

Kualoa Ranch
In 1850 John Morgan's ancestor, Gerrit P. Judd, bought 622 acres of land in the ahupuaʻa of Kualoa from King Kamehameha III. John's family has stewarded the land ever since. His account describes the transitions that this land has been through over the years and the learning curve he had to scale from his first job on the ranch to his current job of ranch manager.

John Morgan I started working at the ranch as a high school laborer in 1971 and worked every summer. At that time we had five employees working the cattle ranch and a small flower operation growing red ginger, bird of paradise, and ti leaves.

At one point my grandmother and my great-aunt each owned a third of the ranch. My great-aunt had a little money, but my grandmother had none. Estate tax rates were 55 percent so we were a land-rich, cash-poor, illiquid operation. At that time, everybody who did work on the ranch reported to my father. He was a hands-on, detail-oriented person, and my mentor. Dad died in 1999, but I had a great relationship with him all my life. He supported me in every way.

I became manager of the ranch in 1981, after ten years of working there as a laborer. My first business venture was that very year. We offered horseback rides but had no visitor operations to speak of and no facilities. Someone said, "You can make money in leatherleaf fern." It is something florists use in flower arranging and which lasts for three weeks. I convinced Dad to sink $100,000 into building a three-acre shade house and getting into the leatherleaf fern business, which promptly failed. It failed for a bunch of different reasons, but I'm the one who takes responsibility. The market analysis, the operations, and the yield weren't well done. There might have been some other management issues, but I was responsible.

Tourism appeared to be the answer to the ranch's problems, as Japanese visitors to Hawai'i was a big industry. It was a gamble, but I convinced my family that we should start an activity business. We formed a separate company in 1984 and opened our doors on April 1, 1985. At that point we had a multifaceted activity business, some of which we subcontracted out. We had the horses, ATVs, some limited tours, jet skis, scuba diving, windsurfing, a gun range, helicopters, and all kinds of stuff! We went from zero to 100 miles an hour in five years and were doing really well.

I'm thinking, "Wow, I've got this wired! This is good. Look at this!" And the family was happy. But if you don't plan it well, everything comes to an end. When the Japanese bubble burst in 1989, things started to tail off. People in the industry found out you could make money doing this, so competition increased. There was the Gulf War. There were all kinds of things that went wrong. We ended up chasing our tails with wrong pricing strategies. By the mid- to late 1990s, we were losing a lot of money.

When we did a SWOT [Strengths, Weaknesses, Opportunities, Threats] analysis, we realized our value proposition was the land, the history, the character of the ranch, nature, and our employees. We got rid of the helicopters, the jet skis, the gun range, and everything that didn't fit with our brand.

I had a plan that required new facilities, but it was a challenge to get approval from some of the family. They weren't all that happy with me at the time, since the business wasn't doing well. Family dynamics are often emotional, and usually emotion doesn't drive good business decisions. In 1991 I asked the family if they would let us bring outside people onto the board. Bill

Paty was one. He was head of the Department of Land and Natural Resources (DLNR), a thinker and an excellent communicator. The next was Richard Kelley, who owned Outrigger Hotels. Outrigger hired George Kanahele, a guru in bringing Hawaiian culture into the hospitality industry. Third was Mike White, who ran the Kāʻanapali Beach Hotel. Mike and the Kāʻanapali Beach received an award from President Reagan for their efforts in bringing Hawaiian culture and employee education into hotel operations.

In the 1990s nothing was paved at the ranch; everything was just gravel. There was just one building and dust all over the place. In order to become a destination we had to look and act like one. Building the Visitors Center in 2004 created a "campus," after which we became a bona fide visitor destination. We created a very long-winded mission statement but narrowed it down over the years. Now, our mission is: Enrich people's lives by preserving the land and celebrating its history.

JG *I came out with some tourist friends to take a horseback ride. While we waited our turn for the horses, we went through the Visitors Center historical displays and I just loved it! I like a museum that is tight, with a lot of richness in a small area, like yours. The graphics of the ahupuaʻa, the overhead visuals of the valley and the peaks, were beautiful and so explanatory. My mainland guests were wowed. Then we went on the horseback ride, which was a fantastic experience! We weren't doing anything dramatic on horseback, moving along on a very slow horse, but we were all so content in our skins. Just to be in that valley and have it surround us was wondrous.*

JM I couldn't agree more. Eventually the movie industry started to discover us. Movies have been a huge help to us in terms of building notoriety. They started filming here as early as 1964, with *In Harm's Way*.

Parts of the original *Magnum, P.I.* and the original *Hawaiʻi Five-O* were filmed here too. Then *Jurassic Park* was filmed in the valley right behind us in 1992. They originally started the movie on location on Kauaʻi until Hurricane ʻIniki destroyed everything. Apparently, Stephen Spielberg was flying over Oʻahu and said, "How about there?" Three days of the filming of *Jurassic Park* were done at Kualoa Ranch.

We make a very concerted effort to be what we call film-friendly. We have a lot of looks; we can be in a pasture, a stream, on steep cliffs, rolling hills, or in a jungle scene. When movie sets have to move their base camp, it is expensive, so if you can film five, or six, or ten, or twelve different things in one place and you are relatively private, it is easier for them. All the location managers know about us and we have great working relationships. We've had over thirty major motion pictures here and just as many TV shows, Including

Lost, which filmed here for six years, once or twice a month.

JG *What do you do with the tourists on their horses and ATVs when you have filming done here?*

JM We work with the producers. Sometimes there are 200 to 300 movie people here. We just work it out.

We have expanded our tours; we now have four tours that go to different parts of the ranch. Each one of them is one and a half hours and we integrate discussions about flora and fauna, Hawaiian culture and history, and agriculture. It's entertaining and informative and of value to the guests, which include locals as well as tourists. For us the home run is if a local person can come out and say, "Wow, that was great! I'm going to tell all my friends who come from the mainland."

We're trying to be more eco-friendly and appeal to a more active market. We have horses, ATVs, and ziplines as well as some electric-assist mountain bikes. We are really looking forward to the advent of the reliable electric ATV because that will get rid of all the noise. This is still a working cattle ranch but we are also a leader in the other businesses. We limit capacity so that the guests don't feel like they are in a hugely busy place. When you went on your horseback ride you probably didn't feel overwhelmed by a lot of people.

JG *There were ATVs way over there when we were on our ride, but other than that, it was just us and the mountain.*

JM Kualoa Ranch is a private nature reserve. Everything is about preserving the land. We thought that while our customers and the public might not want to go see sweet potatoes grow (laughter), if we deliver it to them, they'll get value out of it. We have three main diversified ag hubs, but the majority of the land is used for cattle ranching. If it weren't for the pasture you couldn't see the mountains. In Kahana Valley (to the north), you can't see the mountains because of the trees. We have a piggery, we have sheep, shrimp, tilapia, oysters, and many other crops, which we sell at our Visitors Center. Ag doesn't make money on its own; it is subsidized by the visitor operation. We aspire to improve our operations to actually make money on agriculture. We also consider landscaping to be essential. At a hotel you can't just have super nice rooms and junk landscaping. It's a cost center, not a revenue center, but the agriculture is a huge part of who we are.

We've dedicated a great portion of our land to ag, so our taxes aren't horrendous. We subsidize it a lot, but we think it is worthwhile. We will produce about 500 pigs a year out of our piggery, which is a recycled movie set from

Jumanji. We took down a big warehouse they had built in the middle of the valley, relocated it, and turned it into a piggery.

Another thing we add is employment for this whole area of Oʻahu. We are a big employer in a small community. We are really fortunate that we have an amazing team of dedicated people working hard to preserve this land, make it productive, and share it with the public.

Mac Nuts, Plumeria, and Tiny Ranches

Duncan MacNaughton describes his father's out-of-the-box thinking with regard to agricultural diversification in Hawaiʻi.

JG *Duncan, early in his career your dad, Boyd, worked for C. Brewer & Company.*

Duncan MacNaughton Yes, he worked under Alan Davis for some years and then my father took over as CEO. He retired as chairman and CEO of C. Brewer in the early 1970s. He gathered good people around him and helped the company turn a profit. But it was a challenge. Toward the end of his career he helped with two diversifications.

The Shah of Iran hired C. Brewer & Company to teach the Iranians how to grow sugar. There was a history of sugar cane being grown in Iran, going back hundreds and hundreds of years. So C. Brewer sent some of their management talent to the Middle East and with Brewer's help, Iran reintroduced sugar cane as a successful agricultural business. Eventually the Shah was overthrown and the rest is history. I'm not sure of the condition of anything over there now, let alone the sugar.

The other diversification my father was instrumental in was macadamia nuts. In Australia they were being grown in similar weather conditions as Hawaiʻi. So Boyd introduced macadamia nuts on some of the sugar plantations, particularly in the Keaʻau area, near South Point, which was being converted from sugar. Sugar was still protected by tariffs, but the yields in certain fields were not what they hoped for. So they got into the macadamia nut business. It was slow because it takes a long time for a macadamia nut tree to mature to the point where it produces any quantity of nuts.

JG *A big gamble on your dad's part, I'd say.*

DM No question about it. However, the macadamia business is still around, and sugar is not.

Mary Cooke fondly remembers her father's horticultural genius.

Mary Moragne Cooke My father, William Middleton Moragne, Sr., was a great horticulturalist. Born in Hilo, he was interested in working on the sugar plantations and eventually became the manager of Grove Farm on Kauaʻi.

Plants fascinated him. He decided he wanted to learn how to cross-hybridize plumerias. That is very difficult to do because you run into the difficulty of getting the two parts to adhere because of the slick sap. For ten or twenty years he kept trying to cross a very small dark red plumeria called "Scott Pratt" with a very large light pink called "Daisy Wilcox." Eventually he got a cross with a seedpod of 140 seeds. He named the plumerias he developed for the women in the family. One is called Mary Moragne; two are named after my sisters, Sally Moragne and Katie Moragne; another after my mother, Jean Whiddifield Moragne; and sister-in-law Jean; and then all his grandchildren, Julie, Cathy, and Edi. Many of these plumeria trees still grow on the grounds of the Mānoa Heritage Center.[30]

Kelvin Taketa was close to his grandfather, Tomatsu Sugiyama, and talks about the success he had in business, travel, and cattle ranching.

Kelvin Taketa I was very close to my maternal grandfather. With no more than an eighth-grade education, he started a construction business and was a big success. He built the two tunnels on Maui from Māʻalaea to Lahaina. He built the bridge that goes across Kīpapa Gulch. He built the bridge at Kalihiwai on Kauaʻi. I don't know how in the world he did what he did, but he did it pretty successfully. He also ran a cattle ranch in Maunawili and a ranch in Waiʻanae. Every Sunday, that's where we spent our time. I raised 4-H steers until my ninth-grade year at Punahou. Looking back on it, I am so happy I had that life. It was pretty unique for Punahou, that's for sure.

My grandfather grew up on a dairy farm in Japan and always liked cows. He ended up leasing land in Maunawili from Harold Castle and started a papaya farm. But nobody bought papayas because everybody had them in their yards. So he stopped.

---

[30] Visitors to Koko Crater Botanical Garden can see Mr. Moragne's hybrid plumerias named after the women in his family.

He and my grandmother took a trip abroad every year. They went to Brazil, Colombia, and Peru. At our usual weekend breakfast at the Village Inn he said to me, "Kelvin, when you get out of college, you've got to move to Colombia." I said, "Why?" He said, "Because there is a big Japanese community there." Evidently at the same time a lot of Japanese came to the United States and Hawai'i, many of them also went to Peru, Colombia, and Brazil as agricultural workers. Alberto Fujimori was a Japanese of Peruvian decent when he became the president of Peru.

My grandfather said, "Colombia has got this incredible diversity of natural resources. It's a beautiful country and it reminds me of when I came to Hawai'i. There's going to be tremendous growth." He wasn't wrong about that, but what he didn't predict was that the growth was going to be in growing coca plants for cocaine! On the one hand I was really hurt that he would tell his favorite grandson to move 8,000 miles away. On the other hand, I think he was influencing me to do something different and be an entrepreneur. He didn't say, "Come home and take over the family business." It was, "You've got to go where there is a future for you."

My grandparents all spoke English. They all spoke Japanese as well. But we were not encouraged to learn Japanese. Neither a cattle ranch nor a construction business are good cash-flow businesses, so there would be times when there were twelve of us living in a three-bedroom house. And there were times when we would all have our own houses. When they had to have conversations about money, it was all in Japanese. They didn't want any of the grandchildren to know what they were talking about. ❖

Voices of the Ranchers

Marshall Goodsill

CHAPTER 7

Voices of Laughter

The Last Run of the Oʻahu Railway

My brother found a recording of an interview taken of my father circa 1999. It was wonderful to hear his voice. He talked about the legal work he did in Honolulu in the six months before World War II. One of his first tasks after the war was dismantling the Oʻahu Railway.

Marshall Goodsill The Oʻahu Railway was built to haul sugar cane in World War I. It went as far as Kahuku around Kaʻena Point with a spur going up to Schofield Barracks. The railroad took people to the hotel in Haleʻiwa. During World War II, this was a *very* busy railroad. Sugar was in short supply in the US and was a precious commodity. This railroad was important to keep the sugar moving and they made a lot of money. The Army also used the railroad extensively, hauling troops and other things to Schofield.

In those days, there was an excess profits tax, so Dillingham had a *big* tax burden, which was anathema. If you make a lot of money during wartime, it can be taxed at a high rate to generate funds for the government.[31]

Dillingham had a very smart accountant by the name of Ed Grady, who eventually became a senior partner at their company. He determined that if they abandoned the railroad, they would have a big loss, which they could deduct against the excess profits, which tax-wise was a very sound decision. But this was an awful blow to the Dillinghams. At that time, 1947-48, the Dillingham interests were in two companies: Oʻahu Railway and Hawaiian Dredging & Construction.

---

[31] Investopedia: Excess profits tax is assessed in addition to any corporate income tax already in place. Excess profit taxes are primarily imposed on selective businesses during a time of war or other emergency, or beyond a certain amount of return on invested capital. Excess profits taxes are designed to generate emergency revenue for the government in time of crisis. The tax itself is imposed on the difference between the amount of profit that a company generally earns during peacetime and the profits earned during times of war.

The railroad company was sort of a family patriarchy. Walter Dillingham was the senior brother and chairman and president. His brother, Harold, was the financial vice president. His sons had other positions: Lowell worked in the dredging company, Ben and Lowell both worked in the railroad company. There were all these old-time managers who had worked at the company for years. The offices were at the old railroad depot; it is still there on King Street. We used to go down there and listen to Mr. Walter and Mr. Harold. They always wore suits and ties in their old office, which had Spanish furniture and great big desks.

It was a terrible decision for them to abandon their pride and joy, but they finally decided that economically it was the only thing to do. We had to get the ICC to approve it and there was opposition by some shippers. A pineapple company [Del Monte or Libby, McNeill & Libby] objected. The Army did not want the railroad to leave, there were lots of problems related to what happened to the land, and there were tax problems as well. This was a very big job. I worked on it for a year. By the end I was a railroad expert! (Laughter.)

We didn't have to liquidate the company because it had other interests and a lot of land. Railroads were only a part of their interests; in fact, it was called the Oʻahu Railway & Land Company when it started. They had a lot of valuable land. They left the rails in place at some locations and some of them are still there. If you had the narrow-gauge railroad running now, it might be one of the world's greatest tourist attractions![32]

W. F. Dillingham had a fancy coach built for himself. On the 31st of December 1947, the last day before the whole thing was to be closed down, they had a party for all the people who had worked for the railway,

Ruth and I lived in Waikīkī near the Dillingham fountain on Kalākaua Avenue. Next to the Outrigger Club was the old James P. Castle house; it's now the Elks Club. Next to that was a smaller Castle home which had been turned into an apartment, and we lived there. Ruth didn't know how to drive. One day she was waiting for the bus and Mr. Ben Dillingham, who liked ladies and always wore an orchid, stopped and asked if she wanted a ride. They got to be friends from that encounter. He was a wonderful man.

---

[32] Every Sunday, the Hawaiian Railway Society offers two narrated ninety-minute train rides on six-and-a-half miles of restored Oʻahu Railway & Land Company (OR&L) track running from ʻEwa to Nānākuli. The segment is part of a twelve-mile remnant of Honolulu-to-Kahuku track that is on the national and state registers of historic places. OR&L used this city-to-country route for passenger and freight service between 1888 and 1947. https://www.hawaiianairlines.com/island-guide/oahu/places/activities/hawaiian-railway-society

So, we got on this train; I was wearing my straw hat. Mr. Dillingham came along greeting everybody, and he leaned over me to speak to Ruth, "I'm glad you could bring your poor old father with you today." How we laughed; we were both in our *twenties*!

Fast Friends
As a young mother, Alice Flanders Guild worked at an Ala Moana Center jewelry store owned by an inveterate marketer.

Alice Flanders Guild My first job experience was with Connie Conrad at Security Diamond Company. He hired me as his advertising manager and we stayed together for ten years. Connie inherited the business from his father and although he became a jeweler, his passion was architecture. He was only happy when he was tearing things apart and rebuilding. His two stores at Ala Moana Center and his home were under constant "renovation."

Connie was also a marketer in the truest sense of the word. Over the years that I worked for him it was a tug of war that I never won. Once, he returned from a jewelers' convention and presented me with two little tools that resembled a one-hole paper punch. When I asked him what they were, he explained that they were ear piercing machines and we were going to begin piercing ears in the store the following Saturday. I protested that it was unseemly for a jewelry store to stoop to ear piercing and that we would probably be shut down by the Board of Health. He looked me in the eye and said, "Run the ad—free ear piercing with the purchase of one pair of earrings." I had to eat my words when I arrived at work Saturday to find a mob waiting to have their ears pierced, for free. He created a tremendous market for pierced earrings that was later capitalized on by other jewelry stores.

One year just before Thanksgiving he came to me and said, "We're going to give free turkeys with a jewelry purchase of $250 or more." I said, "We are not giving free turkeys. This is a jewelry store!" He said, "Go out and find a contact for turkeys." We made an arrangement with Foodland to give gift certificates and partnered in the turkey/jewelry business every year thereafter. The lines of people that showed up to get their free turkey were unbelievable! Thanksgiving became one of our biggest sales events of the year.

Diane Paton talks about befriending Alice Flanders Guild when they were children, then shares a story about Humphrey Bogart at the beach at Waikīkī, plus an amusing anecdote from her time working in Washington, DC.

Diane Paton My stepmother, Cecily, conspired with her friend, Muriel Flanders, to provide a companion for poor, friendless me. Alice and I became fast friends and remain so to this day. I started at Punahou School in the eighth grade after having attended a Dominican convent school in California. The first day at Punahou when the teacher came in, I stood up and said, "Good morning, Miss Whatever." Everyone laughed at me. I did not do that again. I'm sure Alice told you that she thought I was a drip. She thought I was the biggest drip she had ever come across! (Laughter.)

The Outrigger Canoe Club became my home away from home, where I attempted to learn to surf early on weekend mornings and breakfasted with club employees on fried eggs over a mountain of rice and shoyu served by snack bar chef Richard, who would often break into a hula while preparing your meal.

The many celebrities who visited Hawai'i seemed to find their way to the Outrigger, the center of water sports, surfing, beach volleyball, and the lore of the beachboys Panama, Sam, Curly, Kalākaua, Rabbit, Chick, and Turkey. We saw Shirley Temple, Douglas Fairbanks, and Doris Duke, and were treated one day to the sight of Hollywood star Humphrey Bogart escorted by the aptly named genial giant Steamboat Mokuahi and a team of burly, barefoot Hawaiian beachboys carrying a canoe across the sand toward the ocean. Bogart—small, pale, fragile-looking, and wearing black socks—struggled to help carry the canoe, to the disappointment of his adoring onlookers!

A Presidential Task Force on the Arts and the Humanities was formed by Executive Order in June of 1982 to determine if the National Endowment for the Arts and the National Endowment for the Humanities should be retained and funded as part of President Ronald Reagan's commitment to America to reduce government spending and bring the budget under control.

President Reagan then formed the President's Committee on the Arts and the Humanities. He appointed as chairman the renowned international and cultural philanthropist Andrew Heiskell, the chairman and CEO of Time Inc. First Lady Nancy Reagan was named honorary chair and I was appointed executive director. In subsequent administrations, First Ladies Barbara Bush, Hillary Clinton, Laura Bush, and Michelle Obama served as honorary chairs of the commission. This major collaborative effort with the Treasury Department focused on protecting and preserving tax incentives that encouraged private sector giving to the arts and the humanities. I can't imagine a better job.

There were difficult and precarious times too, as we worked long hours and received poison-pen letters and death threats when the National Endowment for the Arts funded the highly controversial work of photographer Robert Mapplethorpe.

As executive director of the President's Committee on the Arts and the Humanities, Diane worked out of the grand former postmaster general's office in the Old Post Office Building in Washington, D.C.

DP The offices were located in the clock tower building, the tallest building on Pennsylvania Avenue. My offices were spacious with beautiful wood paneling, including a large conference room with a long conference table, fireplace, and magnificent Hudson River School paintings loaned by a local museum. Alas, those rooms are now the presidential suite in the Trump International Hotel!

Three Strikes
Peter McKenney remembers with amusement his adjustment to being married to a Hawaiian wife, having Hawaiian in-laws, and living in the Hawaiian culture.

Peter McKenney I started my life in Hawai'i with three strikes against me when I married Luanna Farden: I'm haole, I was a mainlander, and I was a Navy military officer.

Luanna's mother was very accepting and took it as her responsibility to teach me about things Hawaiian. Lucy Searle Farden was a remarkable woman. Early in her teaching career she saw a copy of her fitness report, which said, "Mrs. Farden shows great promise as a teacher, considering that she is Hawaiian." That was how she was regarded at the Department of Education! Yet among Luanna's mother's students, I believe, were Senator Inouye, Senator Matsunaga, and Governor Ariyoshi. She taught all of them civics at McKinley High School. She also taught her new son-in-law a lot.

One day Luanna's mother read in the paper that Madalyn Murray O'Hair, the famous atheist, had filed a lawsuit that ended up before the US Supreme Court. Mrs. Farden loved her queen; she loved her culture and was not thrilled by the overthrow. But she also felt "any country that would allow a private citizen to air her grievances all the way to the Supreme Court is my kind of country." She wrote Ms. O'Hair, who was living on the East Coast, to come to Hawai'i to talk to her civics students about being American, her experiences, and her thoughts on the Constitution and its guarantees. I don't know the details, but Madalyn Murray O'Hair did come to Honolulu and talk to Mrs. Farden's civics class!

The rest of the story is that some of the kids went home and said, "Guess who we heard today!" Some parents were aghast! Luanna's mother was called in the next day: "Mrs. Farden, you are fired." And after thirty-two years as a teacher! Lucy Farden and her husband, Carl, went to talk to the governor and told him what happened. The governor picked up the phone and said, "Get me the head of the DOE." And he told him to reinstate Mrs. Farden with full apologies.

Luanna and I were to marry on June 20, 1962. Luanna was back in California, finishing her year as a third-grade teacher. Here I am, sitting in paradise, opposite my about-to-be parents-in-law as her dad squeezed a lime into my gin and tonic. Practically her mother's first words to me were, "Have you ever noticed Luanna's feet?" I hadn't really thought much about her feet. "Luanna is Hawaiian. Hawaiians' feet connect them to the earth. That is where *mana* comes from. You watch the way Hawaiians walk, the grace they show. There is no one else who walks like a Hawaiian does. It is graceful, it is reverent, and it is connected to the earth."

The next lesson came right after we were married at Kawaiaha'o Church. Reverend [Abraham] Akaka's pre-nuptial counseling guides us to this day. Ed Kenney, a cousin, traveled from Broadway to sing at our wedding. For the reception we went to the old O'ahu Country Club. It was magical. Genoa Keawe sang with her trio, and Luanna's father's group, The Three Chiefs, also sang. There was music and hula and flowers. As I entered with my new bride, I was overwhelmed with the joy, beauty, and love.

Suddenly I realized that I needed a special Hawaiian toast and turned to Luanna's Auntie Edna for help. She thought deeply for a moment and then said, "I've got it. *Pehea kou piko*." I said, "That is beautiful. What does that mean?" Auntie replied, "The warmth of the early sun as it burns away the morning mist. That is as your love is to me." I said, "That is beautiful." Her warm brown eyes aglow, she said, "Let me hear you say it." And I replied, "Pehea kou piko." She said, "This is Hawaiian. You need to get it right. More warmth and from the heart. Let me hear it again." So I tried again and again until finally she said, "That's lovely. Go ahead." As I took my seat at the head table next to my bride I asked, "What does 'pehea kou piko' mean?" And she screams, "*What*?" The basic translation is, "How is your navel?" The Hawaiian Dictionary explains: "It is a greeting avoided by some because of its double meaning." My learning started early. I learned what a piko is and learned to be very wary of this auntie.

We lived with Luanna's parents for a whole summer at their home on Front Street in Lahaina. Her dad loved the Sons of Hawai'i. I'm out on my morning bike ride and I see a sign for a Sons of Hawai'i concert in Lahaina. I ran in and bought four tickets. I returned to the house quite pleased with my accomplishment and announced to Luanna's mother that I had tickets to Sons of Hawai'i, and the seats are in the first row. Luanna's mother looked at me and said, "Suppose we don't want to go?" I was angry and disappointed and said to Luanna, who was in the yard hanging up the wash, "Do you know what your mother just said?"

When we cooled down, Luanna's mother explained, "When you are speaking with elders or you are inviting them to something, you ask them, with respect, if they would like to go. You should invite us to join you, not tell us what you have planned for us."

Where I was from they gave gold stars for initiative! Luanna and I are different; I oversell myself and she is very modest. It has been pretty interesting, working it out. Humor has helped!

After five years of our children growing up in Marin County, California, we realized that they knew little of their Hawaiian heritage or the heritage of Luanna's family. We decided to return to Hawai'i. I met a lot of people, mostly through Auntie Irmgard [Aluli] and Luanna's parents, who went out of their way to introduce us to their many friends. I had the privilege of hearing their stories, learning from them, and singing with them. Auntie Irmgard introduced us to the Prince Kūhiō Hawaiian Civic Club. The chorus was led by Kīhei and Anuhea Brown. There I had the chance to practice and perform with some very talented and fun-loving Hawaiians. Practices, performances, interisland trips, "tent cities," laughter, great food, jokes, *jook*, pineapple swipe. What fond memories. That experience deepened my love for Hawai'i.

Luanna McKenney Peter knows so many Hawaiian songs, you would think he had been brought up here. He likes to play bass and we still sing together.

PM Luanna's group is Puamana. When Luanna and I sing for parties we are Manapua. (Laughter.) A white pork bun, but sweet on the inside!

For thirty-two years Puamana has performed for generations of kama'āina parties at the old Willows and they still sing at O'ahu Country Club. Hawai'i has a wonderful tradition of songs being composed to honor a family, their homes, their hospitality, and beloved individuals. When Puamana plays their songs, families rise in acknowledgement and join in the singing and hula of their family song.

The people of Hawai'i have the greatest sense of humor. Parties are spontaneous and fun. I have memories of Uncle Buddy as a Filipino radio DJ, Auntie Annie with her comic hula, and two cousins of ample girth dancing the Filipino bamboo dance using chopsticks. Fun-loving parodies of the Merrie Monarch [Festival] performances, known as the Mini Merrie Monarch, were held in Uncle Buddy's Volcano carport. They were fall-down hilarious, but always respectful.

As I think back on the years that followed our 1975 return to Hawai'i, I've come to better appreciate the importance of Hawaiian humor. The Hawaiian renaissance was underway: voyaging, hula, music, 'ōlelo Hawai'i, 'Iolani Palace, sovereignty meetings and hearings. Humor seems to be the ingredient that kept most of us humble and able to laugh in the racial and cultural diversity of Hawai'i. How many of us remember Sterling Mossman, Kent Bowman, Rap Reiplinger, Andy Bumatai, Keola and Kapono Beamer? The Beamer Brothers' "Mr. San Cho Lee" ends with the lyrics, "One thing I wen notice 'bout dis place, all us guys we tease da uddah race. It's amazing we can live in da same place." Keola and Kapono nailed it.

Today we seem to be a little too cautious, being politically correct. I'm not sure we can return to our exciting and gracious period. Maybe Frank DeLima can help us. Lightening up a bit might lead us through our coming challenges.

How is Electricity Made?

When Tom Williams began talking about his work as a public utility lawyer, he really came alive and was very funny! It came as a surprise to me to learn that having mathematics as a "second language" would be a highly prized skill for an attorney! I also interviewed Tom's colleague David Fairbanks. Stay tuned for Tom's punch line on how electricity is made.

JG *Tell me about Marshall Goodsill.*

David Fairbanks He was a god!

JG *(laughing) He's up there shaking his head, you know!*

DF Well, to us he was a god. I first met Marshall when I interviewed at the firm, in his super-neat and organized, super-clean office, with him impeccably dressed in a suit. I was really amazed he would wear his coat in the office. And his mind—talk about logic! When he was talking out a problem it went just right down the line. And that brilliance was probably exceeded only by his ability to explain the issues to a layperson, so they could understand it. It was just wonderful to see him do that.

Marshall and Hugh Shearer handled most of the utility cases in the 1960s. Very high interest rates were killing the utilities, so both Hawaiian Telephone and Hawaiian Electric had rate cases backed up. Hawaiian Electric had Maui Electric and Hawai'i Electric Light Company as subsidiaries, and the three of them were constantly going in for rate increases.

Public Utility Commission litigation work is highly specialized. You argue and litigate in front of the Public Utilities Commission rather than a jury. The Office of Consumer Protection was the adversary in every rate case.

Tom Williams One of Marshall's skills was dictation. He didn't write things; he dictated. That is a very difficult thing to do, especially for someone who had never done it, like me. Marshall didn't dictate a draft, go correct it, and do another draft; he dictated final versions. I never saw anyone else who could do that. He had an amazingly organized mind.

I was in his office and we were working on something. After he dictated his part, he said, "Well, Tom, why don't you dictate your part?" I mumbled something and when his secretary, Jessie Miller, went out to type it up from her shorthand notes, I went right out with her to see if anything I'd said made sense. (Laughter.) To be able to dictate a brief is difficult! Remember, in those days we didn't have Xerox machines; we had mimeograph machines. If you wanted to change things and do a second draft, you had to cut, tape, and copy. The secretaries didn't like that!

The firm had a lot of trouble recruiting people to work in the utilities area. I showed an aptitude for it and I was interested. There are a lot of mathematical formulas and I understood them easily. Most people became lawyers because they don't like math. The associate who did public utilities work at the firm before I came became an airline steward! (Laughter.)

JG *Tell us why public utility law requires mathematical aptitude.*

TW As part of a rate-making formula there are a lot of calculations. You have to compute the rate base, which is the value of the property dedicated to public use. You have to compute operating expenses, income taxes, and depreciation expenses, which account for wear and tear on the property.

You also had to know what you were doing to work with Marshall. He had to be able to rely on your work. He hired Dave Reber, who is the best corporate attorney in the state of Hawaiʻi and has been for at least the last twenty to twenty-five years. Conrad Weiser was a fantastic trust and estates lawyer. Those were the types of people Marshall liked to work with.

Public utilities law involves both corporate law and rate-making details. It also involves hearings where witnesses are required to be cross-examined. Marshall never liked that aspect of public utilities law, so he brought in Dave (Fairbanks), who was a litigator. Dave liked people and litigation; I liked the math.

The Hawaiian Telephone rate case involved pretty extensive hearings that lasted from 1975 to 1978, so I spent a lot of time with Marshall. I viewed myself as the bag carrier. (Laughter.) That's probably the way the others viewed me too!

It is difficult to explain what goes on in public utility cases. A lot of mathematical analysis is done using computer programs. It helps in this work if you are able to understand the data that is put into the computer in order to determine if the outputs made sense. It was kind of like a foreign language, but I loved it. You have to be able to explain it to the Public Utilities Commission because they are the ones representing the consumers and the public interest.

One day in court the in-house counsel for Hawaiian Tel was arguing with one of the intervener counsels. They were going back and forth, back and forth. Finally the chairman said, "Well, that's all very interesting, but Marshall, what's the answer?" I thought to myself, "I'm definitely on the right side!" If the chairman of the PUC views your counsel as the expert on the subject, you know you are in a good position.

Later in my career, I would talk to an associate to assess if they might be interested in this kind of work. I'd say, "Where does electricity come from?" If they looked at a wall outlet, I would know that they didn't have any concept as to how electricity was generated, transmitted, and distributed. In a sense, they were right that it came from the wall socket, but our job is far more technical than that. We had very bright attorneys who would just throw up their hands.

Mina Morita's coments may not be humorous, but they do support Fairbanks's and Williams's discussion on how the Public Utility Commission works.

Hermina "Mina" Morita Governor [Neil] Abercrombie appointed me to be PUC chair in early 2011. Probably the biggest contribution I made to the Public Utilities Commission was in administration: working to increase its budget, getting new job descriptions written, and cutting out the deadwood to professionalize the staff for the task required. The biggest problem was that for a lot of years the positions were considered patronage positions. Telecom, electric utility, and even transportation, which shouldn't be regulated at all, have had huge changes.

The PUC should be an independent agency but is mistakenly viewed and treated as part of the cabinet and was under the governor's purview all those years. Getting that mindset changed was a task. The kinds of audits and the engineering work they do at the PUC don't fit the typical civil service sector jobs that other agencies do, and that's why it was important to re-do job descriptions and advocate for salaries commensurate with the skill sets required.

Governor Abercrombie picked another commissioner right after me who was highly qualified for the job. Michael Champley, a retired utility executive from Michigan who lived on Maui, knew the electricity sector inside and out. This is when the most productive work was done at the commission. We had a really, really good team. I had Champley and Dr. James Jay Griffin, the current PUC chair. Griffin was a researcher at the Hawai'i Natural Energy Institute at the University of Hawai'i before he started as my chief of policy and research.

Catherine Awakuni, who was the former consumer advocate, became my chief legal counsel. When she left, I was fortunate to hire Thomas Gorak, who specialized in energy and utility issues as my chief legal counsel. For a short time we also had Commissioner John Cole, also a former consumer advocate. My administrative assistant, Brooke Kane, a carryover from the previous administration, was excellent at managing the agency.

The Hawai'i PUC started getting national recognition for setting progressive energy policy. Our biggest challenge was Hawaiian Electric. Mike Champley lifted the veil for us, knowing what should be expected in the operations of a utility. We were able to reorganize all the dockets before the PUC, to give better policy direction in moving to where we are right now. We put out a significant white paper in 2014 called "Inclinations on the Future of Hawai'i's Electric Utilities." It was a nationally recognized, enlightened piece of work regarding energy policy from a regulator. At that time we were so frustrated with Hawaiian Electric that we basically said, "If you don't know where you are going, we're going to tell you where you need to go." And that's what this white paper did.

Child's Play

Peggy Dillingham and I were childhood friends. Since I was with her during many of the adventures she describes below, I can testify to her veracity regarding the dangers of our play areas.

Peggy Dillingham Hannan I called my grandparents Grandpa and Babasan but their real names were Harold G. Dillingham and Margaret Hyde-Smith Dillingham. Their children were Walter, Harold, Henley, Bayard, and Peter. My dad was Bayard Harrison Dillingham and my mother is Carter Randolph Andrews Dillingham Budge.

My grandparents' house was at the base of Diamond Head, on the water. It is now a park. There are two parks on Diamond Head Road near Waikīkī; theirs was on the lot that was closer to the lighthouse. It was an Italian-style house built around a courtyard. The lānai floor was made of coral, which was rough on bare feet. The furniture was Asian with low curlicue tables. The roof was tile and the walls were stucco. It was a big property with tennis courts and a pool. My grandmother was a painter who painted flowers in oil on wood. Since she had no studio, she used the lānai as a work area. Later in her life she painted all the ceiling tiles for the house she lived in. I remember woodroses.

Most of my memories are from a child's perspective. For example, I remember there was a dumbwaiter, a big hand-operated platform elevator made to carry furniture. All three of us children rode in it up to the attic where we would play. I remember being terrified by the large painting of a Chinese emperor, which was on the landing of the stairs leading to the second floor. The emperor had long, dagger-like fingernails. We used to fly around that corner to get away from him!

It was quite formal when we visited my grandparents; we dressed up and behaved ourselves. They had some old toys, like little metal pedal cars, with a horse in the front. I think the legs moved. They were fun.

Walter and Louise Gaylord Dillingham built La Pietra a short distance away. It was also in the Italian style. It is a girls' school now. The fountain on Kalākaua Avenue by the Elks Club was built for Louise Dillingham by Walter.[33]

Judge Walter Frear and Mary Dillingham Frear had a house at Punahou and Wilder Streets, where Arcadia is now. It was not Italian, but more old Hawai'i plantation style. It is sad to me that all these homes are gone now.

Marshall Goodsill Judge and Mrs. Frear had a beautiful colonial house with great big verandas and lawns near Central Union Church. They invited us to a couple of tea parties in their wonderful house. It was like being in the eighteenth century: white suits, Panama hats, and tea.

Peggy Hannan B.F. Dillingham built a house at Mokulē'ia in 1900 or 1901 as a family getaway. There were eight bedrooms! Every other bedroom shared a bathroom, which featured an outdoor shower. The walls of the showers were bushes and the showers watered the plants. In the old days, at the top of the royal palm-lined driveway, was the honeymoon cabin, which was later moved to the side of the main house for the kids to stay in. It had a half-size clawfoot tub. In the main house there was a huge kitchen with a wood-burning stove. Mrs. Shigeoka made great, very thin pancakes for us. Even in the late 1960s she or her daughter were still cooking with that stove. She made breakfast and dinner. There was a kids' table off the kitchen where we ate.

The dining room was formal, and we never ate there that I remember, but we used to blow a ping-pong ball across the table as a game. The player piano was one of our favorite things, with its rolls of music. We'd play musical chairs, waiting for the roll to end.

There was a macadamia nut grove on the property. We used to try crack the nuts, roast them, and serve them to the grown-ups for *pūpū*. We'd smash

---

[33] The Louise Dillingham Memorial Fountain was gifted to the city by the Walter & Louise Dillingham Foundation.

them with a brick, which would mash the shell into the nut and we'd serve these awful things for our parents to eat!

As you left the house you could walk up a wide grass path lined by royal palm trees to the pool fed by a rainwater catchment tank. There was a tennis court too. The Mokuleia Ranch and Land Company ranch hands had horses, which we were allowed to ride on the cane roads along the base of the hills. The Dillingham airfield was nearby.

There was some treachery in our play areas! One wonders how we survived. We'd walk barefoot from the creek to the house over those round pokey ironwood nuts. Then there was that great big old squeaky swing set, which we leapt off of and landed on *kiawe* thorns!

The cane fields were irrigated by flumes which were filled with water. We would walk through the hot, dusty, red-dirt cane field to the flumes where we would lie on our backs and let the water carry us away. That water was *so* cold because it came directly from the mountains. If the flume was full enough, you could slide along in the water and not rub the skin off your back. But if the water was too high, your nose broke all the spider webs.

After rainfalls we'd go mud sliding behind the house. It was a fun slide that would end up in a barbed-wire fence or a *tree*! The red mud, of course, wrecked our clothes. Why did we think that was fun?

However, there were two great big banyan trees in the front of the house and we used to play in the roots as little kids. Each of us had our own little nest of a place in the roots. I don't remember that being too dangerous. (Laughter.) ❖

Carl Farden (left), father of Luanna McKenney, with string musicians of St. Louis College in Honolulu, circa 1918

CHAPTER 8

Voices of Island Music

The Resurgence of Hawaiian Music

I found Judge Moon's comments on the Hawaiian renaissance especially insightful and informative.

Ronald Moon Come statehood, Hawai'i got a governor who was elected by the people instead of appointed by the president. They got a Supreme Court that was appointed and confirmed by the Hawai'i Senate, not the US Senate.

When Bill Richardson became chief justice, he restored Hawaiian customs, which had largely been ignored for economic reasons. Judge Pence generally had a low view of the Richardson Hawai'i Supreme Court because he thought they were messing things up with all these Hawaiian customs. There was real animosity among the large landowners against Richardson for bringing back concepts that they thought were a wrong part of the law.

Hawaiian Homes laws and rules had been largely ignored for fifty years, and in the 1970s people started filing lawsuits about the Office of Hawaiian Affairs not doing its job. It took almost ten years after statehood for these changes to take effect. Local youngsters went to school on the mainland and experienced the civil rights movement, and then came back to Hawai'i. Correspondingly there was a rise of interest in Hawaiian music, paddling, Hawaiian language, scholarship, culture, and hula. There were only a handful of canoe clubs and a handful of hula *hālau* in the early 1970s, but passion about Hawaiian culture caught fire.

This would be a good place for me to pay homage to one of my personal heroes, who participated in the flourishing of island music at the start of the Hawaiian renaissance. The Shingle and Goodsill families lived in the same neighborhood and had sons named Witt and Curt, respectively. A couple of years later Alice Ka'eu'eu (A.K.) Shingle and Jane Marshall Goodsill were born and became childhood friends. Our brothers played together as keiki, *learned to surf together, competed as a doubles team in tennis at Hawai'i Preparatory Academy, and stayed close as they grew older.*

For a time, Witt played music in Waikīkī in the evenings, in what he called a "sawdust-on-the-floor" kind of place. He had an ambition to bring authentic Hawaiian music back into the light. Against all odds, Witt and his friends Steve Siegfried and Lawrence Brown became successful music producers under their Pānini Records label. They were dedicated to improving the quality of their records, prepared thoroughly for local recording sessions, mixed their master tapes in Hollywood, and aligned with performers such as the legendary Gabby Pahinui to create a magical combination of artists and producers.

One night shortly after a huge Pānini album was released, Witt came to dinner and played the album for us, my parents included, while he explained the meaning of the words and the origins of the songs and regaled us with anecdotes from the recording sessions. I remember we laughed at some of the antics and cried at others. I'll never forget how animated and engaged Witt was. It was such a special night!

I am hopelessly biased by my devotion to Witt, who was like a brother to me, but it has always seemed to me that as Pānini Records released one blockbuster after another, the interest in all Hawaiian music seemed to explode. We couldn't wait to get to Andrews Amphitheater on the University of Hawai'i campus to hear authentic Hawaiian music. People wanted to dance hula, learn the Hawaiian language, grow and eat Hawaiian foods, and revive the cultural practices of Hawai'i.

And speaking of the Hawaiian renaissance, Alice Guild offers some background on the revival of local music and dance in this next story.

Alice Flanders Guild I think two major things impacted the Hawaiian culture. The first was the overthrow and the inability of people to *be* Hawaiian because they were pressured to be American. The culture was nearly lost when people didn't speak the language or dance *kahiko*. Then in the 1930s and 40s, you began to see a sort of "yaaka hula hickey dula" Hollywood version of Hawaiian. It was very popular with Hawaiians as well as visitors and local people, because that was all anybody knew. It was fun and it was romantic, but it was not a true representation of Hawaiian culture.

The second thing was statehood and the desire to be "American," particularly for Japanese families, many of whom had been mistreated during the war, who wanted to prove they were true Americans. The legislature was trying to push statehood and, in some ways, Hawai'i became a stage set.

Construction of the State Capitol building began in 1965 and it opened in 1969. Nobody had given any thought to 'Iolani Palace and what would happen to it as this new construction took place all around it. And nobody gave a rip! When the governor approved building the Capitol, there was neither provision nor funding for 'Iolani Palace. Rumors were flying that the palace might be torn down because it was "blocking the view" from some of the legislators' windows. It was at this time that the first real concern for preservation began. So much of Hawaiian heritage, culture, and history had already been lost. Buildings were torn down without any consideration as to their historic value.

This was before the sovereignty movement started. There was no one championing Hawaiian culture. As Hawaiians became more open about their culture, they became more concerned about protecting the palace and other historic sites. And the palace served as the piko for pretty much all things Hawaiian, because it is one of the very few symbols of the monarchy still standing.

About this time there began what was called a Hawaiian renaissance. Pānini Records started recording Gabby Pahinui, beginning a wave of Hawaiian slack-key guitar style. I think this was at about the same time as Woodstock or maybe a little later.

JG *I remember it was music you could hold onto, that felt good, looked good, and sounded good. You could support something local and have pride in it by buying their music and going to their concerts. It began to make us all want more of that. Witt [Shingle] said that one of the things that amazed them was that all ethnicities bought their music, waiting in long lines when the albums were released.*

AG I think you are right that it started with the music. When I was growing up there were no hula hālau. There were a few hula studios where you learned to hula to *hapa haole* songs. Men did not dance at all.

Kaui Philpotts remembers fondly the song-and-dance mentors of her grandmother's generation.

Kaui Philpotts When I was growing up, my mother took me to hula class on Saturday. We just ran around and our *kumu* would whack us on the legs. "Get back in there!" (Laughter.) But now, it's a hālau and you have all these protocols. Who knew! They are very, very serious. More people do their genealogy and claim their Hawaiian blood today. It came out of the Hawaiian renaissance in the 1970s and the Constitutional Convention with "*palaka* power" and all that.

People are more correct about Hawaiian studies and history, and they are more correct in how they practice their culture. More people can ʻōlelo Hawaiian. When they study hula, it incorporates everything in the culture from language to history to genealogy—everything. Maybe I'm just being idealistic, but I don't see people living Hawaiian anymore, in their heart, in their spirit. It's tough living in the world today. I'm thinking of Hawaiian people I knew, growing up, like my grandmother's friends. They were so sassy. They were wonderful.

Within Hawaiian society there was always a caste system. There were the aliʻi and the makaʻāinana in the old days; later there were all the hapas who sort of mingled with everyone. If you look back to the day of Kalākaua and later, there was a lot of intermingling between Hawaiians, and I loved the people who came out of that period. They were still alive when I was a kid and I loved listening to them. They all fooled around with each other and someone would say, "Oh, you know whose kid that is!" I always thought they were so cool! It was kind of relaxed.

There was a huge Hawaiian middle class. Maybe it was because there was so much intermarriage, but there was a big Hawaiian middle class that was educated and lived very well. They had educated kids. And they had dignity. There is no way they would have behaved like so many people today.

ʻIolani Luahine was one of the last court dancers. She was a legend. She came into the Hele On Bar when I was there one night and emptied the place! Sheʻd had a few drinks and started chanting and all the Hawaiians ran for the doors, scared.

A couple of years ago when I was in a hālau, we went up to the Big Island to visit and dance in all these different places related to the songs we had learned. We danced at Hilo Bay. Then we went to Huliheʻe Palace in Kona by the ocean and we danced again. On the way from Hilo to Kona we stopped up in Waimea and visited Queenie and Jamie Dowsett. She was sitting out on her porch and her girlfriend, who was a hula sister from way back when, came over. They were telling jokes and they were dancing. The most rascally songs you have *ever* heard! And they were having so much fun. Everybody was laughing. To me, she and her girlfriend represented the Hawaiʻi and the Hawaiian people that I knew growing up. They can do it with class. It was so natural and so humorous. And it was at nobody's expense. It was like everybody got the same joke and laughed together. It was so delightful. That joy that I used to see in Hawaiian people, I donʻt see much anymore. Itʻs been replaced by more authenticity but also very serious business. But I kind of miss the *kolohe*, you know? They were so fun.

Learning Hula
Luanna McKenney has sweet memories of her youth. Her joy for movement coupled with her shyness in front of people is captured perfectly.

Luanna McKenney I lived with my mother and daddy, Lucy and Carl Farden, and my mare, Zero, on a farm by Kāneʻohe Stream. My parents bought the farm in 1941. They restored the *loʻi kalo* [taro patch] and worked hard on weekends caring for the land. Our cottage was about seventy years old. My mother was a career teacher of English, civics, and social studies at McKinley High. My father was a chemist and statistician at the Pineapple Research Institute at the University of Hawai'i. They commuted to work in Honolulu before the Pali Tunnel was built.

I fondly remember my mother coming into our cool, spacious lānai (originally my horse's shed added on to our cottage) after working in the yard on a hot day. She would sit down, relax, smile, and say, "Luanna, come, dance for me!" And I, bashfully at first, would begin making whatever movements came into my pre-teen mind. Mother would smile and say, "That's beautiful, Luanna!" There was no music. I just began to enjoy moving my body in novel and interesting ways. I made up quite a random succession of movements, repeating those that pleased me. Once I got started, I enjoyed strutting about, watching for my mother's reaction. My dancing seemed to thrill her. I would skip, stride, point my toes and kick; hop; bounce up the stairs; leap; bend this way and that and wave my arms, wrists and fingers; step quickly on tiptoes; look here and there and even cross-eyed for a laugh—whatever came to me.

Dad was an excellent musician, a singer of the old Hawaiian songs. My parents were often invited to parties given by family and friends. I went too. Singing, dancing, storytelling, laughing, and of course, hula. I watched my aunties and uncles hula. So much fun! My Auntie Emma Farden Sharpe, who would become one of Maui's most beloved hula exponents, was my first hula teacher when I was about six years old. I learned for the fun of dancing but was too shy to dance for an audience.

Most of our family potluck dinner picnics were at my Auntie Annie Ryan's house by the ocean at Paiko Drive in Kuli'ou'ou. After dinner was *kanikapila* time. I would run like the night wind down the beach whenever anyone as much as suggested that I dance a hula! When I was about sixteen years old and had just transferred from University Lab School to Punahou School, I asked Mother if I could have formal lessons with the Beamer family (Auntie Louise and Tita). I admired their dancing style and family songs written by "Sweetheart Grandma," Helen Desha Beamer. Within the year I felt ready. At a family party, I stepped up and danced my first "Tropic Trade Winds." My aunties and the guests threw money at my feet when I finished. Mother nodded, smiling, indicating that it's okay, that money is for you!

My hula and music started in an unusual way. I was the only student. I began dancing without music. I progressed with a reverence for nature, slowly but surely making my Hawaiian traditions part of me. I appreciate being trained as a solo dancer, where I can be free to express myself. Hula is a dance to interpret a story. I try to convey these stories with all their poetic feeling.

Whenever I am invited to perform a hula, I find myself grateful to offer a gift of my Hawaiian being. I am sharing a gift that many loving *kūpuna* have given me. I feel my mother's encouraging smile.

Auntie Betty Webster in Kamuela told me a bit about her life and about her various dance kumu.

Betty Solomon Webster My mother was named Mary Agatha Yap [1891-1986]. She was Chinese-Hawaiian from Mākua, at the end of the road beyond Wai'anae, on O'ahu. I was born in 1925. When I went to Maryknoll Catholic school, I stayed with my aunt in Kalihi and I went back home on weekends. Mother worked in the pineapple cannery in Iwilei, in Honolulu. She was a trimmer, trimming areas where the machines did not reach to clean the pineapple. During the summers I worked in the cannery and got five cents an hour.

When I was nine my mother wanted me to learn dance because she had not had that opportunity in her lifetime. She would take my cousin and me to Queen Emma Street to dance with the male kumu, Tom Hiona. He was a nice-looking guy, a good teacher, and strict. He was married to an Oriental lady, Auntie Clara. During the war we went to the military camps and danced hula. Some of them were scattered up in the mountains on O'ahu. We would also perform at places like the Academy of Arts. We did modern and ancient dance, but he was Hawaiian, so we did not dance Tahitian.

Ancient dance is more or less chanting. Performers would not smile; that would not be respectful. The motions are pictures made by our hands—with no movements of the fingers. With modern hula dance you move your fingers gracefully and you smile. That is the difference. The hips and footwork are the same fundamental steps.

I stopped dancing with Tom Hiona when he left Hawai'i. The next kumu was Bill Lincoln. My cousin and I joined his group in his Waikīkī studio. Our performances took place in nightclubs. After that we went with kumu Kent Ghirard. He was haole and we danced mostly modern dance with him. How funny all my kumu were men.

After my high school graduation in 1948 I went straight to Pearl Harbor to work. I did clerical work in the structural shop. In my building there were ship fitters, welders, sheet metal workers, and boilermakers. Another group had inside machinists and service tool rooms. Another one had electricians. Another was outside machinists who went onto the ships to work. I retired in 1986 after thirty-eight years.

I danced all through my married life. And I danced in the shipyard too when there were functions. I taught at one time too, but only kids.

In 1999 Auntie Betty Webster began wearing and collecting novelty glasses while working as a restaurant hostess in Kamuela. She has a Guinness World Record certificate for her running total of 1,506 individual designs, which was verified on October 2, 2015. She showed me her whole collection and we took photos of us wearing pairs of glasses!

Marvin "Puakea" Nogelmeier tells the following story about coming to Hawai'i and falling in love with hula and the Hawaiian culture.

Puakea Nogelmeier One of our good friends in the crafting group was Mililani Allen, a Hawaiian-Korean woman who did beautiful silk batik with Hawaiian patterns. Then we found out that she was actually a kumu hula from the first graduating class of Maiki Aiu Lake, about whom we didn't know much. Mililani explained to us, "I graduated two years ago and I really want to do a men's class but men are *so* gun-shy. Would you guys be in my class?" "Sure!" So all of us characters, a bunch of happy young potheads and a motley crew, showed up at her first men's class.

She was a fun lady, but once we stepped into hālau she said, "When you are in hālau, we do it the way I say it, *when* I say it and *how* I say it." She was like a different lady! But we loved it. I did not know anything about hula. Basically, I did not know anything at all. I remember saying, "Do we ever have to do this to music?" (Laughter.)

I had been in Hawai'i about two years, and I knew a lot of Hawai'i things, but I didn't know any Hawaiian things. And I couldn't tell the difference. To me anybody local was local. We started to learn dances and the very first one we learned was a hula kahiko called "Kawika" but it was for a king, which implied a kingdom, and it was in a foreign language! (Laughter.) Mililani had to explain all this to me. "This is the seventh king of the reign of kings." I didn't know any of that! You don't learn anything about Hawai'i if you are raised on the mainland. When I flew here, I didn't know there was more than one island. I thought of Hawai'i as some big lump out in the middle of the sea, warm and wet.

Hula was an introduction to a whole world. All of her classes were one hour, but the men's class met on Friday at 5:00 p.m. and sometimes we'd go until midnight. It was addictive. We were learning how to make Hawaiian things, how Hawaiian traditions worked, and about Hawaiian history. We were her labor force as she built the social entity of a hālau. If we needed *lei*, my hula brothers and I would go up in the mountains to get maile or *palapalai* fern. She taught us how to pick things. She was a remarkable resource.

She did not speak Hawaiian but the Maiki line was sort of a marriage of academy and tradition. We were learning the hula traditions and we had to keep notes and write down all the words to our hula. Mili made us translate each hula and know what those words meant. There was always a little academia involved.

In 1976 we got put into a new project that was funded by the State Council on Hawaiian Heritage. It was called the Mele Project, to teach young people chanting. Even though hula was having this great reflowering, chanting wasn't, other than the chants that went with the hula. Kumu hula did not *oli*. Nobody oli'ed. Today, there are five-year-olds who are oli-ing; they open the school day with an oli. Everybody has a repertoire of five to ten that they can pull out. Not so back then.

He Mele Aloha Songbook

I was shy about asking Carol Morse Wilcox for an interview because I had read her book, Sugar Water, *and feared she was too famous for a mere mortal to approach. She turned out to be totally charming. Had I known of the fabulous things most of my interviewees had done in their lives I would not have had the courage to approach them either. In this, as with many things, what I did not know gave me an advantage!*

Carol Wilcox Miki Bowers, my math teacher at Punahou, invited me to join their kanikapila[34] group, Hawaiian Sing. We met monthly at a different home. Miki was a dedicated military man, serving in the National Guard most of his life, and he ran Hawaiian Sing accordingly. You were expected to be on time, bring a potluck, and be settled and tuned up by 6:30 p.m. We always started with "'Ā 'Oia," which I never sang because I didn't have the music and didn't know what song they were singing. By the time I found it, the song was over. Everybody had their own three-ring binder of carefully collected music, which usually ran several hundred pages each. There were differences in verses and wording, and discussions about which might be more accurate. You really couldn't participate without having a three-ring binder of your own. Miki gave me a starting binder and I built up my own collection over the years.

Although I grew up singing, I didn't come to kanikapila naturally. I didn't have a natural ear for music or language. I remember singing an entire song enthusiastically in F when the group was singing in C. Couldn't figure out why I was getting "da look." At the end he said, "Well, it works in F too." It was a bit of a struggle. But oh how I loved it. I would leave a kanikapila

---

[34] Puakea Nogelmeier translates kanikapila as "let the music play."

evening full of joy. I joined the Punahou Alumni Choir and learned harmonies. My three-ring binder grew with the choir's sheet music.

It became clear that my three-ring binder was the tool that gave me access to kanikapila, and that there were many people like me who loved to kanikapila and could use such a tool. That was the genesis of *He Mele Aloha: A Hawaiian Songbook*.

While Hawaiian Sing was intolerant of hapa haole songs, and there was some resistance within our ranks, we included them in the songbook. I compiled a list of about 800 potential songs that lent themselves to kanikapila. This precluded chants and difficult solo pieces. Later we honed that to about 370 songs. I developed the format best suited for a kanikapila songbook—big typeface, simple chording, and tablature for each song, plus a lot of margin area for notes.

After about a year I took the mocked-up book to our friend David Sproat, musician and entertainer, and the fire chief for Kaua'i, who had long talked about doing a Hawaiian songbook. I showed him the project and told him I'd be glad to turn it over to him if he wanted to do it, or we could collaborate on it. He said, "You do it. I've always wanted to do this but I know I'm not going to get to it." Sitting in David's kitchen was Kimo Hussey, and he said, "I'll be happy to help you on this book. I have formal training in music, and I'm thinking of starting an academy focusing on the 'ukulele."

I wanted to know if there was community support. I asked Mihana Souza if she thought it was a worthwhile project for me to do, and no one could have been more supportive. Auntie Manu Brand, whom you might know as the sister of Auntie Leina'ala Woodside, and Auntie Mae Loebenstein, who had nurtured me throughout my childhood and adult years, gave their blessing.

With that permission and encouragement I moved ahead with Kimo Hussey, Vicky Hollinger—a musician and entertainer who has a voice to die for and knows every song that has ever been sung—and Puakea Nogelmeier, historian, composer and dancer, Hawaiian language scholar, and voice of TheBus.

There is a long history of Hawaiian music being appropriated for profit, often without permission, fair compensation, or even credit. Our team wanted no part of that history. We agreed that we would participate *manuahi* and that we would donate any profits to a to-be-determined charitable cause.

It was essential that we be as accurate as possible when chronicling an oral tradition, that we use the most authentic lyrics, identify composers and their intent, and describe the context as best we could. While *He Mele Aloha*'s bibliography lists published resources, it does not acknowledge the heavy reliance on dust jackets and liners, or on programs from musical events, or sheet music. Our local libraries were helpful, but it was the Library of Congress's collection that filled in a lot of gaps.

Every Tuesday Puakea would come to our house and review existing translations, or, if necessary, create translations. Every Thursday Kimo and Vicky would come over and they would sing the songs four or five times. They'd decide what key to play it in and I would write down the notes for the songs and put chords up in tablature at the top. If you are like me and you can't remember the fingering for a D, you can look right up there for the tablature. We explained how to transpose if you didn't like singing it in that key.

I visited or spoke to everyone I could to get their *manaʻo* and *kōkua*. I was able to talk story with many composers and artists who were unfailingly generous and kind.

On the legal side of things, much of traditional Hawaiian music was written prior to Hawaiʻi's being annexed, so the question as to whether or not it was covered by United States copyright laws were complex, to say the least. To further complicate the issue was the ever-changing language of US copyright laws, starting with a short time period and evolving into corporations grabbing them wholesale in perpetuity.

By the oddest coincidence, I found a copyright lawyer who loved Hawaiian music and specialized in intellectual property rights. Turned out he was a neighbor! John Overton's usual gig was to protect copyrights; in this case we were looking for public domain material. Copyright infringement is a serious concern. The exposure is huge. With the help of Wayne Pitluck, I set up my own publishing company, ʻOliʻOli Publishing, LLC. We confined ourselves to the lyrics rather than the sheet music or melody, and we approached the families and composers for permission. No one was compensated for the right to publish their work. If they didn't want their work published, it's not in the book. There were only two songs that we wanted that we didn't use. Everyone was generous; even those who were not that enthusiastic about the project itself participated because the profits would go to Lunalilo Home.

It has succeeded beyond our wildest expectations. It's well into its fifteenth printing; it has generated over $150,000 for the Lunalilo Home for elderly Hawaiians. Because it was originally spiral-bound, no one would review it. To this day it hasn't been reviewed. We had problems with the spiral edition, so eventually I put it out in a lay-flat paperbound edition. Most significantly, it has changed the paradigm from Hawaiian music being somewhat proprietary to allowing universal access to it and to the user-friendly ʻukulele.

JG *It's sold 100,001 because I'm getting it for my friend for Christmas!*

CW Excellent! *He Mele Aloha* is a gift on everybody's part and it has been the gift that keeps giving back. We cannot go out without somebody saying, "Thank you so much for that book." It has given and returned nothing but joy and pleasure and aloha. And it was huge fun too.

It should be noted here that Carol Wilcox recently turned all of her resource materials over to the Hawai'i State Archives. ❖

Boat Day, *SS Lurline*, circa 1960s

CHAPTER 9

Voices of Aloha

Welcoming Visitors
Here are three delightful vignettes about travelers arriving in the Islands.

Diane Paton To get a job at Matson Navigation Company, I just went in and knocked on the door. The shipping department office was located on the docks on Nimitz Highway in Honolulu. It was the most favorite, favorite job that I have ever had. I worked in the booking department for the freighters. In addition to their four Waikīkī hotels and their fleet of freighters, Matson had four luxury passenger liners, the *Lurline, Matsonia, Mariposa,* and *Monterey.* My co-workers in the booking department were a wonderful mix of Japanese, Korean, Chinese, Filipino, and Portuguese—the hardest-working, most interesting group imaginable. Their diligence and *esprit de corps* made for an outstanding learning experience.

　　On Boat Days, when the passenger ships docked in Honolulu, they were greeted by the Royal Hawaiian Band, beautiful hula dancers, and bronzed Hawaiian swimmers diving for silver half dollars thrown overboard by passengers. In those days, when Hawai'i students departed to mainland colleges, they were feted by friends and family with onboard send-off parties and heaped with flower lei piled to their eyes. My friend Maili Yardley wrote *Hawai'i's Glamour Days*, describing those years so very well.

　　While training for work at the Matson travel desks of their flagship Waikīkī hotels—the Moana, Surfrider, Princess Kaiulani and Royal Hawaiian—I was sent on delightful orientation trips to the outer islands. When you see a large tour bus marked with the Roberts Tours rabbit logos, they are the fruition of the American dream through the hard work of a kindly Filipino gentleman who would loan his old car to me at his little car rental agency on Kaua'i in the early 1950s.

It was during a day when I was working at the Royal Hawaiian Hotel travel desk that film producer Carl Dudley offered me a leading role in [the film] *Cinerama South Seas Adventure*, which provided yet another dimension to my multifaceted career—with a daily salary that dwarfed my weekly Matson pay.

Kaui Philpotts I lived in Honolulu between 1963 and 1967, working for Tradewind Tours on the tour desk in Waikīkī. I sold tours around the island. The 1960s were a lot of fun because local people still went to the beach at Waikīkī and there was Hawaiian music at all the nightclubs. There were actual hula dancers at the hotels. This was the Waikīkī of the Surfers and Don Ho at Duke's and Kui Lee at Queen's Surf. Tourism was just beginning to boom. You didn't have the mega-hotels yet. The biggest hotel chains were InterIsland Resorts and Island Holidays.

Stuart Ho My great-grandfather, Ho Tin Hee, was from a small village in the Pearl River Delta of China. When he and his brothers immigrated to Hawai'i, he was warned by his older brother not to work on the plantations because the work was back-breaking. So my great-grandfather went to work for the Ward Estate as a day laborer on the land where the Neal S. Blaisdell Center is located today. When my great-grandfather left the Ward Estate he tenant-farmed a large piece of land for rice, at the corner of Kalākaua Avenue and McCully Street. These were the days before the Ala Wai Canal so there was nothing but swamp there. He sold his rice farm in 1915 and moved to "the lanes."

The Chinese social ladder was based on residence. At the bottom of the heap were the guys on the plantations. The low merchant class lived in what Hung Wo Ching used to call "the lanes" off School Street. My grandfather's house is underneath the H-1 freeway near Frog Lane. The next tier up was what they called "Chinese Hollywood," located on the old Bingham Tract, which extended from Pi'ikoi and Pensacola Streets to Date Street. If you were really a high muck-a-muck, you lived in 'Ālewa Heights.

Any yard with a fruit tree in it was owned by a Chinese; the first thing the Chinese did when they moved in was plant a fruit tree. Just drive down H-1 and look on both sides and you will see them.

Ho Tin Hee's brother made a small wartime fortune with a camera and a hula girl on Hotel Street, taking pictures of GIs coming into Honolulu by train at River Street. Because he was shrewd in locating the camera stall, he was able to take pictures of the GIs as they got off the O'ahu Railway & Land train. He sold them prints when they returned to the train station after their leave.

Made in Hawai'i

Puakea Nogelmeier has become the voice of TheBus, Honolulu's public transportation system. If ridership on TheBus has increased, it might be the result of my having told so many people this story!

Puakea Nogelmeier TheBus wanted to initiate an audio service for the visually impaired who might not be able to see street signs, and as an aid to tourists who need a little assistance with our language. The first voice they recorded was that of a man from Texas. In order for him to get the words right, they gave him pronunciation guides. It didn't work so they asked several local folks to do it and it was a mixed bag. They ended up using the voice of one of my students, whose Hawaiian was good, but for some reason there were a lot of complaints. People thought he sounded "grouchy" or sounded like he didn't like their street. (Laughter.) He's a delightful man so this can't be true.

Someone told the guys at TheBus, "I know a guy who can pronounce all of the words correctly, but his voice is probably too low." They said, "Oh, we can fix that. We can digitize it and move the voice wherever we want if the pronunciation is correct." So, we did a test and they liked it. We recorded the entire thirty-hour script in a studio. As it happened, a New York company owned the recording and TheBus had to pay them residuals for its use. It became cheaper over time for TheBus to buy their own equipment and produce their own product. So, we re-recorded the whole thing!

When we did the second recording, the bus drivers said, "Make sure he does it the same way." They loved the way that I said, "Please be careful when exiting TheBus." They said it sounded *so* sincere, so real. (Laughter.) TheBus was adamant about recording it the same way. It was kind of funny.

From the beginning I said, "If you answer the phone with a smile, people hear the smile. Let's record this while smiling." So all of that recording was done on my tiptoes at my highest range. I'd say "Kapi'olani" with a smile and it was still too low, and they had to move it up. But it was done smiling. I'm always surprised when a bus door opens, and I hear, "Aloha and welcome aboard." It sounds friendly.

The important thing is it created a stable public model for the pronunciation of spoken Hawaiian. You can hear "Wai'anae" five ways in the course of a day: on the radio, on the street, in a hotel, on television, in the countryside. You can hear "Wainae," "Waianae," all kinds of pronunciations. On TheBus there is a stable model that says Kāne'ohe and Wai'anae correctly and the same way every day. It has started to affect how people pronounce Hawaiian words.

Someone had a friend visiting from Washington, DC. This man had a nineteen-year-old son working as an intern in a Honolulu law office. Every day he went to the office on TheBus. When the father visited he asked his son to meet him on "Kappy-olani." His son said, "Dad, it's Kapiʻolani. It's not that hard. Just try it. Kapiʻolani." The son was on TheBus every day so his pronunciation was smooth. He only knew how to say it one way. My way! Whereas the father had been hearing it nineteen different ways.

Not long after Puakea told me his story I had the opportunity to drive him to Waiʻanae. The entire drive I had the sound of Puakea's voice in my ear, telling me about the valleys, the ahupuaʻa we were passing through, the names of the towns. It was like my own private TheBus narration!

My very last interview was with Neil Hannahs, an education management expert who spent four decades with Kamehameha Schools. One of his charming stories involved an Island garment manufacturer that made a real difference.

Neil Hannahs I was aware that other indigenous people had received land in settlement of claims against their government and I wondered whether we might benefit from models they had developed. So we set up site visits and meetings with tribes in Alaska and New Zealand to see if we could learn something from their management practices. We asked native leaders, "Do you manage your own lands? What outcomes or returns do you seek from your lands? Does this create opportunities for your people?"

In each case, we learned that their lands were managed by a professional staff with largely Western management skills and objectives. Tribal members represented a very small proportion of the management structure, and their primary goal was to generate income. I asked, "How's that working for you?" They replied, "We hate it!" Then I suggested, "Why don't we change it?"

Consequently, fifteen years ago we joined with Maori and Alaskan tribes in creating and launching a fellowship with the Stanford Woods Institute for the Environment at Stanford University. The program engages early- and mid-career native leaders with an interest in land and natural resource management. To date, nearly 200 fellows have completed the program. Stanford leaders constantly comment on how much this tiny program has changed that big, venerable institution. Imagine that! I went to Stanford as a student thinking that I needed to become like them and today they are learning from us!

We were quite successful in recruiting Hawaiian enterprises to our lands and over time, through their steadfast efforts, lands that were overgrown and in utter disrepair started to come to life and were capable of productive use. I partnered with Kamehameha graduate Lisa Kleissner in co-founding a social enterprise business accelerator called the Hawaiian Investment Ready Program. Lisa and her husband, Charly, built equity in Silicon Valley tech companies and exited their investments with wealth that they used to form a foundation to promote impact investment around the world. When I introduced her to Hawai'i entrepreneurs who were dedicated to healing our lands and promoting community well being, Lisa said, "These are just the types of enterprises we work with in Africa, India, and Europe."

The enterprises that have participated have expressed heartfelt appreciation for our services and for the opportunity to generate the earned income that could reduce their reliance on grants and increase their sense of self-determination. Kealopiko is a good example of such an enterprise. Three Hawaiian women formed this Hawaiian apparel company at a time when most aloha wear design and production was shipped overseas. They started designing Hawaiian content and fashioning beautiful clothing. They produced their line with none of the toxic chemicals that make the garment industry the second largest polluter on Earth, second only to the fossil fuel industries. They find a use for every inch of cloth. They produce and warehouse their inventory on Molokai, an island with high unemployment. Essentially, they have put the "aloha" back in aloha wear.

Agriculture and Tourism
Jim Case's book, Hawai'i Lawyer: Lessons in Law and Life from a Six-Decade Career, *inspired my book, and he was one of my first interviews. Jim claims that his book accidentally turned into an economic history of Hawai'i during his lifetime—a history of sugar, pineapple, and ranching that became the story of how, over time, tourism and financial services took over the economy.*

James Case My thought is that tourism and agriculture can coexist. Tourist resorts invest in land that is not good for agriculture. The best place for resorts is the Kona Coast, which has never been good for agriculture. The best agriculture on the Big Island is on the Hāmākua Coast. Who wants a tourist resort there? Ka'ū can grow sugar cane and macadamia nuts, but it is not a beautiful place to have a hotel. On the island of Hawai'i, tourism and agriculture could coexist—*but* the island of Hawai'i passed a law that you can't grow anything unless you can prove that genetically modified crops (GMOs) won't hurt anybody. This is what we call, in legal terms, having to prove a negative. You can't prove a negative. You can't prove that something won't happen.

They grandfathered in people who were currently farming. But unless they change the law, the farmers will all go out of business. Maui passed the same law, which will mean that farming on Maui will die out. This includes all the land near Pu'unēnē and the (former) Hawaiian Commercial & Sugar land. They are raising cattle on it now. And what about all the farmers in Kula? You have to file a $100,000 environmental impact statement if you want to do anything. Who can afford that? The only thing they can do with the farms up there is live on them.

So I sit here and I moan. Political factors at the moment are controlling the demise of agriculture. [*An update from Mr. Case: Since this interview the courts have held that federal law preempts local law, which means that these laws on Hawaiʻi and Maui islands are illegal.*]

Due to tourism, Oʻahu has the lowest unemployment rate in the state and is saturated with people. That's not true of the Big Island, where there is plenty of room. We have a Hawaiʻi Tourism Authority whose job is to get more tourists. One of our legislators is an independent thinker and has said, "Aren't we saturated with tourists? Yet the Hawaiʻi Tourism Authority is working to attract more." She seems to be the only one asking that question.

The following five passages pertain to water, sustainability, and the changes the jet era brought to the state.

Randy Moore Molokai Ranch is basically a real estate company that owns about 55,000 acres of land, mostly devoted to cattle ranching. The primary motivation for large landowners to raise cattle in Hawaiʻi is to keep property taxes low. Land zoned for agriculture and used for agriculture is valued for property tax purposes at its economic value (for ranching). If you stop ranching and let the lantana and guava take over, the land is valued at "market," which is considerably higher.

You basically don't make money on the cattle. Monty Richards of Kahuā Ranch on the Big Island used to say, "There is a seven-year cycle of cattle prices. You hope your profits are good enough in the two good years to offset your losses in the five bad years—but they usually weren't." After Dole purchased the Libby, McNeill & Libby pineapple business in 1972, and Del Monte closed their Molokai operations in the late 1970s and '80s and ceased renting land from Molokai Ranch for pineapple cultivation, the ranch planted hay on those fields. They harvested the hay and sold it primarily to dairymen on Oʻahu. There are no longer any dairies on Oʻahu, so that business is now gone.

Molokai Ranch owned the towns of Maunaloa and Kualapuʻu, lock, stock, and barrel. Maunaloa had been built by Libby for its Molokai pineapple plantation workers, offices, and shops. Kualapuʻu had been built by Del Monte for the same purpose. Both towns were on land owned by the ranch. When the pineapple operations closed, the ranch inherited the two towns and the infrastructure that supported them—water systems, sewer systems, and roads. After Del Monte announced its departure, the ranch worked with Maui County to subdivide the town as is, and sold the individual homes to the tenants.

Molokai Ranch has had a couple of owners since I worked there in the late 1980s, both of whom had plans for resort and second home development that were stymied by community opposition. The current owner has had the ranch on the market for several years at an asking price of $260 million.

There's not much going on now at the ranch. A tenant rancher has several hundred head of cattle, but the resort on the west end that had been developed by Louisiana Land & Exploration Company in the 1970s—on land acquired from the ranch and subsequently reacquired by the ranch—is pretty much closed. Shuttered operations include two hotels and an eighteen-hole golf course.

William Tam Sumner Erdman of ʻUlupalakua Ranch was on the water commission for a while. He said that when he was younger, the vegetation that used to be at 800 feet is now at 1,300 feet, which has an impact on raising cattle. Many exotic plants don't capture water as well as native plants, so you get more runoff. Therefore, as the vegetation of exotics moves up the mountain, you are getting less capture of water. Pigs and goats tear up the ground.

Erdman and USGS biologist-naturalist Art Medeiros formed this great alliance in Auwahi, an area on Maui that used to be forested and inhabited. Now it is one of the most degraded areas in the state. If you fly over it in a helicopter, you can see all the old sites are now just red dirt. This is toward Kaupō if you're going around ʻUlupalakua on the upper road.

Erdman and Medeiros started an experiment. They took ten acres in a rectangular shape. I asked them why they did that and they said, "So you could see it on Google Earth." They put some check dams in some of the gullies to stop flooding. They fenced it to keep the pigs and goats out. Then they got kids up there to pull out all the exotic plants. They didn't water the land. Lo and behold, the native plants have come back, including some endangered species, which we thought were extinct. A tree has come back that we thought had died out in 1910. The seeds were in the soil.[35]

Kaui Philpotts My grandmother on the Hawaiian side grew up on the Hāmākua Coast. Her father was a luna on a sugar plantation. but her mother lived with the family in Hilo. She was half Hawaiian, half Chinese. The Hāmākua Coast was beautiful. But on Maui, the main plantations were on scrubland. All of central Maui is going back to the brush that it used to be. It's going to be like a dust bowl.

---

[35] Visit Google Auwahi USGS for a TED talk on this topic.

JG *When reading Carol Wilcox's book,* Sugar Water, *I was fascinated with the effort it took to move water from one place to another so that the cane could grow.*

KP Now there's a big fight over water. Should it be used for development or for farmers? Before they develop a lot of homes, there have to be jobs. There are no jobs. There is no industry except for tourism.

I am very, very sad when I go back to Maui. More than any other island, Maui seems to have lost its culture. I grew up above Pā'ia and below Makawao, which was kind of upcountry but not quite. It is lower upcountry. We had sugar camps all over. We lived in what was called Skill Village because it was mostly white-collar workers or management, and skilled labor. My father was an accountant for MA Company [Maui Agriculture]. It is the best climate in the world—it was perfect. They grew cane below our house and pineapple above us.

Jets to Hawai'i

Willson Moore In 1959, statehood came. Hawai'i's attorney general at the time was Bert Kobayashi. He said to me, "With statehood, we have gone from a unicameral system [one house] to bicameral [a house and a senate]. Too many of my deputies have quit to run for public office. The Airport Division needs legal help. Come work for us as a special deputy attorney general."

The state wanted to move the Honolulu airport from the old John Rodgers Airport location on Lagoon Drive to where it is now and that meant a lot of legal work. Tim Ho was the head of the Department of Transportation. Dr. Fujio Matsuda was the head of Public Works and was the big boss. He and I are friends now but back in those days I was a very young attorney. I would never have dreamed that one day I too would call him "Fudge."

I did all of the drafting of the leases and concessions for the new airport. I spent hours and hours and hours with representatives from the major airlines, negotiating the means by which the airlines would pay for their use of the airport. We worked out a system which involved their paying landing fees to the State of Hawai'i whenever they touched down. We made a special allowance for Hawaiian and Aloha Airlines because they landed and took off with greater frequency.

Peter Fithian of Greeters of Hawai'i came to see me. "Willie, I want to provide greeting services for hire. If a businessman can't meet a client coming in, I'll go down and give him a lei and arrange transportation." That sounded crazy but I drafted the concession agreement and of course it proved very profitable for both the state and for Peter.

All leases and concessions went out for bid. Peter Canlis ran the restaurant in the old airport. Peter thought the airport commissioners were automatically going to give him the restaurant and all food concessions at the new airport. They said they were required by law to put it out to bid, which they did. I had nothing to do with it. A Los Angeles outfit called Host International finally won the bid.

A disappointed restaurant bidder from Buffalo, New York—Sport Service Corporation—sued the state. They claimed they were as good or better than Host International and the Airport Commission should have given them the restaurant concession. I was the deputy attorney general assigned to defend the case. I won in the lower court and Sport Service appealed to the Hawai'i Supreme Court, and I won again.

If my memory is correct, in November 1962 the move from Lagoon Drive was accomplished and we opened at the present airport location. Tim Ho asked me to walk through the new airport and report any potential litigation risks so they could be corrected.

On April 28, 1988, Aloha Airlines Flight 243 was en route from Hilo to Honolulu. The skin of the plane partially peeled off. The flight attendant standing near the door without a seatbelt was sucked out of the airplane. Some of the passengers in seatbelts had some debris injuries but the plane made a successful emergency landing on Maui, though much of the top was gone. The British had learned about aircraft metal fatigue in World War II. When fighter aircraft made rapid ascents and descents, the changes in temperature and pressure had a billowing effect on the aluminum skin of the aircraft, creating microscopic cracks. If the skin wasn't repaired, removed, or replaced, it resulted in failure of the fuselage of the aircraft. This was a known phenomenon during World War II but here we were, decades later, dealing with it in Aloha Airlines planes made by Boeing.

Boeing had what we call an AD (airworthy directive) that specifically called for the inspection of the fuselage at various periods during the aircraft's service to try and discover these microscopic cracks. Boeing never realized that the planes that Aloha and Hawaiian were using went up 20,000 feet, landed, then went back up twenty times a day, pressurizing and depressurizing. That was enough to cause the slight billowing effect and create microscopic cracks which propagated back from the doorway on Aloha.

Airports are very dynamic and that was a fascinating time in my legal career. The doorways to tourism opened wide with the introduction of jets and the new airport on O'ahu.

Dennis Fitzgerald Tourism as you see it today couldn't have happened without the changes in technology, communications, and the airline industry.

The first time I came to Hawai'i was on a prop plane. We didn't have jets. The internet allowed improved communication that facilitated the compilation of airline travel and hotel industry data. I think we are up to about ten million tourists a year, and tracking hotel rooms, transportation and local venue data for that number of people is staggering.

Enough is Enough
On Kaua'i tourism issues consumed the Hanalei community as it strove for a balance between economic profit and the loss of its identity.

Carol Wilcox Hanalei is unique, sacred even, in its beauty, cultural landscape, and history. In the 1960s there were no zoning and no building codes on Kaua'i; you applied for a permit and you got it. When the Hanalei Plantation Hotel suddenly appeared on the ridge behind the Hanalei Pier, tarnishing the iconic Hanalei Bay view, it became obvious that Hanalei itself was vulnerable to development.

Kaua'i initiated its first-ever planning process and started with the North Shore Regional Plan in 1971. An individual household survey of North Shore residents ranked community values. Number one, even over economic considerations was: "Preserve the rural and scenic nature of the North Shore." This has guided North Shore planning ever since.

In 1978 Hanalei was a small and traditional community, rich in beauty and history and complex relationships. That year the county adopted the North Shore Development Plan under the leadership of Planning Director Brian Nishimoto. Kaua'i's good planning in general, and Hanalei and the North Shore in particular, stand on his shoulders.

Around 1980 the Hawai'i Department of Transportation (HDOT) determined the need to replace the Hanalei Bridge with a two-lane bridge. They assured us it would look like and creak like the existing bridge, but to meet federal highway standards, the roadway would require realignment, would be widened to include shoulders and rails and pull-off lanes, and eventually would extend to Kē'ē. State Department of Transportation Director E. Alvey Wright asked for community involvement in developing the plans.

We happily responded by establishing the North Shore Belt Road Citizen Advisory Committee, thankfully better known as the "Roads Committee," comprised of representatives of community organizations.

It soon became apparent that the HDOT plan was incompatible with the regional plan's number-one priority to "preserve the rural and scenic nature of the North Shore." Consequently, the Roads Committee requested that

"Historic Preservation of the Hanalei Bridge" be added to alternatives in the Environmental Impact Statement (EIS).

While historic preservation was well established in Hawai'i, it had never been applied to transportation, and if HDOT had its way, it wasn't going to start now. After thirteen years, with the help of HDOT Deputy Director Cheryl Soon and facilitator Peter Adler, the Historic Preservation alternative was added to the EIS and the question of replacing or restoring the bridge was brought before the North Shore community in a public hearing facilitated by James Detor.

The community came out in overwhelming support of preserving the existing sense of scale and slower pace. The opinion of the taro farmers, the caretakers of the soul of Hanalei, was especially important. Karol Haraguchi testified that while her family's farm would benefit from better transportation to get products to market, it would be at the cost of their best taro lo'i. Given that choice, they supported preservation of the Hanalei Bridge.

Safety is always a major consideration. The proposed improvements would handle the larger modern fire trucks. However, a local fireman testified that the fire department had to use a small fire engine on the North Shore to access Hanalei's narrow roads and bridges.

It was decided that the Hanalei Bridge would not be replaced; rather, it was historically restored. Furthermore, Route 560 from Princeville to Hanalei was declared eligible for the National Register of Historic Places.

This decision postponed but did not halt tourism from overwhelming the North Shore. While bridge weight limits prevent large tour buses from passing beyond the Hanalei Bridge, there is no limit to the number of cars or smaller vans and buses. Traffic, parking, and road deterioration have become huge problems.

New problems arose with the advent of commercial boat tours of the Nā Pali Coast. Zodiac companies started in the 1970s at Mākua Beach—called Tunnels—in Ha'ena. By the 1980s, companies began to stage from the boat ramp in the Hanalei River estuary and at Black Pot Park, a small county park by the Hanalei Pier.

A boat tour down the Nā Pali Coast is one of the more spectacular day trips anywhere, no question about it. On some days, upwards of thirty-seven companies were taking more than 3,000 people down the coast. They took up the parking space, the roadways, the park, and toilet facilities. Boats were fueled by hand from containers and launched right off of the beach. The Hanalei Estuary was perpetually covered with a sheen of gas and oil. Cars and trucks were everywhere. Boats sped in and out of the river mouth. It was a mess.

HDOT established the Ad Hoc Committee on Commercial Boating in Hanalei, consisting mostly of commercial boating and retail representatives.

The only non-commercial member of the committee, I was included on behalf of the Hanalei Hawaiian Civic Canoe Club. After a year and a half, the committee agreed on recommending fifteen carefully regulated permits. These were adopted and the DLNR issued the permits.

Then a worse dispute emerged over a boatyard that Mike Sheehan had developed on private land along the estuary banks without a Special Management Area permit. This was a rift that tore the community and its families apart for well over a decade. It is a common story, where jobs and industry conflict with community values and environmental health, but the fact that it's been told many times doesn't in the least reduce the impact on the participants.

Once again, it was the community's job to decide. I helped orchestrate a process to inform the North Shore community about the issues. Four informational meetings were facilitated by Linda Colburn: government rules and regulations, environmental issues, economic benefits from the boater's perspective, and the cultural impacts of boating. All meetings were broadcast on Kaua'i Public Television and the public was invited to attend.

The government presentation was weak. The scientists wimped out. The boaters did themselves no favors. But the final meeting, the one on cultural impact, was riveting. After listening patiently and respectfully throughut the process, well-known and respected local families with generations of history, the same ones who chose "Preserve the rural and scenic beauty of the North Shore" for themselves and their children over all other values, came forward in full force. They said, "We showed you aloha and you took advantage. You are killing us."

Over the four months of this process, islandwide public perception and support of commercial tour boating out of Hanalei went from 80 percent support of the industry to 80 support of the community.

With that mandate, the Planning Department spent the next year developing the Hanalei Estuary Management Plan (HEMP), which limited commercial operation to seven highly restricted permits. Fierce commercial resistance continued. I think there were over twenty-five lawsuits filed, including a SLAPP [Strategic Lawsuit Against Public Participation] suit filed in federal court against county officials in their official and personal capacities for $8 million. None of these suits prevailed, but they succeded in slowing the process and discouraging discussion. Nevertheless, HEMP was passed by the Kaua'i Planning Commission on September 10, 1992, just as Hurricane 'Iniki was bearing down on the Islands.

On the morning of September 11, the Category 4 'Iniki passed dead center over Kaua'i. The hurricane closed down the boating industry for over a year. Eventually the seven permitted operators started up. And then, again, so did unlicensed operations, and protests. It became extremely heated. One day, protesters lined up in the river to blockade the entrance and one of these kids was almost killed. It was a near thing and everyone came to their senses. There was a hiatus.

At that very moment, Governor [Ben] Cayetano came to a fundraiser in Princeville. He had not visited Hanalei before, so later he went with some local guys down to the valley and to Black Pot Park. Hanalei was at its most magnificent that day: the sturdy historic Hanalei Bridge, rainbows, taro loʻi, surfer trucks, sparkling waterfalls, and the ocean. A fishing tournament was staged off Black Pot Park, kids jumped off the Hanalei Pier, local families and tourists intermingled, and most consequentially, as it turned out, many small children were playing along the riverbank.

Governor Cayetano took in the breathtaking beauty of the day, the place, the activity, the joy, and the tranquility. He asked where the tour boats staged. "Right here, in the river mouth, more than 1,000 people a day go in and out right here!" The governor went back to Honolulu and ten days later he came out with an edict. 'There is to be no commercial boating in Hanalei." This was in 1994, twenty years after the first boats started operating out of Hanalei. And that was it. Settled. Over.

It was the right answer for Hanalei, and at some level everyone knew it. It was *pono*. It amazed me that when Governor Cayetano wrote his fine autobiography he never mentioned this event. He saved a community and never even mentioned it. He is a real hero in my book.

I'd like to tell you that the issue was resolved then, but no. First one, then another company came back in, starting slowly, and then growing so that by 2018 there was a fair amount of commercial activity again, although it was much more respectful than it had been in years past. Once again weather made the call. Starting in the afternoon of April 14, 2018, over forty-nine inches of rain fell in twenty-four hours, a national record. The road to Black Pot Park was washed out, along with boats, canoes, trailers, cars, and houses. Black Pot Park was closed for over a year. During that year the county expanded the park to include acreage up the river, restrictions were placed on all commercial activity, and in August 2019, the newly expanded Black Pot Park was opened. Stay tuned. ❖

Alexander & Baldwin office building under construction, 1928

CHAPTER 10

Voices of Development

Stone Houses

Honolulu real estate developer Duncan MacNaughton explained how homes were built from stone quarried on site in the Puʻu Pānini neighborhood near Diamond Head's eastern flank, thanks to the creative genius of plantation manager David Larsen.

Duncan MacNaughton My father became aware of a house called Puʻu Pānini that had been built in 1931 by a guy named David Larsen, who worked for C. Brewer. His hobby was building houses on the weekends. His requirement for picking a location was that it have enough natural rock on the property to build the walls of the house out of stone. Mr. Larsen was manager of the Kilauea Plantation on Kauaʻi, among other plantations, and he built the manager's house at Kilauea totally out of lava rock, again quarried on site. When he was assigned to Honolulu, he built a home that turned into the Crouching Lion Inn near Kahana Bay. The third home he built was right here at Puʻu Pānini.

The rock under the promontory of Puʻu Pānini is a reef formed millions and millions of years ago. It grew underwater around the base of Diamond Head and at some point was raised by volcanic action or uplift. Larsen built four houses at Puʻu Pānini. Nature provided the cliff, which goes half a mile one way and half a mile the other way. He quarried the rock right off the front of the cliff overlooking Kāhala. He started quarrying on the cliff edge and cut off strips of limestone/coral. The quarry site still exists and is now a big pit with a monkeypod tree growing in it.

Coral is the rock at the surface; it is the top of the reef and it has a fairly rough texture. Through wave action the ocean grinds coral into sand. Over time, sand captured on the reef is cemented together by the weight of the reef, turning it into sandstone. The texture on the front of our house is fairly smooth, but if you go to the back of the house it's very rough. The back of the house is coral, and the front is sandstone. I like the rough coral surface better because of its texture.

Larsen used the quarried stone differently from house to house. Some houses were made primarily of sandstone. Another was actually stacked sandstone, which is entirely different. You harvest sandstone in horizontal layers as opposed to vertical layers.

In 1931 Mr. Larsen finished this house and lived in it until he died just before World War II. Mrs. Larsen said to the military, "If you want to use my home during the war as an officers' club, you have my permission." The military took over a lot of properties like this on Oʻahu and turned them back to the owners after the war. Mrs. Larsen didn't want to move back into her house after the war and put all four of the houses up for sale.

My father was interested in living here because it was fee simple versus leasehold at Kāhala. Fee simple means that the person who buys it owns the property outright. They have legal title to the dirt. Leasehold means a lessor owns the dirt and gives you a lease to use the property for somewhere between fifty to sixty years.

Before the Bishop Estate leases in Kāhala expired around 1999, a state law came into effect that the lessee had the right to buy the leasehold at a price that was acceptable to the lessor. If there couldn't be a meeting of the minds, the state had the right to condemn the lessor's interest, an appraisal would be arranged, and everybody would go away happy.

At some point in time, Punahou School had been given all the property that now makes up Puʻu Pānini Circle. My father approached Punahou and bought it. One of the reasons my father reached out to buy all this property was he had seen the city subdivision plan for this area, and he didn't like it. Each lot had a house at the front of the lot and one at the back down a long driveway. They were called "flag lots" because of the long driveway, like a pole, that had two flags flying on it. He convinced the city to allow him to subdivide the property the way you see it today.

JG *Was your dad the one who figured out the layout, the elevations, and the dimensions of the lots? He must have had fun doing that!*

DM Yes, he did all that and the park was his idea. The paddle tennis court, however, was my mother's idea.

A Realtor Remembers

Jeanne "Frankie" McDonald Anderson Licensed in 1956, I am probably the longest licensed Realtor in the state of Hawaiʻi. I have specialized in oceanfront properties in Kāhala, Black Point, Portlock, and the Gold Coast, along with equestrian estates and Kona resort properties.

My mother, Marion Blair, came to Hawaiʻi in 1938 and became an extremely successful businesswoman. She was more than a Realtor, advising numerous condominium developers and representing buyers in every building along the Gold Coast. She also served as the listing broker for the developers, working hand in hand in designing their floor plans and providing sales strategy and promotional expertise.

She marketed the Diamond Head Ambassador, The Kainalu, The Sea Breeze, The Tahitienne, the Castle Surf, and the Rosalei apartments in Waikīkī. She wisely purchased a prime unit in each project. She worked with numerous developers including Rudy Tongg and Fred Daily and several architects such as George Wimberly and Hal Whitaker. I believe my mother sold Henry Kaiser his first Waikīkī property on John 'Ena Road.

After college, my first job was working for Betty Wilder writing for the *Honolulu Star-Bulletin* society page, meeting many celebrities and world travelers like Peter Lawford and Richard Boone. This led to traveling to Australia to do publicity work on the film *Kangaroo*. From 1950 to 1953 I worked at MGM in Los Angeles as a publicist. In addition, I wrote articles for *Life* magazine and worked for *Sports Illustrated*, answering letters to the editor. I provided fashion show commentary for Carol & Mary at the Royal Hawaiian for many years as well.

I met my husband, Robert Alexander Anderson, Jr., on the beach at the Outrigger Canoe Club in 1953 and we were married in 1955. Bob is the eldest son of Peggy and Alex (Andy) Anderson, who was a businessman and president of The Hawaii Corporation (formerly Von Hamm-Young). He was also the composer of several of the most famous hapa-haole hits: "Haole Hula," "Lovely Hula Hands," and "Mele Kalikimaka." Their family goes back many generations in Hawai'i. George "Dad" Center, Peggy's brother, coached Duke Kahanamoku in three Olympic Games. Alexander Young, who built the Young Hotel, was Bob's great-grandfather.

The Diamond Head Ambassador on Kalākaua Avenue was the first cooperative apartment built on the Gold Coast and my mother was the selling agent. It is a development that consists of three buildings, on three separate but contiguous lots, with two owners and joined by Japanese-inspired bridges between them. The two outside lots were owned by the same individual, while the middle lot had a separate owner. The thought was that after the fifty-five-year lease expired, the owners could remove the bridges and have three unique properties. Of course this did not happen. They consolidated into one lot and eventually bought the fee on the land.

Another prolific developer, Charlie Pietsch, brought my mother aboard for his Regency at Kāhala project. I was one of only three sales agents. On the initial day of sales, I was late to work on the day sales opened. (I had been visiting the Kona Coast with Richard Boone and his wife, Claire). I arrived at the sales center at 10:30 a.m., only to discover that the building had sold out between 8 a.m. and 10 a.m. People had received the marketing material, loved the location, and wanted in. I learned a valuable lesson from that experience—never be late for an appointment!

My most interesting and favorite real estate transaction involved an oceanfront parcel on Royal Place where Kāhala Beach meets Black Point. There was a large estate, which had been formerly owned by members of the Shingle family. It was leasehold and had to be sold on an agreement of sale because of stipulations of the sellers' family trust. The actor Lee Majors wanted to purchase the home. Majors' attorney, David Flynn, came to town with his actress wife, Jane Seymour, and said, "We can't possibly buy this—it's leasehold! Do you think I'm a fool?! Lee would not own the land!" They did not purchase the property.

The next day I saw Jimmy Reynolds driving up Black Point Road. I stopped him and asked if he knew of anyone who'd like to buy on Royal Place. He said, "I have wanted that property all my life! Is it for sale? I'll buy it! My attorney, Mitch D'Olier, will call you tomorrow morning." They purchased it for around $1.2 million. He bought it on a handshake, basically. Reynolds only recently sold the property.

Real estate is something everyone loves to talk about, and conversations with friends and acquaintances have produced a number of sales over the years.

Real estate trends? I came across an old contract for Richard and Claire Boone on Black Point Road—it was one page! Today the contracts are seventeen-plus pages with numerous addendums attached. What a monster we have created!

The one thing I know is, if you want to be secure in your old age, buy real estate while you're young!

Ala Moana Center
Several people I interviewed had good stories to tell about Ala Moana Center. Here, Walter Dods and Alice Guild talk about the inception of the development, and Duncan MacNaughton adds a story from the present day.

Walter Dods I worked for Dillingham Corporation at the beginning of my career. Dillingham was different from the Big Five.[36] All those companies

---

[36] The term Big Five refers to the following companies: C. Brewer & Co., Theo H. Davies & Co, American Factors (Amfac), Alexander & Baldwin, and Castle and Cooke.

originated with sugar and then each went into other businesses. But all the way back to the founder, Benjamin Franklin Dillingham, the Dillinghams were kind of renegades. B.F. Dillingham wasn't from missionary stock. He came over as a sailor and broke his leg right before the ship was to sail, so he ended up staying in Hawai'i. He borrowed $5,000 and bought a used dredge and dredged what today is known as Pearl Harbor.

B.F. was an entrepreneurial non-agricultural person. Ultimately the company got into construction and that became Hawaiian Dredging. Then they bought Hawaiian Tug and Barge and Young Brothers. If you were to rank the Big Five by real size and real profits, Dillingham would have been one and two, not six. The Big Five had their day, but Brewer and Davies were pretty small. You also had Castle & Cooke, Amfac, and Alexander & Baldwin. Ultimately the only one that survived was A&B.

Dillingham was more modern looking. They developed Ala Moana Center by taking a duck pond and creating one of the world's largest outdoor shopping centers. I had a chance to join the company during an economic surge in which they were building half of the hotels in Waikīkī. I was there from 1965 to the end of 1968.

I started as assistant public relations director. Six months later the advertising manager who did all the marketing and the ads for the Dillingham buildings got fired. The next day they made me advertising manager. I had less than zero background in advertising.

I was at Dillingham for four very exciting years. I remember that once a month I crawled through all the rafters of Ala Moana Center while it was being built, taking photographs for the Equitable Life Insurance Company, who made the big loan that created Ala Moana. My job was to take these big photographs and create a handmade book. Once a month I'd paste the pictures to the cardboard, put the binding on, and send it to Equitable to show them the progress of the construction. Obviously there were engineers writing reports, but mine was the photographic display of Ala Moana Center.

This account by Alice Guild is one of my favorite feel-good stories about how things worked behind the scenes in the old days.

Alice Flanders Guild Morley Theaker was the general manager of Sears, which was down between Young and Beretania Streets. There were all these satellite stores around it, such as Slipper House and Crack Seed Center. Lowell Dillingham approached Morley, asking Sears to be the anchor tenant for Ala Moana. Sears was the logical choice because they were freestanding. At first, Morley didn't want to move, and then he said, "Well, if I move Sears, you have to take all the little stores that surround Sears, because they will never survive if Sears moves!" He built that into the deal, and that is how all those small shops got into Ala Moana.

This was before any of the downtown stores such as Carol & Mary, McInerny, Liberty House, and Ross Sutherland moved. None of them came in that first wave. They all came in Phase II. It was all these little shops that were part of Phase I. Shirokiya and Iida were two of the original stores and they brought in local flavor. Right from the beginning the developers put in incredible sculptures, landscaping, fountains, and ponds with koi fish. Phase II, with Liberty House as its anchor, started building as soon as Phase I was completed. You could shop outdoors and still be comfortable and not be pounding the sidewalks. When the two phases were completed, it definitely had an island, Hawaiian feel.

Ala Moana was a success from day one. It was built in the late 1960s with the idea of getting the local people to come shop. It wasn't for the tourists, but the tourists came because it was where the local people shopped. People liked it because it was so different. All of these stores were in one place with tons of parking.

When I was there, we figured that every man, woman, and child in Hawai'i visited the shopping center five times a year or the equivalent. And remember, the tourist industry was very small in those days. Ala Moana attracted more people than Disneyland. It was a phenomenon.

My job was to promote the center, which meant organizing the merchants so they would go along with sidewalk sales and other events. There were at least two major promotions a month with full-page advertising sections. And there was always a crisis of some sort to handle. A boy gets his shoelace caught in the escalator at Penney's, for instance. One of the worst was a hurricane that hit on Black Friday, the biggest shopping day of the year. This was before cell phones, and our communication was very primitive. We called all the merchants and told them we were going to close the center at noon, so people could get home to their families. We also told all the radio stations and TV stations that the center would be closing at noon. Some of the big stores refused to close! Finally, at about 2:00 p.m., when there were *no* customers at all, they closed.

Ala Moana Center was a mega-success. However, eventually it moved out of the hands of local ownership. It's very hard for people who aren't familiar with island ways to "get it." Most of the merchants who came to Ala Moana in the beginning were local. Some were first generation; most were second generation. Their parents had worked in the cane fields and then finally opened their little shop. The whole family worked there. You could go in the back and all the kids would be there doing their homework every day. They may have moved uptown, but they still operated the same way. All the merchants knew each other and took care of each other. They watched each other's stores.

Now the people who work there don't even know who owns their store. That's nothing against Ala Moana; that's just the way of retail today.

I was curious about new developments in a community that is mostly already built out.

JG *Duncan, am I right that developing on Oʻahu now doesn't require finding vacant land, but taking something existing down and building something new?*

Duncan MacNaughton Yes. An example of that is the Park Lane project. General Growth now owns Ala Moana Center, and they were expanding the center where the former Sears store was located. The property on the makai side of that expansion was an old parking deck. It was untouchable as long as Sears was there, because they had the right to the parking areas around their store forever. With Sears gone, those rules no longer applied. We made a deal to buy the property, but in order to do it, we had to tear down the existing decks and rebuild them with a new, completely up-to-date structural system. Then we built a condominium project on top of the newly built parking deck. We have two floors of commercial parking, two floors of residential parking, and six floors of residential condominiums.

The Groundbreaking Ilikai
My high school friend Willie Lum helps out at the family's manapua *shop in Chinatown. Spotting Stuart Ho there one morning, Willie told him about* Voices of Hawaiʻi *and asked Stuart if he'd like to participate. Stuart should write his own book, as should nearly every one of my interviewees. Here is just one of his stories.*

Stuart Ho For my father [Chinn Ho], building the Ilikai apartment and hotel complex was the biggest milestone of his career. When it opened its doors in 1964, it was the world's largest condominium. It also quietly changed the way business was done in Hawaiʻi with respect to the relationship between haole bankers and non-haole businessmen, and the threat of mainland bankers eyeing Hawaiʻi.

In the 1920s Walter F. Dillingham's construction company was the successful bidder in an effort to drain swampy Waikīkī and create the Ala Wai Canal. Dillingham made a deal with the territorial government to fill the shoreline on both sides of Ala Moana Boulevard with the spoil he dug up. He owned and maintained these undeveloped flats of pure white coral for decades before they became the sites for Ala Moana Center, Fort DeRussy, Ala Moana Park, the Hawaiian Village, and the Ilikai.

After statehood in 1959, the Dillingham Company, which now included (Walter's sons) Lowell and Ben, decided to get into real estate development. They hired a smart guy named Don Graham, who built an organization with bright, young managers. Graham's grand vision was to move retail from Honolulu's crowded downtown nearer to Waikīkī's hotels. But he needed cash.

Federal law limits banks to short-term lending because the FDIC only guarantees short-term deposits and the feds want to be sure that banks will always have cash on hand to pay depositors demanding cash. In the case of a home mortgage, the long-term take-out lender is normally the FDIC or FNMA. But commercial loans are another matter. The kind of take-out loans Graham was looking for were customarily provided by large insurance companies, which invested for the long term and were continually searching for long-term investments.

No one in New York knew anything about Hawai'i except what they saw on travel posters. Graham had begun educating Willis "Bill" Holtum, the executive vice president of The Equitable Life Assurance Company of New York, about the virtues of investing in Hawai'i. Bill listened, but he had a board presided over by the huge figure of James Oates. Like the famous *New Yorker* cover illustration, the typical New Yorker's view of the world was the sun setting over the New Jersey Palisades. Chicago was a pin in the far distance. California was nowhere in sight. Hawai'i…

As Graham cast his eye on developing the Ilikai, Puerto Rico enacted a law incorporating a French legal concept—the condominium. Graham could visualize selling cubes of apartments in the sky, needing only to be walled, floored, and ceilinged as the project sold. He commissioned John Graham & Associates of Seattle, designers of the Space Needle, to design the original three-corridor Ilikai—which was named by Napua Stevens.

Graham called on two mainland developers, Guy Harrison and James Driver, and gave them an option to buy the five-acre site. If they could deliver on the sales of units, Hawaiian Dredging, a subsidiary of Dillingham, would build the 1,000-plus apartment condominium. Harrison and Driver had a tough time marketing the new concept, but they found someone to buy them out—Chinn Ho. I remember my father coming home the afternoon he made the deal. I had never seen him so excited.

Dad signed a fixed-cost contract with Hawaiian Dredging to build a one-million-square-foot building for $14 million. The round numbers make the math simple: build a building for $14 per square foot; sell it for $29 per square foot. That meant a two-bedroom, 1,000-square-foot apartment would have to sell for an average of $29,000.

I don't know how Dad planned to pay the $14 million, as he was starting from scratch. He didn't even have a sales organization, but he did have one future Ilikai sales star, Andy Friedlander.

The building specifications called for piles to be driven until "refusal;" i.e., they could be driven no further. Five hundred thousand dollars of the $14-million contract had been budgeted for pile driving. It was soon obvious that the cost of driving the piles would exceed the budget allocation by a significant amount.

Sales were moving at a good pace, thanks to Canadians with sandy feet, but it was not enough to cover any foreseeable budget shortfall. Dad flew to New York City to discuss his troubles with his younger brother, Philip, a stockbroker with J.R. Williston & Beane. Uncle Philip introduced Dad to Ed Palmer at Empire Trust, and Palmer pointed him to what one would have thought was a very unlikely character, Samuel Silverman. Silverman was a suave, kindly, middle-aged gentleman who worked out of a townhouse at 20 East 65th Street with the sometime assistance of a secretary.

Sam Silverman was more than he appeared. He was a mortgage broker but he also originated complex financing for the Columbia University treasurer's office. Columbia would step into a short-term gap to facilitate the financing among triple-A credit parties, lend its considerable credit to fill the gap, and walk off with a fat fee while not having to put up a penny. Sam was a money machine for Columbia, and Columbia's treasurer, William Bloor, was an even bigger money machine. Sam didn't really need a secretary because everyone in the New York financial community knew whom he represented. Sam often wrote out drafts of Columbia's "standby" commitment in neat longhand on a plain piece of paper perfectly covering—without all the "hereinafters"—all the essential points a good lawyer would look for. Later on, someone coined the phrase "mezzanine financing," which more precisely described some version of what Sam and Bloor often did.

Dad discussed the Ilikai situation with Sam. Normally, a reasonable cost overrun would be covered by an extension of credit, provided that sales were progressing satisfactorily. But Sam's New York City-educated nose smelled rats, or so he told me twice in later years. One was that Hawaiian Dredging would probably like to see a foreclosure on the Ilikai project. The second was a realization that local banks were reluctant for mainland banks to encroach on their domain; they were not eager for New York lenders to discover Hawai'i as a place to make money.

Dad brought our entire family to greet Sam when he arrived at the old John Rodgers Airport. Sam disembarked, resplendent in a white Panama suit and white shoes. When Dad invited Sam to a large cocktail party, Sam asked who would be there. "Pretty much everyone in Honolulu's commercial and banking community," Dad replied. Sam asked if he could bring a guest, and

Dad said of course. Sam called the head of real estate at First National Bank of Boston, a guy named King Upton, and invited him to fly to Honolulu, all expenses paid. Upton asked what he had to do. Sam replied, "Do nothing; just drink all the mai tais you want." Upton came.

The party went something like this: Dad circulated, introducing Sam as his New York financial advisor, and Sam introduced Upton as head of First National of Boston's real estate lending. Rudy Peterson, head of Bank of Hawai'i from 1961 to 1963, was Dad's lender. He observed from afar and, as usual, didn't miss a thing. Rudy Peterson was one of my idols. He was the only CEO of a big bank [Bank of America, 1963-1968] ever to answer his own phone without a secretary giving the caller the third degree.

After that party, credit was extended by Bank of Hawai'i to my dad for the Ilikai project and it was built to huge success. And Bill Holtum's Equitable did the take-out on the Ilikai.

Another of my father's advisors during the development of the Ilikai was his lawyer, Matsuo Takabuki. "Matsy," a combat veteran of the 442nd Regimental Combat Team, went to law school on the GI Bill. He was brilliant in a quiet sort of way and capable of absorbing complex financial strategies from the New York legal and banking talents. Later he was appointed a trustee of Kamehameha Schools, over the objections of many Hawaiians, and is widely credited with putting the school on a more solid and diversified financial footing.

The Rusting of Aloha Stadium
Here, Willie tells a fascinating story about rust!

Willson Moore One day, two lawyers from the Los Angeles law firm of Adams, Duque, and Hazeltine came to my office. They represented Charles Luckman, a very famous architect and developer in Los Angeles, who designed Cape Canaveral, Madison Square Garden, and other huge projects.

Luckman wanted to do something unique in designing Aloha Stadium. His idea was to use weathering steel, not solid concrete, because he envisioned a design whereby stadium sections could be moved on a film of air. Since weight was a consideration, rather than using heavy solid concrete, he wanted to use a product called Corten made by US Steel.[37] The steel companies advertised that this material, when exposed to the elements, rusted only

---

[37] Also made by Bethlehem Steel under the trade name Mayari.

slightly and then developed a patina of a microscopic amount, which protected it from further erosion and has a lovely brown color. Or so the architects thought.

Chuck Luckman wrote to US Steel and in essence said, "Here is the location. We're a thousand yards from Pearl Harbor; there are no waves in Pearl Harbor but the site is fairly close to salt water, which surrounds the island of Oʻahu. We want to use Corten steel for the framing." He got a letter back from US Steel saying, "Admirable application of our product." Bethlehem Steel was more tepid but agreed. Therefore, Luckman used weathering steel extensively in Aloha Stadium. It turned out it was *not* a good product and cost the state millions of dollars because it started rusting and did not stop.

The first lawsuit was filed by the state against the general contractor, Dillingham, for delays and cost overruns. Dillingham joined Luckman, claiming design problems were to blame. The stands were originally designed to move on large slick runways with machinery made by Rolair. The plan was to move back and forth between baseball and football configurations. The stands worked originally but over the years settlement caused the runway platforms to get out of kilter and the stadium became frozen in the football configuration.

The cost overruns had many, many facets. There were electrical problems, plumbing problems, and soil problems, which involved many years of lawsuits. But eventually the weathering steel became the major litigation issue. When the Corten did not perform as promised, the state filed a lawsuit for failure of the product, suing both Chuck Luckman individually and Luckman Inc., plus the two steel companies.

I was involved in the Aloha Stadium case, defending Chuck Luckman, for nineteen years, from 1974 to 1993. The reason for that was that the state of Hawaiʻi is represented by the attorney general's office. The state of Hawaiʻi, unlike many other states in the Union, does not have a permanent attorney staff—no career attorneys in the office. The deputies tend to come on board, work for two or three years—I did four—get experience, and then go out into the community and make more money. A new deputy attorney general assigned to litigation would come in, open the doors to multiple rooms filled with Aloha Stadium documents and say, "I think my successor can handle this better," thereby ducking the problem.

Finally, Warren Price, a very fine man and lawyer, became attorney general. Warren had been with the law firm of Goodsill Anderson Quinn & Stifel. Warren said enough was enough, and he hired Goodsill partner David Dezzani, a first-rate trial attorney, as a special deputy attorney general to prosecute all of the state's claims against all of the defendants. As soon as all the litigants in the weathering steel claims were identified, I had a meeting in my office. I had a platter-sized piece of Corten rust from the stadium, which showed how extensive the corrosion was. I passed it around the room and said, "Gentlemen, this is what we are facing." This was probably 1989 or 1990.

Finally, in 1993 the case went to trial. After the jury was selected, my primary opponents in the trial were Dave Dezzani for the state and the attorney for US Steel. I renewed my offer to settle the Luckman interests. Dave and I agreed to and did settle out all the Luckman interests. Part of the deal was offering some of our witnesses to Dezzani and he used them. To my surprise, Dave went to trial and lost. Dave was convinced that there were errors made by the trial court that would be sustained by the appellate court. He talked to Warren, who okayed the appeal, which was taken, and the lower court verdict was reversed, and the case returned to the lower court for retrial. By then Margery Bronster was the new state attorney general and settled with the steel companies, thus ending the case.

There is a fun side story to the start of the 1993 Aloha Stadium trial. I was there as one of the attorneys to pick the jury when the large panel of prospective jurors filed into the courtroom. The trial had been predicted to be a lengthy one, hence the need for a big jury panel from which to choose. One of those was Mary Lou Brogan, wife of a fellow golfer and retired hotel executive. As soon as Mary Lou spied me, she called out "Hi, Willie!"—whereupon the trial judge promptly excused her from jury service. She probably got out of a month-long trial!

Chuck Luckman was not only my client for nineteen years but he became a good friend. He gave me a copy of his autobiography, *Twice in a Lifetime*, and his inscription was both warm and complimentary. ✤

C. Brewer & Co. administration building at Fort and Queen Streets circa 1940s, currently the offices of the Hawai'i Community Foundation

CHAPTER 11

Voices of Philanthropy

Enriching Hawai'i
Here is a story about individual philanthropy in Hawai'i involving Dwayne Steele. I am very devoted to Dwayne because when we were taking care of my father toward the end of his life, every day about 2:00 p.m. Dwayne would appear on our lānai like a ray of sunshine. Sometimes he'd have his 'ukulele.

Puakea Nogelmeier When I was teaching in the department of Indo-Pacific Languages at the University of Hawai'i at Mānoa, there was this guy who was diving into learning the Hawaiian language. The first fifteen to twenty minutes of class were all in Hawaiian, often with me on some diatribe. Then we'd talk grammar. One day I came in and I was angry because I had just gone to the fundraiser for the Pūnana Leo immersion preschool, which was a brand-new thing. I had just learned about the pitifully small donations given by a few large organizations in town. I had donated $300 at the fundraiser, which was a lot of money for me at the time.

To participate in my monologue, you had to speak in Hawaiian. I'd only answer questions that were asked in Hawaiian. We finished the class and Dwayne came to me and said, "I didn't understand everything you said, but does Pūnana Leo need help? Maybe I can help." I told him to get in touch with them. There were only two Pūnana Leo then, one on O'ahu and one in Hilo. It turns out that he contacted them *that* day and gave each of them $5,000, a computer, and some other things.

In 1989 we were going to start up a radio show called *Ka Leo Hawai'i*.[38] It was a weekly interview with native speakers and a huge resource for language students. Dwayne was in my class and we didn't have a radio show for students

---

[38] Larry Kimura had started it with UH's *Hui Aloha 'Āina Tuahine* in 1972. In 1986 Larry moved to Hilo, so the show folded.

to listen to. I said to the organizers, "One of my students is a businessman. We could ask him for ideas." We needed $12,000, which was $1,000 a month for the show. I asked him, "Nakila [Dwayne's Hawaiian name], we need $12,000 to start this radio show. We want to go to twelve businesses and get $1,000 from each one. We'll give them lots of PR; all the commercials can be dedicated to them. Can you help us think of businesses that would be supportive?" He said, "I'll pay for the first year and give you time to find the businesses. You never have to mention my name; you never have to mention my company. We'll just cover the first year." So we started.

The very first Sunday night we brought Mrs. Lindsey, a native speaker from the University of Hawaiʻi, as our first guest. Monday morning Dwayne was in my office, saying, "I listened to the program last night. I am *so* excited. She's wonderful. You're wonderful. I'll pay for next year!" And he paid for Ka Leo Hawaiʻi for the next ten years! It became part of his passion. And he supported us. (Smiles broadly.)

Hawaiʻi's Foundations
Hawaiʻi's major philanthropic efforts often begin with nonprofit corporations and trusts, as Mitch D'Olier explains.

Mitch D'Olier The Tax Reform Act of 1969 separated charities into the categories of private foundations and public charities. Each entity needed to decide which it was. It was a very interesting specialty niche in legal practice in Hawaiʻi because there was so much philanthropy: the missionary philanthropy, the Native Hawaiian philanthropy, and all the other types of philanthropy.

I spent a lot of time as a lawyer getting determinations from the IRS that we were right about what status we wanted. It was better to be a public charity than a private foundation. Generally nonprofit organizations are exempt from paying taxes but if they engaged in certain kinds of transactions, they would have to pay taxes. Determining whether they would pay tax as ordinary income or capital gains was an important distinction. Some big businesses, like hospitals, were tax exempt so they needed to figure out which of their activities were taxable and how to minimize their tax exposure.

I got a call from James Castle McIntosh, asking me to be the first non-family president of the Harold K.L. Castle Foundation. John Baldwin had just passed away, and J.B. McIntosh wanted to make the foundation into a community asset, not a family play toy. I have incredible respect for them; you can visit castlefoundation.org and see that we are the most transparent foundation in Hawaiʻi. You can see everything, including everybody's salary and what we do.

Issues of major importance to the Harold Castle Foundation include: In public education, how do we close the achievement gap for under-resourced kids in the most challenged communities? I truly believed the foundation could be a force to improve public education, so I got involved. Baldwin and McIntosh were both concerned about the environment, so the ocean shorelines became a focus. How do we improve the nearshore marine health of the main islands? And how do we build strong communities in Windward Oʻahu?

I'm a regional chair for Teach for America. The Castle Foundation funds part of the local Teach for America effort. It's a national movement, founded in 1990, to close achievement gaps. We bring the best and the brightest teachers from around the country, about one third of them from Hawaiʻi schools, to teach in Title 1 schools. We have seventy teachers in Waiʻanae and Nānākuli. We have teachers on the east side of the Big Island where we are most heavily concentrated. We have 400 teachers in Hawaiʻi right now. Our son, Jordan, spent his six years teaching in Waiʻanae and chose public education as his career because of Teach For America.

The Castle Foundation also supports Mālama Maunalua. We are trying to improve the health of Maunalua Bay. Their vision statement is: "A Maunalua Bay where marine life is abundant, the water is clean and clear, and people take *kuleana* in caring for the Bay."

Kelvin Taketa and I went to high school together. Fifty years later we sat together for this interview. I was dumbfounded that "kids like us" could grow up to have had such responsible jobs!

Kelvin Taketa Community foundations are a type of philanthropy first established in 1913. Hawaiʻi Community Foundation, having started in 1916, is the fifth-oldest of about 800 community foundations. Community foundations were intended to be places where citizens, other than the fabulously wealthy, could put in money through their estate plans and during their lifetime to supporting the community in perpetuity. Endowments were managed by an entity similar to a trust company that was exclusively for philanthropic endeavors. Community foundations are an aggregator, or warehouse if you will, of philanthropic funds.

When I started with the Hawaiʻi Community Foundation, we had 200-plus funds with about $200 million in assets, and we gave away about $15 million a year. Twenty years later we had about 700 funds with assets of $600- to $700-million and we gave away about $60 million a year. That last statistic is most meaningful, as money doesn't do a community any good when it is sitting in our coffers. It only creates value when it is deployed.

The Hawai'i Community Foundation funds everything from early childhood to elderly care, private education, public education, and scholarship programs. We are the third-largest scholarship funder and financial aid provider for post-secondary education in the state, behind the University of Hawai'i and Kamehameha Schools. We fund everything on every island in every community.

In the 1980s there was no voice for the philanthropic nonprofit sector in Hawai'i. None. People would say things like, "We shouldn't pay these nonprofit executives so much money. They should be doing it for love." I said to Don Horner, who was running First Hawaiian Bank, "Why is it that in this community there are bank executives who make a million dollars a year and we don't think anything about it? And yet, if a nonprofit executive who runs Queen's Hospital were to make close to that amount, everybody would be upset. Which one of those people has a more profound effect on the people of Hawai'i?"

The nonprofit community employs about 15 percent of the entire population of this state. It is a critically important sector in our state but woefully underappreciated. We started our own research and communication strategy, to be the voice of the nonprofit sector. That led us to address really large shortfalls in the capacity and resiliency of the sector, through leadership and board development programs and capacity building grants that cut across all parts of the sector. People came to understand that the Hawai'i Community Foundation could be an effective advisor because we were broader than just one cause. This approach attracted a lot of people who cared deeply about our community,

On September 12, 2001, there were literally no planes flying to Hawai'i. Jeff Watanabe said at a board retreat, "The whole world just changed and we can't pretend it hasn't." We agreed and arranged forty community meetings in twenty-three days. We talked to everybody in the community about what was happening and what people were worried about. We put about one million dollars of our own money in reserve and we put it out into the community immediately.

When the recession hit, a lot of funders were trying to figure out how we could help the working poor, people who were still going to work every day at the hotels but had their hours cut from forty to twenty. In about thirty days, we raised over $4 million from a dozen funders, and sixty days later we had it all out on the street. Pooling those funds under one roof and grant-making process made it easier for the donors and, more important, for the agencies. If those agencies tried to approach the twelve funders separately, it would have taken months to raise and deploy those funds.

That's when we started creating multiple funder collaboratives. We organized groups of funders either around a theme, a project, or an initiative. We started an environmental funders group at a time when there were very few institutional funders of environmental issues. That group has grown to about fifteen funders and has been a great success story. We went from $30,000 a year in environment funding to a group of more than a dozen environment-focused foundations and donors who meet and share ideas and experiences and collectively provide millions each year.

And the corollary to that was the establishment of a collaboration among agencies we called networks. Each focused on a shared goal with careful measurements to track progress and spur innovation. Homeless families, middle school at-risk kids, and preserving and building our resources for fresh water are just a few of the ones that were launched and continue to be active today.

I believe that in the twenty-first century the primary currency of organizations like the Hawai'i Community Foundation is not money, but the ability to organize and create intellectual capital and distribute it in an open source way. I think that has much more leverage than money does. For the most part people talk to us because they see a need in the community. Our approach is that no matter how crazy or ill-founded an idea may be, it shouldn't stop us from trying to guide them by giving them ideas, resources, places to go, or sites on the Web to read. I am proud that many organizations who do *not* get grants from HCF still speak favorably about the encouragement and help they receive from the foundation.

When I look back on my tenure at the foundation, there isn't any one thing that we *did*, it's the *way* we did it that is most meaningful.

'Iolani Palace

A docent, historian, and past director share the history of—and their devotion to—'Iolani Palace.

Willson Moore In ten years as a docent I guided over 6,000 people through 'Iolani Palace. I talked about palace history, monarch history, a little bit about Hawaiian culture, and generally showed off the absolute masterpiece of King Kalākaua's showplace. It was completed in 1882; the overthrow came in 1893 so the monarchy reigned there for eleven years.

Between 1955 and 1959 I was deputy attorney general for the Harbor Board. If the legislature passed a bill that affected harbors in any way, I had to investigate. I then wrote a report to Governor Bill Quinn, the first governor after statehood, to explain the situation and recommend an action. Up those 'Iolani Palace stairs I would climb, to meet with Governor Quinn in what was once, and is now again, King Kalākaua 's bedroom.

The building was a bloody mess. Palace contents had mostly been sold, and the lovely chandeliers had been taken down and stored at Bishop Museum for safekeeping. Fluorescent lights were put in and each room held two temporary add-on wooden offices. Back in those days everyone smoked inside, so it reeked of smoke. After statehood the legislature met in what is now the Blue Room and the Dining Room and the Throne Room—tight quarters. It was a palace in name only!

As an office building it got heavy use. I've been told there were eight to ten layers of paint on some of the wall surfaces. The lovely koa wood floors had not been covered with rugs, and between termites and the damage from use when it was the seat of Hawai'i government for seventy-plus years [1893-1969], the floors needed to be replaced. The floors now are pine and fir, and yes, we have rugs and people on tours wear booties.

As we enter the palace with a tour, we say, "Come join me and let's step back in time." Of course, we start with King Kamehameha I. He died in 1819, long before the palace was built. The only monarchs that ever actually inhabited the palace were King Kalākaua and Queen Lili'uokalani. There was a lot of pomp and ceremony, and servants, and an air of grandeur about the place that we can't completely duplicate. We have the portraits and we tell them which monarchs were residents of the palace. We show them artifacts and try to re-create the era for them.

Zita Cup Choy very nicely shared her time and experiences with me in several meetings.

Zita Cup Choy I joined the first docent class at 'Iolani Palace on June 24, 1977. We trained for eleven months while the palace was being renovated. We did course work and wrote papers such as, "How did Kamehameha unify the islands?" and "Name the key political, economic, and social events of each of the monarchs." We visited other museums to see how they gave their tours. We did practice tours in empty rooms. In March 1978 the palace was rededicated, and it opened to the public in May 1978. In 1980 a few pieces of furniture were installed.

By 2003 I had been a volunteer docent for twenty-three years and they had a need for someone to do a docent-training class, which led to a part-time position. In 2004 Stuart Ching hired me to do the data entry into the palace's new collections database. I was excited about that and I learned a tremendous amount about the collection!

The curatorial staff made cards for each item and gave it a number. I was responsible for putting every item into the computer. One accession was 929 pieces of stationery! And you have to enter each individually. These are treasures with the Hawaiian coat of arms printed or embossed onto the paper.

When the monarchy ended and the provisional government moved in, a government official may have decided he couldn't bear to throw this stationery away or use it as scratch paper, so he took it home. His grandchildren ended up with it and brought it to us.

John Lorring was in Ireland looking for antique wood and found himself in the rain near a farmhouse. The owner said, "Bring your picnic inside." There in the parlor was a portrait of Kamehameha II and his wife. It matched the portraits hanging in the Grand Hall of the palace. On the back was a label indicating who the prime minister of England was when Kamehameha II visited. John bought the paintings for the cost of a load of antique bricks and donated them to the palace.

One Kamaʻāina Sunday someone on a tour asked me about the bed in the king's bedroom. This young college-aged man was the grandson of the woman who gave us the bed. He said, "It belonged to my tutu and she was born in that bed."

In 2007, when most of the database work was done, I started working full-time in docent education. Because of my knowledge of the monarchy period and my decades of involvement with the Friends of ʻIolani Palace, my title recently changed to historian.

King Kalākaua passed the bar in 1869, something we tell visitors to the palace who are in the legal profession. When the US Supreme Court justices came to Hawaiʻi for the Jurist In Residence program I was asked to conduct tours for Justice Alito, Justice Sotomayor, Justice Breyer's wife, and President Owada from the International Court of Justice in the Hague. As historian, I looked through the records so I could tell them whom King Kalākaua entertained. When Japanese lawyers come to Hawaiʻi for workshops, they come to the palace for tours. I found out about the first lawyer from Japan who was licensed to practice law in Hawaiʻi during the monarchy period, which I shared with them. When the Asia-Pacific Economic Cooperation (APEC) was here, we searched to determine if Kalākaua had entertained anyone from the APEC countries represented. Unfortunately, sovereignty groups disrupted things and the palace had to be shut down the entire week APEC was here!

Hawaiʻi was an independent, internationally recognized nation that was educated and ahead of its time in technology. When Captain Cook arrived, Hawaiians saw wonderful metal tools that could cut the time they spent taking a tree down to make a canoe, so they adopted this new technology. Some see that as moving away from ancient Hawaiian traditions; some see it as a clever adaptation.

Decolonizing museums is a current trend. We should not be talking about the museum from a white Anglo-Saxon perspective. That history should be told from the perspective of the indigenous population. This is what we do. We talk about King Kalākaua wanting more for his people. Some in the museum community criticize us for that. They might like us to tell the story from the perspective of the servants at the palace. But there were no servants; they were staff. To work with and handle aliʻi clothing and food, you had to be connected to the aliʻi rank, although the king did hire a lot of non-Hawaiians to cook for his foreign guests. During the monarchy period you could not get onto the property unless you were invited, worked here, or knew the password.

Many people want us to tell the angry Hawaiian story about the overthrow. Jim Bartels, the first curator at ʻIolani Palace, urged us to consider that on any given tour we might have a descendant of an annexationist, a descendant of the royal family, or a descendent of a monarchist on the tour, and the other sixteen have no clue Hawaiʻi was an independent nation. You want to educate them all and give an honest rendition of history that represents all perspectives, not just one. It is a difficult balance to attain.

When I asked Alice Guild to tell me how her family first came to Hawaiʻi, there was a l-o-n-g pause followed by, "Probably on the first canoe." She estimates she has given fifty years of her life to the renovation of ʻIolani Palace. Here are several of the stories she told me.

JG *Tell me about the recovery of items originally in the palace. Where had they been in the interim?*

Alice Flanders Guild Many items had been given as personal gifts to the royal family, and in some cases these items went back to those who gave them. Many of the families that had those things were reluctant to return them, as they feared they might get in trouble if they came forward. After many assurances that people could turn things in without being identified, things started drifting in.

Anything that had been purchased with funds of the kingdom was confiscated after the overthrow as state property by the provisional government. The majority of these objects were sold at auctions that were staged when ships came through, either from the Orient to the mainland or vice versa. In those days the harbor was much closer to the palace and people walked from the pier to the palace and bought two forks or a teacup or a table at the royal auction.

One of my jobs at the Junior League was to illustrate the objects that we were trying to recover. I did black-and-white drawings from old photographs. In some cases, we might have a single place setting of silver and we were looking for fifty more! The furniture was very distinctive. It was made by Davenport and Company of Cambridge, Massachusetts. They are the same company that made the furniture for the White House. In fact, it is very similar. It looks like Eastlake furniture, but every piece had the royal crown on the top of it. I did illustrations of all kinds of items that were missing from the collection.

The restoration philosophy was we would use the original wherever possible. If the original was not available, we would use period pieces that were as close as possible. The last resort was using a reproduction. We thought the palace would end up with many reproductions but as it turns out, most of the furniture is original! To my knowledge we only reproduced one set of benches. When people started coming through the palace, they recognized things: "Oh my goodness! My mother has a plate like that." And two months later a plate would arrive. I don't know how many serving pieces are in the serving set now, but most of them came back one or two at a time.

A family came on a tour and saw a picture of the original furnishings of the king's bedroom. One of the little tables had been purchased at an auction and it ended up in a mainland governor's mansion. Jim Bartels wrote them asking for it, and they refused to return it. This kid went back to his school and told his class about this table and they bombarded the governor with letters, saying, "Return the palace table." Those kids pressured the governor until the table was returned. It can now be seen in the king's bedroom.

The restoration took ten years. The palace trained docents to give "empty palace tours," which were absolutely wonderful. You had to use your imagination as there wasn't a stick of furniture in there. The docent might say something like, "Now, just imagine the king and queen coming down the grand staircase while the Royal Hawaiian Band is playing. The women are dressed in their ball gowns and the men are wearing their royal orders and they are bowing to the royal couple. The Throne Room doors are thrown open, the carpets have been rolled up, and the king and queen lead the guests into the ballroom, where they dance until dinner is served at midnight or two o'clock in the morning. And they don't go home until the first cock crows."

Alice also reminisced about the volunteers who removed layers and layers of industrial paint from the beautiful wooden shutters on the palace windows using only wire toothbrushes!

The Mānoa Heritage Center

On the twentieth anniversary of the founding of the Mānoa Heritage Center, Mary Moragne Cooke[39] shared with me the story of the center's journey.

Mary Moragne Cooke My husband's grandfather was born weighing two and a half pounds, and his parents hired a *kahuna lāʻau lapaʻau* named Kaʻahaʻāina Naihe to care for him. She kept him alive and because of that he had tremendous aloha for Hawaiian culture, and he took care of Kaʻahaʻāina for the rest of her life. He graduated from Yale University and his specialty was land snails. Each valley had its own land snails, which grew in trees and were endemic to that area. He could recognize the difference between a Mānoa land snail and a Pālolo land snail.

In 1992, my husband, Sam, and I bought the Kūkaʻōʻō Heiau, which abutted our home. It was in terrible shape. There were two huge banyan trees on the mauka side of the *heiau*. Within the heiau walls there were eight volunteer rubber trees growing. The heiau was restored stone by stone by Hawaiian experts led by Billy Fields. Then we decided to remove every non-endemic plant from the area around the heiau and replant with native Hawaiian plants. We had *one* tree left after we did that. We hired Jim Nakata to re-landscape all the paths around the heiau with native plants.

We don't have big exhibits, we don't have anything flashy, or any fancy technology. The splendor of the outdoors is the highlight of our tour. Most schoolchildren are in their classrooms day after day and go on only two field trips the entire school year. When they come here, they get off the bus and run across the lawn, they ask questions, they grab lizards, they pick up leaves, and find kukui nuts. They are on a high, just from being outdoors. No electronic devices!

How do we give tours? First, we introduce the house and the Cooke family, who built this house. Then we wander over to the heiau. "What is a heiau? What is it used for and how was it built?" Then we wander through the native plant garden. "What is a native plant, as opposed to an introduced plant? Indigenous? Endemic?" We talk about the way Hawaiians managed the valley in historical times as an ahupuaʻa, the Hawaiian land division. "What does all that mean and how did Hawaiians live and survive in this valley?" The kids get to imagine all this culture and history and even the geology of how the valley was formed. We also have a newly built educational center where the children can learn about Hawaiiana and participate in learning crafts.

---

[39] Watch KIKU TV's interview with Mary, "The Wisdom of Hawaiʻi's Elders: Mary Moragne Cooke."

Our mission statement is: "Mānoa Heritage Center recognizes the historical and cultural value of the site and is devoted to maintaining and sharing it with the public." To that end, we have always encouraged the Native Hawaiian community to visit. One time a group of lāʻau lapaʻau plant experts came and performed a chant at the heiau. Another time a Native Hawaiian language immersion school came and wanted to be on the site and perform chants. We are able to say "yes" to everybody. In the very beginning, the Hawaiian community was not sure if it was going to be a "yes." One group called ahead to make a reservation and I said, "Please come." They said, "But we have seventy kids." I got special permission from the protocol committee for this Hawaiian school. A big group came and gathered on the lawn. They wore their *kīhei*, the cloth tied on the shoulder.

Sam always flew an American flag above the porte cochere at our house. He put the flag out every morning and brought it in every night. The group came carrying a Hawaiian flag, which was upside down, which means distress. They said, "You'll have to take the American flag down." They didn't want to visit the heiau unless the American flag was down. Sam said, "No problem!" and I was relieved! He took the flag down and invited everyone in. The whole group of seventy kids surrounded the heiau and performed the most beautiful chant I have ever heard. They know how to speak Hawaiian and they know the intonations because they are taught by experts. Above the heiau they would call out and below they would answer back. It reverberated in the valley and was quite an experience.

As they left, they were very formal. But the next day they reappeared and gave us all tee shirts as a thank you. They were so friendly when they came back. That was the only slightly sensitive incident, and from that time on there's never been a problem.

Sigrid Southworth has a passion for passing on knowledge She did this in her professional life at Kamehameha Schools and in her volunteer work at the Mānoa Heritage Center.

Sigrid Boyum Southworth After I retired from working as the librarian at Kamehameha Schools, I was invited to take a tour of the Cookes' gardens. At the end of the trip I said to Mary Cooke, "You can't get rid of me!" I attended the very next docent class and have volunteered there for ten years. I like being outdoors in a beautiful garden and sharing knowledge of Hawaiʻi.

The heart of what we try to share is the history and significance of Mānoa Valley, its *wahi pana* [celebrated places]. Kūkaʻōʻō Heiau is in spectacular condition. It is one of only twenty-two vestiges of heiau left on this island out of an original 139. There are a few others that are in semi-good condition and many that are tucked away, completely overgrown by vines, out of sight and falling apart. It has been rebuilt, we think accurately and faithfully by Billy Fields, the best Hawaiian stone mason. He used every rock available to him and needed no more. His work was based on two excellent archaeological surveys. When people ask, "How do you know what you are doing?" we think the right experts were involved. In ancient Hawaiʻi, if a rock fell out of the wall of a heiau, it would have been replaced.

The stewardship of Kūkaʻōʻō by Mary and Sam Cooke has been very special. And since the house will become a museum when Mary no longer wishes to live there, it will be preserved forever, as will the heiau and the land.

I interviewed David Lee because I knew firsthand of his relationships with people who were older than him. My parents had a goal as they aged of keeping up friendships with people younger than they were. Juliet and David Lee were two of their specific choices in that effort.

David Lee I was born in 1949 at Kapiʻolani Hospital and grew up in Mānoa Valley. My parents were older, and I spent a lot of time with my grandfather, who was seventy-five years older than me.

One of my first mentors and lifelong friends was Patsy Mink's husband, John. We met when I was an intern in Patsy's office in Washington, DC, in 1971. John was a brilliant scientist, war hero, and a hydrologist who developed mathematical modeling of groundwater resources. We had a great deal in common although he was twenty-five years my senior. I gave a eulogy for him when he died.

Juliet and I met the friendly and outgoing Sam Cooke at a cocktail party. He liked people and was a hysterical storyteller who could tell a scathing story but tell no names. Sam was also quite a serious scholar. We became close friends and I somehow found myself giving tours of the Mānoa Heritage Center and being on the board. I have no idea how I ever agreed to either of those things.

It was sad for so many islanders when Sam Cooke died, and David Lee's eulogy at his funeral was a welcome balm. David also spoke at the funerals of Marshall Goodsill and of the Vietnam-era general and community leader Fred Weyand. ✤

Voices of Philanthropy

Gateway lithograph by Ida Perkins

CHAPTER 12

Voices of Architecture, Literature, and Art

Hawai'i's Modern Design Legacy
Having grown up in a house designed and built by Vladimir Ossipoff—and because this celebrated architect and his family were close friends of the Goodsill family—I couldn't resist including some stories about Hawai'i's modern design legacy told by Dean Sakamoto and Bob Liljestrand.

Dean Sakamoto[40] Yale was my alma mater. They have a great library with architectural journals going back to the beginning. I looked up Vladimir Ossipoff and there he was! He was published in almost every important architectural journal from 1949 to 1975.

In early 2000 modern architecture was being reappreciated. The National Historic Preservation Act states that any building or structure or work of public art that is fifty years or older is eligible for historic status. So modern architecture was now historic.

While volunteering at the Cranbrook Art Museum, I met Jocelyn Snyder, whose father, Sid, was one of Val Ossipoff's partners. Years later Sid discovered that I had been the architecture curator at Yale University for a show on Eero Saarinen. Sid said, "Dean, Val died two years ago, and friends and clients are asking me to do something to commemorate him. I don't know how to do that. I'm an architect. But you apparently do know how to do that. Why don't we go to the Honolulu Art Academy [now the Honolulu Museum of Art] and I'll introduce you to George Ellis, the director." George said, "I'm retiring in a year. Write me a letter about what you're talking about and I'll leave it on my desk when I leave." The new director was going to be Stephen Little, who came from the Art Institute of Chicago.

---

[40] Dean Sakamoto points out that the phrase "historic preservation" is associated with the National Historic Preservation Act, which has created national standards and laws on how to register, preserve, maintain, and fund the restoration of significant structures and places. While he does this professionally he does not consider himself a "historic preservationist."

A year later I'm shoveling snow in New Haven, when the phone rings. It's February 5, 2003. Stephen Little says, "I found your letter about the show on Vladimir Ossipoff. What a brilliant idea. When can you start? We'll fly you back to Honolulu." One of Stephen's first projects as director was the architecture show on Ossipoff.

I had four years to understand Ossipoff's sixty-eight-year body of work. There were some oral histories at the AIA, but there was no book, no authority on modern architecture in Hawai'i, and no biography of Ossipoff. Among those I called upon were Linus Pauling, Jr., Dr. Howard Liljestrand, Marshall Goodsill, and Sam Cooke, chairman of the board of the art museum.

The exhibit opened in November of 2004. It was called Hawai'i Modern, a name I made up. Yale Press agreed to publish the book. I had never written a book, just articles and shorter things. I never did anything so hard in my life. Fortunately, I didn't write it all myself; I had contributors.

As director of the Yale Architecture Gallery, I was able to get the Hawai'i Modern exhibit as the inaugural show at the newly renovated Paul Rudolph Hall at Yale.[41] Then it went to Frankfurt, Germany, where I was on the advisory committee of the German Architecture Museum. Bob and Vicky Liljestrand went with me.

Sam Cooke blessed the Ossipoff project, and not six months into it, he called and said, "Dean, the National Tropical Botanical Garden (NTBG) on Kaua'i needs your help." The Wichmans—Chipper and Hauoli—headed the NTBG, a nonprofit that is chartered by Congress to be the nation's center of research for tropical botany. It's a real jewel. They have multiple gardens: two on Kaua'i, one on Maui, one on the Big Island, and one in Florida. Val Ossipoff did the master plan for the research campus but the one building he didn't work on was their botanical research center. It includes their library, rare book collection, and research center, which they had to raise money to build. It took years and Val died in the meantime. He left just one sketch. Sam said, "The board has been trying to choose an architect for the last five years, but it has to be unanimous and they couldn't decide. None of them know anything about Ossipoff. They don't even know who he was. You do. Go over there."

This was the biggest project I had ever done, and it was important. I was writing this book at the same time. I don't know how I survived! Luckily, I was in New England, where I had no distractions and the Puritan work ethic is in the air there; everybody just works. The Hawai'i Modern show and book got

---

[41] Hawaiian Modernism, By Way of Russia: https://www.nytimes.com/2008/09/28/nyregion/connecticut/28artsct.html?smid=nytcore-ios-share

really good reviews in journals and in *The New York Times*. All of a sudden, the world realized that Hawai'i had important modern architecture and that the architect named Ossipoff was someone they should all know.

The botanical garden turned out well. It was a $12-million project and we were able to get it built under budget. They like it because it's robust, made out of concrete. It is built around that very special rare book collection. They keep important and unique plant samples in the herbarium.

In 2011, I decided to leave Yale when the University of Hawai'i and the Department of Urban and Regional Planning got a grant to develop the National Disaster Preparedness Training Center. The faculty professor who got the grant to create the center felt like he needed someone to teach a course on hurricane-resilient building design. He had heard of the Botanical Research Center. Since I had had to design a building that would withstand a medium hurricane, he said, "I want you to create the program for FEMA to train other professionals in how to design sustainable hurricane and storm resistant buildings." They gave me a faculty job with the promise of giving me a faculty position in the architecture school, but that never happened.

I created this national program on hurricane-resilient design. We finished it just before Hurricane Sandy hit in 2012. I've offered this program for architects' national conventions around the country because it is an important topic for architects. I could write a book on that if I had time to do it. Ossipoff was very aware of the power of nature. He survived the great earthquake in Japan in 1923, and he always designed with the climate in mind. The work for FEMA is an extension of learning to design for what nature can throw at you, and that's related to what Val Ossipoff was interested in.

Architecture in Hawai'i really needs direction. There is such incongruity between the sky, the ocean, the mountains, and what we have built. It has been *so* insensitive to all that beauty. In addition to the beauty, I am interested in how to create buildings informed by the context, the place, the culture, the people, and the humanity of this place. I think that was one of the things that Mr. Ossipoff knew how to do well—make things function but also blend in. The Hawai'i Modern show for me was about helping to establish a foundation for the future of the build environment in Hawai'i.

Bob Liljestrand Many family issues arose around the idea of preserving [the Ossipoff-designed Liljestrand House on Tantalus]. Some felt, "It's just a wooden house. There is absolutely nothing special about it." We had created the Liljestrand Foundation, but it went dormant because we couldn't transfer the house to the foundation until we had the estate settled. The IRS was problematic; they denied our limited family partnership the usual partnership discount, so a huge bill hit us that we didn't expect and hadn't budgeted for.

My brother and I sold all our assets to get the money to bail us out of our tax liability. After eleven or twelve years we got it all worked out, not to everybody's satisfaction but we got it all worked out.

Since it was now ten years since the foundation had been formed and my brother had died, we had to rewrite the articles of incorporation and bylaws and update our website. Then our foundation accountant retired, and I learned that foundation accounting is a very specialized part of accounting and very few accountants actually do it. We had a hell of a time finding an accountant. But we did get house transferred and we went about the business of figuring out how to support it.

We had small weddings and parties and gatherings. We've developed a good relationship with Philip Richardson, who runs Current Affairs, a very elegant party planning business in Honolulu.

When the Ossipoff show came along at the Art Academy, they wanted to do tours of the house, so we started those. Then I was contacted by the Docomomo [Documentation and Conservation of the Modern Movement]. It is a worldwide organization headquartered wherever the executive director happens to live; at the moment, it's Lisbon. They asked us to become a partner, which we did, and we have their logo on our website.

Another organization, the Iconic Houses network[42] headquartered in Amsterdam, catalogs historic houses all over the world. These houses have to be open at least one day a year for tours. If you were in Lisbon you could go to their website, click the little flag on Lisbon and every house you could go to in Lisbon will come up. They contacted us and said, "We'd like to invite you to join our network."

It turned out that they have a pretty major conference every other year. The Getty Foundation financed the one in 2016 at the Getty Museum. We went to the conference and met Richard Neutra's son and (Charles and Ray) Eames' granddaughter. I never saw *The Big Lebowski* but we had a reception in the house that was featured in the film, famous because it is so over-the-top, designed by John Lautner, who designed Bob Hope's house in Palm Springs. Those who signed up for the conference were asked to submit a one-page essay on what they were doing with their iconic house and four were selected as case studies. We were one of them!

We ended up hiring the woman who was the keynote speaker at this conference to help us take our foundation to a higher level. With her assistance we restructured our board, developed an advisory council, created partnerships, and hired an assistant director.

---

[42] Learn more about the Iconic Houses network at www.iconichouses.org

We established a partnership with the Merwin Conservancy, which brings poets from all over the world to do readings. They are based on Maui but wanted to expand to Honolulu. Unfortunately, it became too successful and they moved to the Doris Duke Theatre, a larger venue.

We have what we call a Design Conversation Series. A number of noted architects and artists from as far away as Egypt have given lectures at the house.

The University of Iowa has what's considered the finest writing and journalism program in the world. They sponsor the Iowa Writers' Workshop, a two-year residency program. They have created a series that focuses on issues of the Pacific area titled Margins of the Sea. For this conference we have developed partnerships with the Matsunaga Institute for Peace and Conflict Resolution, the East-West Center, the Doris Duke Foundation via Shangri La, and the Halekulani Hotel.

Architectural historians love this house, not only because of the house but also its contents and documentation. For example, at the Jean Charlot Residence [in Kāhala] there is a wonderful bookshelf, but the books are gone. One wonders what books he read. Our house is complete. When touring the house, a PhD professor of ceramics was taken with our glassware and ceramics. Scholars in Chinese art get excited about the bronze pieces. I said to one of them, "You know, these bronzes are probably hundreds of years old. My grandparents were missionaries in China and bought them in China 100 years ago." She said, "More likely they are thousands of years old." Everything is here. The paintings are here. My mother wrote detailed letters to her parents and said, "Save these letters because I am writing the story of a house." My parents photographed everything too; the whole process of building this house was photographed.

Richard Neutra was a superstar of mid-century modern architecture. He was a draftsman and intern architect in Frank Lloyd Wright's office when Wright designed Fallingwater for the Kaufmann family. The Kaufmann family later decided they wanted to build a house in Palm Springs. They chased down Richard Neutra and did not hire Wright. Wright was so incensed he never spoke to them again. The Kaufmann house in Palm Springs that Richard Neutra designed is probably his best-known work.

I once saw a photograph of Val Ossipoff and Neutra together. I don't know why they happened to be together. There were four who were the superstar architects of the Los Angeles and Palm Springs areas in the 1930s: Neutra, Rudolph Schindler, John Lautner, and I've forgotten the fourth. Val was obviously influenced by them. Val graduated from the University of California, Berkeley architecture school in 1931. He came to Hawai'i because he had a roommate at Berkeley who was from here and who convinced him to come.

Val took the principles of modernism—simplicity, no unnecessary ornamentation—and added deep eaves and pitched roofs because of the rain in the tropics. Modernist houses could have a cold feel. He warmed them up and made them more comfortable. And he highlighted remarkable orientation to the outdoors.

The woodwork and the quality of the woodwork in this house is Japanese: the notching at junctions of wood members. Nowadays they simply use a Simpson tie. There is beautiful built-in work in the master bedroom and architect John Hara, a scholar of Japanese architecture, pointed out that Ossipoff probably never drew this. He used Japanese carpenters and he probably just discussed it with them and told them what he wanted. They *knew* what he wanted.

Many noted people in the design world would come and spend a day with us in the house, including a man named Kageyama, who flies all over the world doing *tatami* rooms—he's *the* Japanese building consultant. There's an interior corridor the length of the bedroom wing and a balcony on the other side of the wing that acts as a secondary corridor. I've always thought it reminiscent of the *engawa* of the Japanese house, the cantilevered area outside the exterior wall. I asked these experts, "Is it fair to be pointing this out as reminiscent of Japanese architecture?" "Absolutely," they'd say. Also, the entry foyer is similar to the *genkan* [traditional entryway] in Japanese architecture.

Harold Koda, a superstar in the world of design, is retired now but was previously the curator of the 38,000-item costume collection at the Metropolitan Museum in New York. He spent two days in the house.

Hawaiian Historical Writing
Puakea Nogelmeier's contribution to preserving Hawai'i's written history is well known. Here is part of the story in his own words.

Puakea Nogelmeier Our project is now called Awaiāulu but it started off as Hoʻolaupaʻi: Hawaiian Newspaper Project. There are over 100 different Hawaiian newspapers that span 114 years with a million pages worth of text. For my PhD, I was able to show that we've only used three percent of it, while 97 percent sits there, dusty!

Because of improvements in digital technology, in the late 1990s we were able to search Hawaiian newspapers, government documents, and letters for the first time, in a way that showed their incredible value. Digitizing and optical character recognition (OCR) allowed us to search quickly and to compare texts easily. The Hawaiian repository of native-language publications is bigger than all the indigenous publications in the Pacific combined. It is a historical novelty that a very small, very literate, independent nation used the published word as their shared narrative. These newspapers are unique in the world.

JG *I would guide people to your TED talk online. I learned that a researcher could find descriptions of people, places, events, and even climate on a specific date, in these documents.*

PN Thank you for mentioning that. Dwayne Steele was our primary funder, and Oswald Stender helped the project get some federal funding, at which point we moved to the Bishop Museum and were called Hoʻolaupaʻi ["to generate abundance"]. We hired Kauʻi Sai-Dudoit as the director of a dedicated team, and she made it all happen for nearly a decade.

The Niʻihau community became a real concern for Dwayne. It is the last living community where Hawaiian is the language. When their kids went into English school, they were put in the English as a Second Language program or were considered learning-disabled. Dwayne decided he wanted to hire the Niʻihauans for their Hawaiian language skills. They were employed doing construction or gardening, but nobody was engaging them for their own language. He said, "Have them type newspaper text to make it searchable. So it's slow—so what?" I go to Kauaʻi with a Macintosh computer and a microfilm reader and do typing tests on a group of Niʻihauans at Dwayne's expense. That was an absolute stitch. They were terrible typists. It would take 300 years to redo what took only 100 years to publish! We gave up on that idea.

Then we were introduced to a new OCR that had worked for the Maori historical newspapers, producing better text. Kauʻi and her Hoʻolaupaʻi team were assembled.

Dwayne was traveling a lot for his work and said to me, "I can do it on my laptop on the planes." I said, "If you're in the office I can measure your time. If you're going to do it on your own, then we can pay you only by the page. I'll give you ten dollars a page." He said, "For Christ's sake, it takes me four hours to type a page!" I said, "Well, then, you have to get better." And he said, "You know, you are spending *my* money!" I said, "Which is why I have to be *very, very* careful about it. If I overpay you, then *everybody* will expect that." He said, "I'm making like $2.50 an hour!" I said, "So if you get better at this, you can make five!" He got regular checks. I really paid him. It was his money! He would be up in first class on a flight to London and checking pages. He said, "It offsets the cost of my airfare." (If a twelve-hour flight cost $60!)

We were able to keep it going until 2009 but the project lost its biggest cheerleader when Dwayne passed away [in 2006]. It is such a huge undertaking that it was hard to find support for it. We are only 10 or 20 percent complete."

Continual progress is being made on Awaiāulu. As of 2020, almost three-fifths of the 125,000 newspaper pages are online, along with thousands of other Hawaiian documents.

Riánna McCarthy Williams is one of those people who flies under the radar. I was amazed at the depth of her research. Riánna moved to Hawai'i from Chicago in 1958 to attend the University of Hawai'i. She volunteered for nine years as a docent at 'Iolani Palace, where she became very close with the curator, Jim Bartels. Riánna started doing research at Jim's request and never stopped. Kimberley A.K. "Tweedles" McKeague introduced me to Riánna.

Riánna McCarthy Williams: I've always considered myself fortunate to have had Jim as a friend and mentor. He was part Hawaiian, born and raised here. He was drafted into the Navy and served in Vietnam for three years. He started volunteering at Bishop Museum when he was in high school, reading whatever he could get his hands on. He got a paid job at 'Iolani Palace when it was in the early stages of becoming a museum. He eventually became the curator. When Alice Guild left, he became the director. Then he left there and went to Washington Place. He was fifty-seven when he died of cancer. I'm positive he had more knowledge of the monarchy period and other extraneous Hawaiian historical things than anyone else. When he died it was a *huge* loss to Hawaiian history.

For my part, at the State Archives, I read 440 letters—probably 400 to Mary Dominis and forty to her son, John Owen Dominis. I transcribed Queen Lili'uokalani's diaries, Queen Emma's diaries, and some early letters from Charles Reed Bishop. The letters were in English and I put them onto the computer so the public could read them without handling the originals. (I had to do it twice since the first version was lost!)

When I left the palace, I started doing my own research on all kinds of oddball things that nobody but me was interested in, such as passports during the kingdom of Hawai'i, the forging of Queen Lili'uokalani's will, the Honolulu Military Academy in Kaimukī, a small biography of Fraulein Wolf, the Queen's German teacher and supposedly a spiritualist or medium. I also wrote several articles for the *Honolulu Advertiser*'s "Reader's Journal" section in the 1990s.

I wrote *Queen Lili'uokalani, the Dominis family, and Washington Place, their home*. The book begins with Captain Dominis, then moves to his son, John Owen, who married Lili'uokalani long before she became queen. The first part is "Lili'uokalani, Citizen and Queen" and the second part is her life in Washington Place. It also covers the governors who lived in the house through Governor Abercrombie. I didn't include Governor Ige, except for his photo, since he had just become governor when the book came out in 2015.

Some topics from the table of contents: her childhood, her education, her other homes, her birthday celebrations, her musical genius, her religious beliefs, her home life, her stubbornness and pride, her animals and pets, Boy Scouts and Girl Scouts, flags, the Red Cross, servants, and babies. She wrote about why she never had children. She could have sexual relations, but she had a physical condition that prevented her from becoming pregnant. She loved children. After she and John had been married sixteen years, she *hānai*'ed a baby girl that she named after herself, Lydia, but kept the girl's last name, Aholo. Lydia lived to be 101 and never married and had no children.

Four years later, the queen hānai'ed a little boy, Kaipo Aea. He died in his early thirties. He was a scamp and a problem, but she loved him dearly. She was always lecturing him about drinking too much and consorting with low women. He was also unmarried with no children. A few years later the queen's husband, John, had a child by another Hawaiian woman and the queen took that child too. He married and had three children, from whom we have Dominis descendants today. So essentially, she had three hānai children. I wrote a play about the personal life of Queen Lili'uokalani.

I am not Episcopalian, nor do I go to the cathedral, but I knew Saint Andrews had an interesting history that had not been fully recorded, so I wrote *The History of Honolulu's Saint Andrews Cathedral*.

I was sitting in the library/archives of Bishop Museum doing research and suddenly realized that when the ali'i died, you'd see two sentences here and then a sentence there and maybe a paragraph somewhere else. There was no cohesive story about each death and funeral. This led me to research the deaths of twenty-two ali'i and write a book entitled *Deaths and Funerals of Major Hawaiian Ali'i*. It was fascinating learning about the deathbed scenes, which included Hawaiian and English/Western rituals. For Queen Lili'uokalani's funeral, 40,000 people lined the streets between Kawaiaha'o Church and the Royal Mausoleum in Nu'uanu Valley to watch her casket go by. A newspaper article said they were hanging out of windows and sitting in trees. *Pau Lili'uokalani, pau ali'i!* It was the final wail from her servants Myra and Wakeke as the gates clanged shut behind them.

In 1996 I wrote a children's book called *Mahealani and the King of Hawai'i*. There are two sections to the book, one celebrating the king's fiftieth birthday and the other celebrating the king's coronation. It is the voice of a little girl whose parents worked for the king. She struggles to find a gift for the king for each occasion. What is a little girl with no money going to give to the king? Other people are giving him crystal and silver; what is she going to do? She finally finds a gift at the end of both stories.

Kaumakapili Church is a protestant church in Chinatown, near Tamashiro's Market. I had done the Saint Andrews Cathedral book, so I researched and found interesting stories about Kaumakapili.

I'm a mainland haole and that's against me in some people's minds. I would second-guess myself. "Did I write that correctly?" I would go back to the source, whether books or the State Archives or Bishop Museum, three or four times to make sure I understood it and got it right. Nobody could afford to pay me for my research time! My research and publications are a way that I can give back for the wonderful life I've had in Hawai'i. It's my way of saying thank you for allowing me to be here and participate in my tiny corner of Hawaiiana.

I've heard it said that Hawaiians feel their history has been written primarily by white men, and as such is probably skewed because of the clash of cultures. The newest trend is relying on the history that Hawaiians wrote themselves, which can be found in the newspapers that Puakea Nogelmeier and his crew are translating into English. However, historians like Riánna, who have spent countless hours reading the diaries and documents of Hawaiian monarchs (which were written in English), are also of great value in preserving the voices of Hawai'i.

Paintings and Artifacts
When I was interviewing Corky Bryan and Carl Carlson about ranching on the Big Island, I stopped at the Isaacs Art Center in Kamuela. To my great delight, I stumbled upon the largest collection of Madge Tennent artwork in the world. Mollie Hustace, the center's director, is also the AP art history teacher at Hawai'i Preparatory Academy and a docent for the Laurance Rockefeller Collection at the Mauna Kea Beach Hotel. Her husband, James Hustace, the senior certified art appraiser in Hawai'i, was at the gallery when I visited.

James Hustace Hawaiian art is different from the art we appraise from the US mainland, Asia, and all parts of Europe, as it tends to be more site specific. For example, hula dancers at the Merrie Monarch Festival, pa'u riders on Lei Day, the misty Ko'olau Mountains, the beautiful gardens at 'Āinahau—Princess Ka'iulani's Waikīkī home—fishnets hanging to dry along a windward O'ahu shoreline, romantic views of Diamond Head, dramatic views of snow-capped Mauna Kea, volcanoscapes of fiery eruptions at Kīlauea, and more.

Along with my eldest son, James Edward Hustace, who is the president of the large Waimea Community Association and also an internationally certified fine art appraiser, we wrote *Painters and Etchers of Hawai'i—A Biographical Collection—1780-2018*. Every artist of importance to Hawai'i is documented with pertinent information and a selection of images. When we produce our appraisals, we always try to identify the location and subject matter for each artwork. Any personal story adds relevance and value to the art.

For instance, Peter Hayward lived at Punalu'u on the windward side of O'ahu. His paintings are so alive that you can almost feel the wind through his coconut trees. When I was a young boy, I'd see him on the neighboring shore with his easel. He'd set up right in front of US Navy Commander William Kanakanui's coral beach wall. Every afternoon the retired naval officer would take his swim towards the reef as I was out sailing. Years later I discovered that some of Hayward's paintings featured my old sailing canoe.

Eight women who were "society" painters formed a plein-air group in the 1970s and contributed their work to hospitals, schools, charities, and other worthy causes. My sister-in-law, Diana Pietsch, told me: "First they were known as the Screwy Hui because they drank screwdrivers when they finished painting and had their picnic lunches. They were having a benefit show at an admiral's home at Pearl Harbor, and they overheard the admiral's wife talking to a friend on the phone, saying she couldn't meet that day for lunch as she had this group of "Roving Rembrandts" at her house for a benefit show. The name stuck. One of the "Rembrandts" is still with us, the well-respected landscape artist Betty Hay Freeland. Her paintings grace private club collections, businesses, and private homes.

The great landscape master Lloyd Sexton started painting florals before moving on to mesmerizing island scenes. Current artist Harry Wishard, who was taught by his uncle Lloyd, specializes in landscape realism and maintains a fine gallery in Hāwī.

Perhaps Hawai'i's most internationally known artist, Madge Tennent, was just thirteen when her parents sent her from Great Britain to Paris to study in the famous salons with teachers like William-Adolphe Bouguereau. Years later she came to Hawai'i for a two-day visit and never left. She received a lot of criticism for making her Hawaiian women so large in scale, but her intent was to illustrate their elegance and importance in the Hawaiian culture. Isaacs Art Center has close to 180 of her works, some of which have been displayed in the Metropolitan Museum of Art in New York City and the Smithsonian in Washington, DC.

Not to be neglected are Jules Tavernier and D. Howard Hitchcock, two pillars of vintage Hawaiian art.

We appraise international art, from works by Gustav Klimt to Marc

Chagall. Many of these require that the owners provide authentication documents. We enjoy the challenges of appraising top-quality American paintings, like Bennett Bradbury's work entitled "Garrapata." The artist at one time had a studio at the Royal Hawaiian Hotel and later gave painting seminars at the old Ward Warehouse. He retired to Carmel, California, where he produced wonderful and powerful seascapes. Bradbury's brother was the well-known science fiction author, Ray Bradbury.

We also work with treasures of the South Seas and Hawaiʻi such as rare Niʻihau shell necklaces, *kapa* bark cloth, stone and wood artifacts, varieties of magnificent wood calabashes, colorful feathered lei, quilts, sculpture, Hawaiian furniture, royal treasures such as horse hitching posts and whaling try-pots, Hawaiian musical instruments, and *lauhala* hats. We have been tasked with appraising Murano glass, sculpture from Israel and Hungary, Northwest American Indian (First Nations) art, solid koa wood Steinway pianos, Imari and Kutani dishware, Ming pieces, Gump jewelry, Chinese tapestries, Western cowboy sculptures, Thai temple rubbings, European wall and floor tile from cathedrals, and even a "Hidden Stitch" cloth from Beijing. As the saying goes, you just never know what might walk in the door for an appraisal. ❁

Voices of Architecture, Literature, and Art

Hanalei Valley

CHAPTER 13

Voices of Natural Resources

The Nature Conservancy
I allowed the process of finding interviewees to unfold organically, simply trusting the process. As a result, I sometimes heard more than one voice from the same organization—in this case, The Nature Conservancy (TNC). I had known Kelvin Taketa in high school and kept hearing about his grown-up career, so I asked him for an interview. Another interviewee suggested I talk to TNC's Audrey Newman.

Kelvin Taketa The mission of The Nature Conservancy is to preserve the biological diversity of the world. The job of The Nature Conservancy is to preserve habitat, to save all these species. My job was to put aside land for preservation.

When I returned to Hawai'i from law school in 1980, there wasn't a single CEO of a Big Five company who didn't answer his own phone. Maybe you had to go through the secretary, but they picked up the phone. Now it is much more difficult to navigate. When I was raising money for The Nature Conservancy in the 1980s, I had to be able to walk both sides of Bishop Street. We had to get First Hawaiian *and* Bank of Hawai'i to play if we were going to raise money in any significant way. We also had to get to the private family foundations like Cooke and Atherton and others. And we had to get to the Big Five since they, or others like them, owned a lot of the land we were interested in preserving.

Hawai'i was, and is, the endangered species capital of the United States. And the list of species in Hawai'i that are threatened or endangered or actually extinct grows every year. Part of that has to do with our isolation; some species here are found nowhere else in the world. Because of this endangered species extinction crisis, the US government put a lot of resources into bringing field biologists to Hawai'i. The US Forest Service, the Fish and Wildlife Service, and the national parks have robust research arms here.

Herb Cornuelle and Sam Cooke basically built The Nature Conservancy in Hawai'i. They were both mentors of mine, and I cannot speak highly enough of them. Sam Cooke and Phil Spalding ran Molokai Ranch and helped TNC protect Pelekunu Valley, the Kamakou rain forest, and the Mo'omomi dunes. On Maui, we were interested in preserving the native forest that surrounded Haleakalā National Park and the watershed lands on West Maui above Lahaina and Kapalua, both of which were controlled by the Baldwin family. They helped TNC establish the Waikamoi preserve as well as the West Maui Mountains.

Mary Cooke remembered me from Punahou. Sam said, "That name sounds familiar. I think he was this young Communist who was going to Punahou at the time Mary was a trustee." (Laughter.) But he and I became best friends.

The Nature Conservancy would talk to people, make presentations, and negotiate a deal. In some cases, we would do what's called a "bargain sale"—they gave us the land at a discounted price along with what rights they retained and what TNC held. They gave us options, so we had time to raise the money against a deadline. The Nature Conservancy would own the land outright or co-own the land through a conservation easement with the fee owner. They were pretty complicated deals for that time.

By 1987, I was working in Washington, DC, for the new president of The Nature Conservancy, Frank Boren. I ran government relations, fundraising, membership, communications, and marketing for TNC. I was lucky enough to work for The Nature Conservancy during a phase of hypergrowth. We took the membership from about 360,000 to over 600,000 in three years. I then returned to Hawai'i to launch the conservancy's work in the Asia-Pacific region for eight more years. TNC went from being a small part of the conservation world to becoming the largest conservation organization in the world and one of the ten largest nonprofits in the United States. I witnessed that period of dramatic growth and innovation.

Audrey Newman I started at The Nature Conservancy in 1985 and stayed twenty-five years. Kelvin Taketa was the head of TNC at the time, and my boss was Alan Holt. They were both very important mentors to me. The first thing I did was build the Heritage Program's database on Hawai'i's rare plants, animals, and ecosystems. This data was used to map places that were important to protect and places that were okay to develop. If you were a biologist or a conservationist or a birder, you'd go straight to where all the dots were on the map. If you were a landowner or developer, you went straight to all the open spaces. There is something for everyone on the maps.

The Heritage Program's first big contract was with the Campbell Estate. We mapped all the rare plants and animals on Campbell Estate land at Honouliuli. We also mapped plants and animals statewide, to determine the importance of the populations on their land. I bought the first computer at The Nature Conservancy for this project.

There were some very special findings to report to the Campbell Estate board and beneficiaries, as Honouliuli, on the southern end of the Waiʻanae mountain range, is one of the most biologically rich places in the state. The beneficiaries were over the moon about this: "Of course, we want to protect it!" And they did.

In the 1980s we were learning that invasive species were a critical issue for our Hawaiian forests. This included the ungulates[43] that degraded our forests and the weeds that moved in after them. After a while, we realized that we couldn't just take care of the invasive plants and animals in the forest; we had to take care of problems before they got to the forest.

Alan Holt and Susan Miller documented how agencies were protecting Hawaiʻi from new invasive species. They looked at threats to our economy, agriculture, human health, and environment. Turns out our protection was like having a ten-foot-tall, two-foot-wide solid barrier in some places, but right next to it, there was a big gap, then another barrier and another gap. The Coordinating Group on Alien Pest Species was created.[44] They brought together the feds, the state, some county reps, some nonprofits like TNC, as well as business interests like the Farm Bureau, and started systematically plugging these gaps. However, many still remain! It is a constant effort.

Alan and I helped create the Hawaiʻi Conservation Biology Initiative to bring scientists and managers together. Today it has grown into the Hawaiʻi Conservation Alliance. In 1982, I was invited to a gathering of almost all the people working in conservation in Hawaiʻi; there were about forty of us. Now there are more than 1,000 people attending the annual Hawaiʻi Conservation Conference, and that is just a fraction of everyone working on conservation across the state.

In 1990 Kelvin asked if I would take the job of director of protection, the best title I've had in my whole life! I negotiated land deals to buy land or create agreements with landowners to protect key lands. I was also responsible for working with the legislature on TNC's priorities

The conservancy had set up preserves on almost every island and we had more landowners who wanted to work with us, but we couldn't raise the money to manage any more land. Colin Cameron of Maui Land & Pineapple was on our board and had a gorgeous piece of land called Puʻu Kukui in West Maui. It is one of two places in all of Hawaiʻi where ungulates had never stepped foot. It was untouched and intact. Colin said, "I know TNC can't

---

[43] Pigs, deer, goats, cattle and other hooved animals
[44] CGAPS celebrated its twenty-fifth anniversary in 2020.

afford to manage another piece of land and this land is too important to risk. I want an easement so the land will be protected forever, and I want TNC to teach us how to manage it."

The cost of keeping animals out of a large, remote, and rugged area can be significant. First you have to fence it, and then you have to remove the animals. Otherwise you have just created a pigpen. Then you have to keep the animals out. And you have to control weeds and other things that are invasive, so they don't move into the most special, native parts of the forest.

TNC trained Maui Land & Pineapple staff to do all these things, and the company bore the cost. This paradigm shift in our way of doing conservation work led to our asking the legislature to create the Natural Area Partnership Program and the Forest Stewardship Program. If a landowner made a permanent commitment of their land for conservation—it had to be important land that we had identified as a natural area—the landowner would pay one third of the management cost and the state would pay two thirds. That tripled the amount of money available for management.

The state was willing to invest in these places because they were home to Hawai'i's unique native plants and animals, they had huge cultural significance, and the native forest is the best watershed. It captures, processes, and produces most of our fresh water.

I am proud to say all the environmental organizations supported this as did the Land Use Research Foundation, the realtors, and the business community. This was the first time we all came together at the legislature. The affordable housing folks even partnered with us. We created a special fund, and with the help of realtors and big landowners, we established a small increase in the conveyance tax. Half of the increase was earmarked for the Natural Area Partnership/Forest Stewardship Fund and half of the increase went to affordable housing.

TNC's director on Maui, Mark White, pulled all the landowners of the East Maui watershed together and said, "Why don't we work together? Let's design our fences, get funding, and build our fences together. We'll save money and be more effective." The model took off because it made so much sense. It brought the landowners together, including the Board of Water Supply, the state, and the federal government. Over time, the new fund supported watershed partnerships. That made it possible for the East Maui Watershed Partnership to be replicated on every island.

Successful conservation is about people much more than about science. Ultimately, conservation means changing the programs, laws, and funding to support special places and species.

When I became Kelvin's deputy director for Asia-Pacific in 1992, we were going to build a conservation program for one third of the world, starting with a staff of twelve! Kelvin led the region, including fundraising and internal and external politics. My job was building the conservation program and hiring people to manage, create, and run our country and crosscutting programs. Our experiences in Hawai'i were the foundation for all our Asia-Pacific work.

Let the Rivers Flow
Carol Wilcox is dedicated to causes that the rest of us often let others fight for us. I'm grateful to her for her persistence and passion!

Carol Wilcox The Water Roundtable is one of Hawai'i's most inspirational stories. In the 1980s a number of emerging island leaders gathered to draft a water code for Hawai'i. Based upon traditional Hawaiian law and practices, court decisions, and the Hawai'i State Constitution, it started with the premise that water is a public trust resource. That is, water cannot be privately owned; it belongs to the people of Hawai'i. In 1987 the Hawai'i State Legislature passed the Hawai'i Water Code and created the Commission on Water Resource Management in HRS174c.

Nationally, it was increasingly understood that free-flowing rivers had intrinsic values that were easily compromised by human intervention. The Hanalei, Lumaha'i, and Wainiha were some of the last publicly accessible free-flowing rivers in the Islands. Despite this, the Hawai'i State Legislature was preparing to issue special purpose revenue bonds to Utah-based Island Power Company, to build hydroelectric plants on the Hanalei, Lumaha'i and Wainiha rivers.

The proposed hydroelectric projects didn't withstand scrutiny. The access, construction, water availability, and energy production figures were unsupported and unrealistic. The impact on taro cultivation, the Hanalei Wildlife Refuge, and the issue of the narrow roads and fragile one-way bridges had not been addressed. The projects were suspiciously vague, speculative, and showed little intent to actually build, rather creating perceived value with a permitted project.

Mina Morita, Helena Santos, and I joined forces to argue against the special-purpose revenue bonds (SPR) at the legislature. Senator Anthony Chang was supportive. He advised me to fit the request on one page. When I did so he busted me for reducing the font and expanding the margins. I got it right the third time.

Kaua'i's Senator Richard Kawakami, lead proponent of the SPR bonds, passed away unexpectedly, and with him, the legislative support. Island Power gave up on Lumahaʻi and Waimea but pursued a DLNR permit for the Hanalei hydroelectric plant.

The Department of Land and Natural Resources held a hearing in the Hanalei Cafeteria under chairman Bill Paty. When asked how they would access the site, the developer responded, "We're going to bring the materials up the river." The only way to access the site was through a mile-long, partially collapsed tunnel. The Hanalei hydroelectric project died that day. We then went back to the legislature and advocated for a 1988 amendment that expanded stream protection in the new Hawaiʻi Water Code.

HRS 174C-31(c)(4) identifies rivers or streams, or a portion of a river or stream, which appropriately may be placed within a wild and scenic rivers system, to be preserved and protected as part of the public trust. For the purposes of this paragraph, the term "wild and scenic rivers" means rivers or streams, or a portion of a river or stream, of high natural quality or that possess significant scenic value, including but not limited to, rivers or streams which are within the natural area reserves system. The commission shall report its findings to the legislature twenty days prior to the convening of each regular legislative session.

The fact that the Hanalei, Lumahaʻi, and Wainiha Rivers were some of the last free-flowing rivers in Hawaiʻi was not widely recognized. In order to get them protected as part of the public trust, an entirely new project was required. The Water Commission agreed to participate in an inventory of Hawaiʻi's rivers and streams in collaboration with the National Parks Service. Thus began a new two-year stream assessment project.

Sallie Edmunds and I were the project co-managers. Because of Hawaiʻi's small scale, we replaced "river" with "stream." Together we inventoried every perennial stream in Hawaiʻi, recorded their physical attributes, in-stream flows, and whether or not they were diverted and/or channelized. We established committees to assess the ecological, recreational, scenic, and cultural resources of each stream.

Audrey Newman facilitated the Aquatic Resources Committee. Under her leadership, government, university, and private-sector aquatic scientists worked together to develop a list of indicator species of native aquatic fauna that suggested the stream's health. Through literature review and field study, they developed a sadly small list of streams with a healthy complement of native aquatic systems. That list raised the awareness which helps protect aquatic resources to this day. The aquatic scientific community collaboration continued for at least a decade through regular symposiums hosted by Bill Devick of the Division of Aquatic Resources.

In 1990 we submitted the Hawaiʻi Stream Assessment: A Preliminary Appraisal of Hawaiʻi's Stream Resources to the Commission on Water

Resource Management. The commissioners paged through it in silence while we waited in some apprehension. Water Commissioner Michael Chun finally broke the silence, "Well, it's nice to see real work." The Hawai'i Stream Assessment is still a go-to reference in Hawai'i.

Sallie Edmunds is currently the Central City, River and Environmental Planning Manager for the City of Portland, Bureau of Planning and Sustainability. No hydroelectric plants have been built on the Hanalei, Lumaha'i, or Wainiha rivers.

Hawaiian Fishpond Heritage

One day, Valerie Ossipoff took me to Kānewai Fishpond, one of the ponds stewarded by the Maunalua Fishpond Heritage Center. I had no idea what to expect, except that if Valerie thought it was a good place, it surely was. I fell in love with this little gem of a place and became friends with the center's executive director, Chris Cramer. He turned out to be interview number seventy-three of seventy-five, and what an interview it was!

Chris Cramer When [the developer] Henry Kaiser came to Hawai'i Kai and "fixed things," we lost Polynesia's largest fishpond. The Maunalua Fishpond covered 523 acres in Hawai'i Kai and held millions of mullet.

Many consider these fishponds to be Hawai'i's equivalent to Egypt's pyramids. The *ali'i nui* might bring thousands and thousands of *kanaka* from different islands to build the ponds. It could take a labor force of 10,000 to construct them, passing stones one by one out into the ocean to wall off giant fishponds and to create barriers to surround freshwater sources in the bay.

Auntie Laura Thompson is one of my heroes. Her family was the konohiki of their ahupua'a.[45] She has a picture showing the horses drinking fresh water in Maunalua Bay. They are *way* out by the reef and their heads are buried

---

[45] Wikipedia: The lands of the ruling chiefs of Hawai'i were divided into radial divisions of land when possible. These divisions were under the control of other smaller chiefs and managed by a steward. Land was divided up in strict adherence to the wishes of the ali'i nui. The island was called the *mokupuni* and was split into several *moku*. The moku (district) parameters ran from the highest mountaintop down to the sea. These divisions were ruled by an *ali'i 'ai moku* who would have been appointed by the ruling chief. Each of these mokus were further split into ahupua'a, named after the dividing boundary altar where taxes were collected for each area during the Makahiki. Each ahupua'a was then run by a headman or chief called a konohiki.

in a lens of fresh water. Seeing that picture, people could envision the concept of freshwater springs in the middle of the bay. Fresh water is carried by underground lava tubes from the mountains out into the bay. It has been said that whalers used to come and fill up their casks there in the old days. I can totally envision Auntie Laura riding her horse in the ocean all the way to Koko Head.

The whole coastline in East Oʻahu once teemed with springs and fishponds. There are Hawaiian families in this area who cared for these lands for generations, maintaining that cultural connection to the sea. By 2004, those traditions were facing extinction.

One day I saw an article in the newspaper that the state was going to auction "remnant highway parcels" along Kalanianaʻole Highway. Peeking through the brush I was surprised to see not land, but water. I was looking at one of the last Hawaiian fishponds in Honolulu. They were publicly owned and about to be auctioned. One pond even had approval to be filled in. I felt something had to be done.

The Reeves ʻohana has been respected stewards in Niu for generations. Angela Correa-Pei from the Reeves ʻohana had the idea to start a 501(c)(3). I had no clue what that was! Jeannine Johnson and I soon founded the Maunalua Fishpond Heritage Center. Jeannine's ʻohana hails from the Hawaiian fishing village of Miloliʻi. Although these last fishponds were closed off to Angela's and Jeannine's generations, our vision was that the next would be able to grow up caring for these special places. The only problem was that the state was about to auction them!

Kalauhaʻihaʻi Fishpond was the name of one of the fishponds scheduled for auction. Tadayoshi Hara had been its keeper until it was taken over by the Hawaiʻi Department of Transportation. He was originally from ʻOpihikao Village on the Big Island near Kalapana. He moved to Niu into a home that had a glass floor over the fishpond at Kalauhaʻihaʻi. He could see the fish swimming right under the glass of his living room floor. Three fish came to know him and would come up when he tapped the glass. There was every kind of fish and prawn in that pond. He could drink the sweet water. Big sea mullet would swim right up to the fishpond *ʻauwai* (channel). At night, Mr. Hara would shine his flashlight down and looking back at him were the glowing red eyes of the *ʻōpae lōlō*, the really large shrimp. Back in the day his kids would dance disco on the glass!

In 2007, his former fishpond property was being readied for auction by the Department of Transportation.[46] The first time I called Mr. Hara, we talked for about a minute and he said, "The state, they're dirty buggahs!" He

---

[46] https://www.staradvertiser.com/2010/08/02/business fishpond-protected-by-law-may-yet-be-sold/

was so upset he hung up the phone. I called him a few months later and we became friends. Filmmaker Ann Marie Kirk and I recorded Mr. Hara, and his story moved everyone. Ann Marie created a website, maunalua.net, that featured his story. It shifted the way people looked at historic and cultural sites like this because finally people could hear directly from kūpuna.

Mr. Hara's father had passed away when he was a young boy. Next door was an old Hawaiian fisherman with one arm; his other arm had been blown off while he was fishing using dynamite. The old man hānai'ed young Hara and taught him things never usually shared outside his family.

Hara described to us the traumatic day in the mid-1990s when the state ruined his pond. "The Department of Transportation was widening the road and hit the lava tube that fed the pond. My neighbor called and I left work to arrive in time to see my whole pond go dry. The floor was covered with fish. The last ones still alive were flopping in the lava tube. I felt as if someone had stabbed me in the heart, and I had a stroke on the spot. I tried to fight the state from the hospital." It was a very bitter experience for Mr. Hara. The state initially said they would fix it. Later they said it could not be fixed. Mr. Hara and the neighboring Lee family received a small compensation and left their homes, never to return.

Mr. Hara had old pictures showing the pond filled with the most crystal-blue water I had ever seen. He was able to point to the lava tube that flowed under Kalaniana'ole Highway and fed his pond. We worked with Joe Kennedy, a bold young scientist from the University of Hawai'i's School of Earth Science and Technology, and Lisa Pezzino, a visiting researcher from San Francisco. They were part of a group who bucked the conventional science of focusing on streams and rain instead of understanding groundwater. Hawaiians in the past knew all about underground water systems, but that knowledge had been largely overlooked.

After three years of searching for the fresh water shown in Mr. Hara's pictures, Jeannine Johnson sent a one-word message—"Eureka!" meaning, "I found it!" She had been reading a huge sewage project report. A line on one page said, "Segment C has over 1 million gallons a day of infiltration." Segment C was directly in front of the fishpond. When the lava tube was broken, the water found the lowest nearby point, which was a cracked sewer main. Fresh water was entering the sewage pipe and being piped miles to Sand Island to be treated as sewage.

The city claimed that it was seawater, not fresh water, but agreed to go with one of the young scientists to Section C at 3:00 a.m. when no one flushes the toilet. They popped open the manhole cover to find it was full to the brim. As soon as the lab opened, we took over the sample. It was fresh water—almost no salt at all!

As the city relined the main line, the scientists monitored it. Every day they lined that pipe, we saw water come back into the pond. It went from dry mud to ankle-deep water, then knee- and hip-deep. After twenty years, water flowed back into the fishpond! The leak wasn't completely fixed from the lateral lines, but it was a big leap forward. I called Mr. Hara and told him the good news. He was elated.

The state was still preparing the fishpond lands for auction. Over the years drug addicts had begun to live in these overgrown jungles. There were "No Trespassing, Government Property" signs all over. We would be arrested if we put one toe onto the property, but the squatters could live there and use the place as their toilet. Someone had sprayed the words "Smoke Ice" [methamphetamine] next to a roll of toilet paper. I remember visiting with Lieutenant Governor Duke Aiona and his cabinet. They couldn't get in because the squatters had changed the locks! The cops said one of the drug addicts even put the fishpond as his address on his ID.

We tried unsuccessfully to work out a transfer of the land to the Hawaiian Studies program. I finally asked HDOT for the exact auction law so I could read it myself. I found a loophole related to public interest determination. Several years later that route proved successful.

Things got desperate before they got better. We drafted a bill prohibiting the sale of publicly owned fishponds. Tony Costa was the leading advocate for the fishermen at the legislature. The fishermen did not see eye-to-eye with the environmentalists, but this was something that wasn't going to take anything away from the fishermen or from the environmentalists. I practically lived at the legislature for two years. At the very end of the first year the politicians held the bill hostage, horse trading back and forth. The second year this bill to save fishponds all across Hawai'i unanimously passed both houses and went to Governor Linda Lingle for her signature. She sided with her staff at HDOT and refused to meet with the community members. Instead she put the bill on her veto list. We were devastated.

Days before the veto deadline, the governor was on Mike Buck's radio show. I called the station and was the last caller they put on. I shared with her that these were the very last fishponds in East Honolulu that hadn't been destroyed. It would be a travesty to sell them at public auction and let them be filled in. I didn't have much time to talk, but evidently something got through to her. She took the bill off her veto list and let it pass without her signature.

The resulting 2010 law said that you could not sell publicly owned Hawaiian fishponds, at which point the state declared, "These are not fishponds; these are water features." First they called them remnant parcels and then they called them water features. When William Aila became head of the DLNR he said, "That's a *mākāhā*, the gate to a Hawaiian fishpond. Anyone seeing a mākāhā knows it is a fishpond." He brought about a change such that these lands are now under the Department of Land and Natural Resources.

Kuliʻouʻou Lagoon is actually an ancient fishpond. When we first started going there, it had no water in it. It was filled with upside-down jellyfish, which flourish in stagnant water with no circulation. When we unblocked the lava tubes and cleaned up the fishponds, fresh water began flowing through them and the overflow entered the lagoon. Over time the lagoon became healthier and the jellyfish left.

We wanted to preserve the home with the glass floor, but it had been so damaged by the neglect of the Department of Transportation that it was falling apart. Kalauhaʻihaʻi Fishpond is now an open pond that we use as an ocean classroom for community learning and fishpond restoration.

A block away, with the community's help, we are also restoring Kanewai Spring. Our community has united around these last fishponds in a beautiful way!

Endangered Forests
Neil Hannahs and Gary Gill spoke independently about their efforts to save different Hawaiian forests.

Neil Hannahs For years, koa forests on Bishop Estate land were cut for lumber, furniture, musical instruments, flooring, canoes, and crafts. There was seldom a requirement to replenish the forest after harvesting the wood. In one 5,000-acre block of land, as much as one and a half million board feet of koa forest is dying due to lack of regeneration, as well as animal, human, and weed infestation.

Working as a consultant to Paniolo Tonewoods,[47] we came up with a plan to revive this forest by harvesting koa to make into musical instruments. The length of the lease was twenty five-years. Under a stewardship agreement, compensation for the wood (stumpage fees) is reinvested to improve the health, biodiversity, and regenerative capability of the forests.

The value created by milling the koa into guitar tonewood will allow us to expend around $20 million in regenerating the forest. By making this investment in stewardship, we project that the site will host around nine and a half million board feet of koa in twenty-five years and over thirteen million

---

[46] Paniolo Tonewoods is a partnership of Taylor Guitars and Pacific Rim Tonewoods.

board feet of koa in thirty-five years. The projected financial value of that future inventory is head-turning, and the projected health of the land and resources is heart-warming.

This abundance will have been accomplished with private investment. The principals of Paniolo Tonewoods, Bob Taylor and Steve McMinn, take a long-range view of their businesses and do not want future harvesters and luthiers fighting for the last board foot of koa. They are committed to being stewards of the land and assuring a robust supply of koa long after they are gone. How can we mobilize more commercial capital for investments that create a thriving environment and a just society? I am keen and energized to deploy, prove, and promote this model.

Gary Gill came to my attention because of his conservation efforts on the Pālehua ridge on Oʻahu.

Gary Gill At one point, the Campbell Estate owned thousands of acres of land on Oʻahu. As time passed and the trust expired, they were required by law to dissolve the Campbell Estate family trust and become the James Campbell Company. As a real estate company, their focus was on commercial and residential property; therefore, they sold agriculture land in Kunia, Kahuku, and ʻEwa.

In 2007 one of the last parcels they had was the mountaintop called Pālehua, above Makakilo. A branch of it goes from the coastline in Nānākuli all the way up through the summit of the Waiʻanae Mountains to Schofield. It's about 7,000 acres.

My grandparents made a really good business decision in 1933. My grandmother, Lorin Tarr Gill, received a small inheritance from her West Virginian grandmother, an early pioneer in the Ohio River valley. My grandmother had been threatened with being disinherited because she married that "savage" from the Sandwich Islands, my grandfather. But before she could be disinherited, her grandmother died, and Lorin inherited a few thousand bucks. In the middle of the Depression this was like winning the lottery! She and my grandfather purchased a small parcel of undeveloped, dredged, coral-spoiled land on Seaside Avenue in Waikīkī.

My grandfather, Tom Gill, was an architect in Honolulu. He pooled his resources with my grandmother, and they built a number of little duplex apartments on their half-acre, creating a boutique hotel. Grandma would pick up people on Boat Day at Honolulu Harbor in her Model A and drive them to the Gill Apartments on Seaside Avenue.

Ultimately, my generation sold that property, which meant we had a small pool of money with no idea what to do with it except that maybe we should put it into some other land. I asked a friend who was an attorney for the Campbell Estate if he had any ideas. He said, "Well, we're selling a mountain." I said, "We don't have that kind of money!" But as it worked out, the Trust for Public Lands had raised public money and Ed Olson, a large landowner on the Big Island, became involved. My family threw in everything that we had from the sale of the Waikīkī property and our *hui* (group) bought 7,000 acres from the Campbell Estate. The Ed Olson Trust has just under one-half of the acreage on the east side of Pālehua Road, and Gill Ewa Lands, LLC has the western portion of the property along Nānākuli Ridge.

With a once-in-three-lifetimes opportunity that barely came together and serendipitous timing, we leveraged half an acre of Waikīkī into 1,600 acres of agriculture and conservation land in Wai'anae. The property includes the coastline just before the Nānākuli Homestead. Between the Kahe power plant and the homestead there are a couple of hundred yards of shoreline, and then the property goes all the way up to Mauna Kapu at 2,700 feet in elevation.

Our land includes a number of the historic cabins that were built with various degrees of permitting, including the Ossipoff cabin. The cabin and guest house were in very poor repair, and restoring them has been an expensive but stimulating adventure. I just restored the guest house deck. The structure was nearly destroyed by termites. I cut some eucalyptus and we redid it in natural wood. In the main cabin there is tatami, which has rotted. Xandra Ossipoff's daughter, Keira, is helping to come up with some way of constructing *faux* tatami that will not mold.[48]

In addition to overseeing the restoration of these historic cabins, we are constructing fences to protect the remaining Hawaiian forest. I was up there with students from Kapolei High School, building a hog-wire fence around a grove of *lama* trees—Hawaiian mahogany sacred to the goddess Laka. It is a very slow-growing tree. I don't think it is on the endangered list, but it is rare and special and it's in decline. We have a lama tree that the botanists say is the oldest one they've seen. It is hundreds of years old and has a few keiki to its side. The tree is right by the ranch road and is threatened by grazing cattle.

We've had three fires in ten years. All fires on O'ahu are man-made; there are no natural fires. A big fire in 2014 was started by seven-year-old twin boys playing with lighters in their Makakilo Heights house. They burned the biggest grove of *wiliwili* on the island.

---

[48] An excellent article by Michael Adno with photos by Chris Mottalini of the Ossipoff house can be found at: https://s3.amazonaws.com/external_clips/2287888/AL_07_Travel_Ossipoff_Cabins_Chris_Mottalini_LR.pdf?1485629299

Some residents are concerned about how the forest fires are going to impact people's houses. My concern is how the people's fires are going to impact the forest. Nobody wants to see their house burn down, but you have insurance to rebuild a house after a disaster. Once burned, wiliwili trees are gone forever. So I'm building firebreaks and designing a water system to help prevent fires from coming into the forest. The fire department has been involved and they hope to do wildfire response training.

A 2016 forest fire burned out the entire back of Nānākuli Valley. We have to keep our lower agriculture land grazed. When the grass catches on fire, it burns fifty feet high in a firestorm, and there is no stopping it until the fire gets up to the edge of the forest. Then you can try to fight it. That fire burned the conservation area, which was not grazed, and then went down into the agricultural land that we had fenced to protect the sandalwood from the cattle. We kept the cattle out but we didn't keep the fire out. Fortunately, most of the sandalwood has come back; suckers came up from the roots. It was a quick burn, so the trees got burned but the root system survived.

We are building fences to keep the huge population of pigs out; they do huge damage on the mountain. The ʻelepaio, a native Hawaiian endangered forest bird, has habitat on our property and is being managed by the Army Natural Resources Program under the Endangered Species Act. With our permission they are trapping rodents and we are fencing, culling exotic plants, and growing natives.

This is what I'm doing these days. It's a full-time job! ❋

Honolulu Star-Bulletin special edition, March 12, 1959

CHAPTER 14

Voices of the Media

Society Columnists
As a young girl I seldom read the paper, but I always liked the photograph of the glamorous Lois Taylor at the head of the society column.

Lois Taylor Clarke I went to the University of California at Berkeley during World War II and there were few men attending, so I had few distractions. The school figured if you were strong enough to play football you should be carrying a gun, so there were no sports. Consequently, I got a very good education. I majored in journalism.

The Farringtons owned the *Star-Bulletin* and I had to have a personal interview with Mrs. Farrington. They knew I could write, but I guess they didn't know if I knew how to use a fork. I was duly inducted into writing the society column and worked there for almost thirty years!

I stuck with the society column for about twelve years and then there was a feeling among the editors that society writing was kind of dumb, so I shifted over to interviewing, which I'd wanted to do all along. The hotels would call and say, "So-and-so will be here; please arrange an interview." One of my interviews was with Howard Cosell. I'll never forget it. He said he would meet me by the pool at the Royal Hawaiian at 3:00 p.m. At 3:00 p.m. the photographer and I went in. There were three men sitting there and I could not tell which was which. I went up to one of them and said, "Mr. Cosell?" He stood up and said, "I am Cosell!" He was very arrogant but very pleasant. We talked about football, a game about which I knew virtually nothing.

Cobey Black, who was a friend of mine, worked for the *Advertiser* as a columnist. Sometimes we interviewed the same celebrities. I would type out the story and the editor would read it and make corrections. Then the city editor sent it to the typesetters in the back shop. They set the type in hot lead in wooden forms. They would set up the whole page, make one print copy, and send it back to the editor for review. If it was okay, with no typos, they would run the presses and print the paper.

They often spilled the lead on the soft pine floor. It ended up making the most beautiful floor you could imagine with these silver spots embedded in the wood. Years later, when the building was gutted, one of the photographers who had a house on the Big Island took that wood for the interior of his house. He sanded it down and it was absolutely gorgeous.

All day long every day, the wireless came in and if it were a big story, we would hear *ding ding ding*. Ordinarily it was one *ding* with a report that there had been an earthquake in some place you never heard of. One day in November it rang four times, *ding ding ding ding*, and news came over the wireless that President Kennedy had been shot and was probably dying.

Ours was an evening paper, so the deadline was early in the morning. But the deadline was 9:00 p.m. the night before for the issues that went to the outer islands. Those papers were printed at night and then flown over on the early morning planes along with the loaves of bread from Love's Bakery.

On the morning that President Kennedy was shot, they slammed shut the presses because they were going to have to lay out a whole new edition to print. Ordinarily they shut down the presses slowly, but not that November morning. The presses were so huge and so heavy that when they stopped, the whole building shook!

I worked at night a lot, because if the mayor was going to give a party the photographer and I would slog along. (My husband) Stan was a stockbroker and got up at the crack of dawn because of the time difference between here and New York, where the stock exchange is. He left the house for work at 5:30 a.m., then came home to take a nap so he could have dinner with the kids. I was often just leaving, all dressed up to go someplace when they were eating dinner. But during the daytime, when the kids were growing up, I spent most of my time in the carpool! Thursday was my day to drive. And if I broke my leg, the ambulance was to drive from (my home on) Maunalani Heights, swing by Punahou School, pick up the kids, buy the kids an ice cream, send them home, and then take me to the hospital. Betty Long drove Tuesday and Maris Gray had another day. We never switched days.

Kaui Philpotts clearly loves being a connector of people and a collector of stories.

Kaui Philpotts I worked for the *Maui News* from 1974 to 1989. I started out selling ads and because I would go all around town, I knew everything that was happening, including all the gossip. Everybody would tell me stories. "I remember your mother," they'd say. Somebody on the staff told me I ought to write a gossip column. And I thought, "I could do that!" So I did. It started a lifelong career.

I was kind. I never said bad things. I had good sense. "So-and-so is just back from a trip to X and they found this for their store." I reported on who got married and who was visiting. Probably because I was a mix of haole-Hawaiian-Chinese, all kinds of people talked to me. People also love seeing their name in the papers. Pretty soon I was hearing that people were buying the paper every Wednesday for my column, which was in the business section because I mostly talked about who had new things, who was closing their doors, or who was moving.

It grew into a full-on feature-writing job. The paper was growing and we had a wonderful editor, Nora Cooper. Lynne Horner was our graphic artist and a terrific writer. The two of us would do the feature and entertainment section.

Christopher Hemmeter had just started to build the Hyatt Regency Maui, and Colin Cameron, whose mother and father owned the paper, was building the Kapalua resort. A&B was building the Wailea resort. Maui was exploding in the luxury area. You can't imagine what being there at that time was like. Everybody wanted to come to Maui. They eventually bypassed Honolulu. I met people I would never, ever have met if I had worked anywhere else. I had lunch with Yoko Ono. John [Lennon] had just died and she had a portfolio of his work that she wanted to get into the art galleries in Lahaina. I interviewed Cary Grant on the *USS Constitution*. I interviewed the top Napa and Sonoma winemakers, who would bring me wine and invite me to stay at their vineyards.

I didn't know any of the celebrities, but I had the guts to call them up and say, "Can I interview you?" They often said, "Sure. Come to lunch." Do you remember Mrs. Fields' Cookies? My girlfriend and I went out to Kapalua where her husband had purchased a place and she baked us her cookies. The paper even sent me to Japan to do a series of stories on Japanese tourism, which was just beginning.

Anybody who was anyone at that time and came to the island, we interviewed them. Carol Lawrence had been in *West Side Story* and had just gotten a divorce from Robert Goulet. It was amazing what people would say to you when they thought you were safe. I think they forgot where they were and what I did for a living. I never wrote half the things they told me, but oh my goodness!

Maui had started to grow so much that I was getting nostalgic about the old days. I wrote many features about people who had grown up on the plantations. I was so touched by them, by their wisdom. I always got so much from them in their simplicity. I really loved those people and hearing their stories.

Hawai'i's First TV Anchorwoman

Linda Coble's mother and my mother were college friends, and my mother kept an eye on Linda's career from the moment she arrived in Hawai'i. Linda became a very popular television reporter, then an anchor, before she moved to radio. She told me about the early days when she had no name and no experience.

Linda Coble I got hired at Hawai'i station KITV the day the US landed a man on the moon. My job was not glamorous; I would take the men's dirty suits to the cleaners, I would answer the phone, I would sweep the film off the floor, I'd tell the reporters when their film was almost finished in the giant machine.

One day there was a car bombing at Holiday Mart [now Don Quijote, near Ala Moana Center] and I was the only person in the newsroom. I had on a pink *mu'umu'u* with little puffy sleeves. They said, "Just go with a cameraman and he'll tell you what to do." I said, "Okay" (voice quavering) and suddenly I was the reporter. I got out of the car, my cameraman was behind me, and I'm dragging the length of my microphone cord through the traffic and over the yellow tape that said, "Do Not Cross." They thought I was someone who knew the victim or lived in the apartment and was trying to get to my car. I went right to the window of the car. The victim was still in the front seat. His leg was almost blown off and he was swearing. I peeked my head around with my microphone and I said, "How do you feel?" That's the last time I ever asked that stupid question! He said, "How the (expletive) do you think I feel?" Obviously, I couldn't use that sound bite. But I was there! I got all the video that nobody else could get.

I was the secretary at the station and one night they said, "Linda, Barry Goldwater is coming back from his big trip to Cambodia and Vietnam and he's going to stop over at Hickam. They said it was okay for the cameraman to go, but he has to have a reporter with him." I said, "Okay, I'll go." So out the door we went.

Goldwater had gone down the steps of the plane to smoke. I walked over to the Navy guy and said, "Would you please tell Barry Goldwater that Linda Coble is here to see him." He looked at me like I had to be kidding. And I said, "Linda Coble." He walked across the tarmac all the way over to where Barry was, and I could see Barry crane his neck and walk toward me. He kept coming closer until he could yell out, "Linda, how the hell is Bob?" He and my dad, Robert P. Coble, had served in the Air Force together. I knew there weren't that many Cobles, and I knew they were close. I got it on camera the first time Barry said, "We should have nuked the hell out of them." It was front page news on the mainland when he finally got home.

In a few months, I was reporting. I also started to fill in as an anchor. Bob Sevey, who was the news director at the CBS affiliate here, KGMB, never wanted a woman on the air. He said women just didn't have authority in their voices. But he saw that it was becoming popular and I was "it." I was the first female reporter/anchor in Hawai'i. I was very proud of that. So he hired me; stole me from Channel 4! That was 1972. Al Michaels had been my sports guy at KITV, and Chuck Henry was also there. There were great mentors at Channel 4 and I had wonderful training.

Sevey was one of those who made sure we always had both sides of every story, unlike today where there is a lot of opinionated discussion before and after clips. If I came back from a city council meeting where 90 percent of the people were against and a few people were for something, and I had concentrated on the "against," I had to get back in the car and go find someone who was "for" and interview them. That was the way we were. Both sides of every story.

Gerald Ford came to town right after he became president. When Air Force One and Two came in (Air Force Two had all the reporters from the mainland) they'd go scurrying to their cars while the locals had to sit in the bleachers. I found a guy in a white uniform and said, "Why is it they get to sit in the cars and go with the president, and I don't?" He said, "Linda, take car 26." I ran under the bleachers and tugged on my cameraman and said, "Come with me. Leave the tripod, bring the camera and your bag." Pierre Bowman, who was a *Star-Bulletin* writer, was the only person who saw me do this. He came running up to the car as I was getting in. The man in the white uniform was standing there. Pierre said, "Why does *she* get to go, and I don't?" "Because you're too fat." And he shut the door and off we drove. (Laughter.)

We were with the president's team and all the mainland reporters following the president on his rounds. It was December 7th, so he was out at Pearl Harbor. Nobody could talk to him; we just "shot" him as he went around. Back at the airport, the Kamehameha Singers were performing. I was trying to get a cord straightened so I could get sound from the singers. I was bent over, digging in my bag, and I stood up just as the President of the United States was walking past me. He didn't see me. When I stood up, I hit his chin and nearly knocked him out. If his tongue had been anywhere near his teeth, he would have bled to death! (Laughter.) All the Secret Service were running at me like I had done it on purpose. My head hurt! But I had my microphone in my hand, so I stuck it out and said, "Mr. President, what were your feelings when you were on board the Arizona Memorial?" I got the most beautiful sound bite.

One time my cameraman and I were driving along and heard on our car radio that an accident had happened on the H-1 freeway. We were right there when a big truck drove under the Middle Street overpass and flung its wrecking ball over the overpass into the opposite lane of traffic going 'ewa. The wrecking ball smashed into a vehicle with two people in it. They were driving out to visit a location where they were going to be married the next week. I'm walking with my cameraman along H-1 toward the car.

The cops, who all knew and liked me, said, "Linda, don't look at this. We have it covered." I looked down the way and saw the truck. I said, "C'mon, let's go." As I got closer to the truck, I turned to my cameraman and said, "Turn off the light." I walked up to the window and the truck driver was slumped over the steering wheel, sobbing. I walked to the passenger side, climbed in and sat with him for about twenty minutes until somebody showed up. He was just sobbing, "I didn't lower the boom, I didn't lower the boom, Linda." If I had gone up there with a microphone and stuck it in his face, that would have been the most unkind, ugly thing to do. I would have had a great story but the red light in my brain clicked off forever, right then. People were more important than the story. Who they were, rather than what they were involved in, became more important. It was the turning point for me. I think that's one reason that by 1988 I was okay to leave. Sevey had just left. And I was ready.

I worked in radio for ten years. I took an offer to be the newsperson for Perry & Price, the number-one radio show on KSSK-AM and FM. I sat across from Michael W. Perry and Larry Price, with a window separating us. On radio I could be a little bit more vocal with my thoughts and I knew a lot of backstories. Every time there was a discussion, I would throw my two cents in. It was great. I could share stories and talk about things that mattered to me. We had huge ratings. It was the second most-listened-to morning show in the country.

Radio and TV
John Fink has so much energy that I could see how he was so effective as an announcer for sporting events! He certainly made the radio and TV industries come alive for me.

John Fink My father had been stationed in Hawai'i for six months during World War II. He fell in love with Lahainaluna and Spreckelsville, the local lifestyle, and traditions. This mainland haole from New York "got" what the local people were all about; he seemed to understand the soul of the people.

In 1975, Mom, Dad, and my younger sister moved to Honolulu from the Chicago area. Dad lived to be eighty-eight. My mom passed twelve years later at eighty-nine, having lived here for forty-five years. Dad was an independent jewelry sales representative who sold jewelry to stores throughout Hawai'i. Until he was seventy, he was literally dragging big bags of jewelry drawers around to buyers!

I attended UH for one semester in 1976 and then finished at Wesleyan University in Connecticut. My first job in Hawai'i was public relations director for Team Hawai'i of the North American Soccer League. I was responsible for press releases about the team. There were three major TV stations: KGMB,

KHON, and KITV. At KGMB, my main contact was the sports anchor, Joe Moore, who became a local institution. My contact at KHON was legendary sportscaster Les Keiter, affectionately known as "the General" due to a role he had played on the original *Hawaiʻi Five-O* TV series. After one season, Team Hawaiʻi sought greener pastures in Tulsa, Oklahoma. I opted to stay here—a smart move.

My next job was at KAHU/KULA radio in Waipahu, housed near Waipahu High School in an old World War II bomb shelter, changing the reel-to-reel music on tape machines. We played Top 40 hits and oldies.

In 1982 I moved to television as a salesman at KGMB, the CBS affiliate in Hawaiʻi. In 1986 I went to KHNL as the general sales manager, a position I held for ten years. No station in Hawaiʻi was regularly covering college sports in the early 1980s, and very few schools had any presence on TV in a big way. But KHNL put UH sports on TV, first in 1984 with baseball, and soon thereafter airing over 110 sporting events annually, from September through May, the most telecasts for any college team in America. We were one of the first entities in America to really push women's volleyball, softball, soccer, and basketball. I did play-by-play for Wahine soccer for twenty-five years on KHNL and KFVE. We even covered one or two UH women's water polo games each year. This was all well before gender equality became a big issue along with the much-needed Title IX.

Jim Leahey handled play-by-play for football road games as well as all the other sports. Because he had conflicts with weekend home matches, I was asked to do play-by-play for Wahine volleyball when Jim was on the road. Punahou School Athletic Director Chris McLachlin was the color commentator. I learned the intricacies of the game from Chris. I call him Mother Teresa, as he has helped so many people on their life journey. He and his equally amazing wife, Beth, have taken kids in and let them live in their house. The two of them are truly uniquely positive and passionate people. When he was offered a position as an assistant coach for the US women's volleyball team in the Olympics, he said no because he had three young kids at home. Beth is in the US Volleyball Hall of Fame. She was on the Women's Olympic Volleyball team in 1980, the year the United States boycotted the Summer Games in Russia, so she didn't get to play. She was part of the original UH Wahine team involved with Title IX, which was enacted through the valiant efforts of Hawaiʻi's own [US Representative] Patsy Mink and Dr. Donnis Thompson, which is a great story in itself.

The job of the play-by-play guy is to explain what is going on in the game. After the play ends, the color guy throws in commentary about what happened during or because of the play. Chris was the volleyball expert and I was the one inserting the action. When UH Wahine volleyball ratings came out, we realized there were over 100,000 people watching on KHNL. The 1986 season ended and the next year general manager Rick Blangiardi, who brought UH sports to TV in a big way here, said, "Why don't you do all the games in 1987?" So I did play-by-play for women's volleyball with Chris over the next ten years. I became known for a time as "the voice of Wahine volleyball." It was a great honor.

I took over as the general manager of KHNL and KFVE in 1996. We had just debuted the first all-digital newsroom in the world. Needless to say, it was a tech mess with beta tests and reboots for months and months. In late 1999 we were bought by Raycom Media, a company that owned twenty or so TV stations.

KHNL took over the management of KFVE in 1993 and moved UH sports there. The FOX network was not too happy about getting preempted for sports on KHNL, so shifting UH sports to KFVE made sense. Taking over KFVE, which had been struggling, allowed us to move UH sports and some of our local music specials such as the Nā Hōkū Hanohano Awards and music shows like "Hot Hawaiian Nights" to a separate broadcast station, thus allowing KHNL to be the full-time home of FOX. KFVE quickly became known as "The Home Team" and had great success for the next twenty-five years as an independent broadcast station, eventually airing more local, non-news programming than any other TV station in the country.

I believe strongly in the power of broadcasting and television, especially at the local level. Citizens need TV, radio, and newspapers to keep an eye on what locally elected officials are doing or not doing. If local media dwindles, we are in for a tough world, without vetted information sources. Twitter, social media, and web trolls are not the answer. Through local TV, one has the power to inform, entertain, educate, and even change people's lives, which is wonderful if it is used properly and responsibly.

The Merrie Monarch Festival is watched annually by almost a half million people locally and another half million throughout the rest of the world via live internet streaming. People in more than 120 countries annually watch this incredible cultural celebration of dance, music, and storytelling. KFVE's coverage of the Hōkū Awards and the Keiki Hula Competition help to preserve, perpetuate, and promote the future of Hawaiian music and culture. Being a part of this growth and the renaissance of our unique local culture via television has been an honor, a passion play, and a true pleasure for me over the past four decades.

The Librarian
Sigrid Southworth worked as a librarian at Kamehameha Schools for thirty-seven years. Sigrid spoke with me about how she got the job.

Sigrid Southworth One day when I was in graduate school, I walked into the student lounge at Simmons University in Boston and there was a three-by-five card on the bulletin board that said Mr. Kimber Moulton of the Kamehameha Schools would be coming to interview. I got all dressed up and walked in and said, "*Aloha. Pehea ʻoe?*" He said, "Where are you from?" And I said, "Well, where do you think?" It was pretty flippant, but we went on to have an absolutely wonderful interview. By the end of it, I wanted to work at Kamehameha, and he wanted me. I spent thirty-seven years there.

I started in 1964 when there were still two separate schools—one for girls and one for boys. I was the Girls' School librarian. The next year the schools were co-educated but we still had to maintain a Girls' School library and a Boys' School library for several years. It was about 1970 when we merged the two libraries. When we put all the books together, I realized what a phenomenal Hawaiian collection we had.

When Punahou School was founded in 1841, there was a dictum that a copy of everything published in the kingdom should be placed in the Punahou library. We didn't have such a collection but the very first librarian was very good about acquiring things about Hawaiʻi. The collection was started in 1887, when Kamehameha Schools was started. Many much older publications have been acquired in the years since.

Eventually the Hawaiian collection in the high school library couldn't contain both the academic collection for schoolwork and the archival collection for the history of the schools. So we lobbied for and got an archivist hired, and a true archive was formed. We moved all the archival material about the school out of the curricular collection. The curricular collection is comprised of everything about Hawaiʻi that the students might use in study.

After we opened Midkiff Learning Center in 1977, I worked with both Hawaiian Studies classes and with regular classes; I was primarily responsible for the Hawaiian Collection. In a research project for an English class studying etymology, we would survey the many types of dictionaries. Or in a history class studying the Civil War we would go to our Civil War materials and learn the difference between primary and secondary sources. We would discuss how to find specific information, such as what kind of boots they wore in the Civil War. The teachers often created individual research projects for their students. One teacher came up with really creative assignments for his physics class where the students had to pick some activity of ancient Hawaiʻi and look at the physics involved with pounding kapa or the physics of a heavy board sliding in on the waves. Students used the Hawaiian collection to gather data about the activity, and physics/physiology books to understand the physics.

A required assignment for all ninth grade Hawaiian culture classes was called wahi pana (celebrated places). Students would research their home community. A student would come up to me and say, "There's nothing about my part of Hilo." "Okay, let's look at a map. Oh, there is Railroad Street. Why do you suppose that's called Railroad Street? Let's go look at the train books about Hawai'i." Or, "Why is Mountain View called Mountain View? What was there that made the view important?" It was one of my favorite assignments of the whole year. They had to learn the winds, the rains, and the songs written about their place.

When we opened Midkiff Learning Center, Janice Williams and I wore pedometers and discovered we averaged thirteen miles of walking a day. So, librarians do not just sit at desks and read! (Laughter.) We are very physically active and busy.

I hear both Punahou and Kamehameha are drastically reducing their book collections. They are turning the libraries into big, open study spaces. Each child has their own laptop and that is the source of their information. What was on our library shelves had been vetted; we read reviews by the millions and chose the best books. We might have 350 books on the Civil War and they are all accurate sources, whereas on the computer you might get 3,500,000 hits, and who knows the authenticity of some of them.

Once the internet came along, if a teacher suspected plagiarism, we could do a search and often find verbatim what the student had copied. We also got to the point where we could say, "Hmmm, that sounds like the Britannica yearbook." Plagiarism was a major no-no.

For thirteen years I lived on the Kamehameha Girls campus as a faculty boarding advisor. I would frequently take girls hiking. In the early 1970s Chuck Burrows, who started teaching at Kamehameha the same year I did, was teaching biology and he started the Environmental Task Force Club. His biology classes would go to Kualoa Park where they would conduct twenty-four-hour, around-the-clock testing of temperature, wind, oxygen in the water, and salinity in the water. They were learning field science. They had so much fun that Chuck decided to create an extra-curricular club through which they could do field studies more often. He asked me to join him as an advisor and we attracted both boarding and day students. As the activities grew in popularity, the name of the club was changed to Hui Lama. Hui means a group and lama is one of our endemic trees. Kamehameha is located in the ahupua'a of Kapalama. In ancient Hawai'i, lama branches were bundled together and burned to form a torch by which they got minimal light. By extension *mālamalama* means understanding, comprehension, enlightenment.

Hui Lama became one of the most active and significant clubs on the campus. We spent one week every year on a different island. We took field scientists with us and the kids called them by their first names, rubbed shoulders with them, and learned how special field science can be. Many of the Hui Lama members have gone into environmental endeavors as adults. We took them to places where you had to have permission, a four-wheel-drive vehicle, somebody who knew the way, and a key. Then we began going further afield. They had a three-week field trip to the Four Corners area—Arizona, New Mexico, Colorado, and Utah— to compare Hawaiian, Hopi, and Navajo cultures. Then we had three weeks in Alaska where we studied the *kōlea*, the Pacific golden plover, which flies between Hawai'i and the Arctic. It's a 3,000-mile flight that they do in three days. We went to New Zealand for three weeks and did a study of flightless birds, because we had so many skeletons of flightless birds in Hawai'i that were extinct long before modern habitation. Finally, we went to Rapa Nui (Easter Island) for three weeks of comparing that Polynesian culture with our own.

Newspapers in old Hawai'i were all written in Hawaiian. Bishop Museum has a wonderful collection of them but many of them have not been translated. I think we stand to learn a great deal when they do get translated and doing so may provide jobs for many of the college students who are majoring in Hawaiian language.

Gavan Daws, in his interview with Leslie Wilcox on [her PBS Hawai'i program] *Long Story Short*, says he is criticized today by Hawaiians because his book *Shoal of Time* has a Western point of view. He said yes, he is Western and that was what was being written at the time. "Go ahead and write another point of view. We need them all. Just do it."

By the time I retired from Kamehameha, we had over 14,000 volumes in the Hawaiian collection alone. Fourteen thousand is much bigger than most high school libraries. We have over 100,000 volumes in the library. It was a large and very carefully built library. You go through and weed out a general collection periodically and do some discarding. It is not a sin to throw a book away. But we did not delete much in the Hawaiian collection. Not everything there is totally accurate, but it was important to keep a representation of what has been published.

There is no longer a School of Library Science. It's the School of Information and Library Science. Every year for thirty-seven years there was a new challenge. When I started, electric typewriters were the newest thing. Later, learning to do computer cataloguing when I was new to word processing was huge. Twelve-, thirteen-, fourteen-hour days were not at all uncommon. I worked with students almost constantly from 7:30 a.m. until 3:30 p.m. The cataloguing, which is deep-thought work, had to be done before or after that. I would frequently go in at 5:00 or 5:30 in the morning to work, when I was fresh and it was quiet, with no interruptions. But it was a wonderful and fulfilling career. ❖

"Clearing Sky," etching by Huc-Mazelet Luquiens

CHAPTER 15

Voices of Inspiration

These final stories are among my favorites. Each one includes something that left me really inspired. I'm delighted to share these voices of inspiration, a fitting conclusion to Voices of Hawai'i.

Success at a Sears Kiosk
No matter how many times I read it, the last paragraph of Peter Ehrman's story always chokes me up.

Peter Ehrman I was born in Hawai'i and went to Punahou School from kindergarten to twelfth grade. I played a lot of sports, but by high school I was in love with volleyball. I was very lucky that UCLA recruited me to play volleyball. I was there from 1978 to 1982 and the team won two national championships during that time. I played with two of the most famous names in volleyball history in the US. One of them was Karch Kiraly, currently the US Women's Olympic volleyball coach. He is the greatest volleyball player the US has ever produced. The other was Christopher Saint John "Singin'" Smith, who was also outstanding.

    I had the good fortune to rent a room in the beautiful home of a retired UCLA professor who lived across the street from campus. He was a very serious investor in the stock market, and nearly every day some of the athletes who lived in his house would go through the *Wall Street Journal* with him as he shared his investing ideas. This was my first introduction to the world of economics and finance. Because of him, when it was time to select a major, I choose economics.

    After I graduated it just so happened that the Honolulu office of Dean Witter (now Morgan Stanley) was expanding. There was an ad in the newspaper for a stockbroker position, which I answered, and I interviewed with Paul Loo. He offered me an entry-level position as a stockbroker trainee. He was a brilliant man who taught us to stick with high-quality, dividend-paying securities that would be around for a long time, as opposed to trying to find the next great home-run investment.

My second mentor was Sam Cooke, who was, in my opinion, the most successful investment advisor at Dean Witter. He was deeply rooted in the community; his grandfather was involved with the founding of Bank of Hawaiʻi and his grandmother founded the Honolulu Academy of Arts, now the Honolulu Museum of Art.

You asked me about things that are different now than when I started; one of them is the speed of business. It used to be that you discussed an idea with a client, and they'd say, "Send me some information on that." You would print up reports and mail a nice packet to them. Then you'd call a week later to review it. Today it's all done in a matter of minutes. You download the information, email it to them in a single PDF, have a two-minute phone call, they respond instantly, and you make the trade. This is a radically different way to do business.

When I first started in the business, Sears had just acquired Dean Witter and Allstate Life Insurance Company. They thought it would be a great idea to have little kiosks in Sears stores manned by an Allstate person and a Dean Witter person. My assignment was manning a shift at a kiosk at either Sears Ala Moana or Sears Pearlridge. Some days I'd sit all day and not talk to a single person. Other days someone with no experience with investing whatsoever might walk by looking for guidance. At the end of the conversation they might tell me that they had $250,000 that they had just inherited and wanted to invest. They would say all this standing next to the car batteries and tires at the auto section in Sears!

Most of the people who came in knew nothing about investing so it was a lot less intimidating for them to talk to a live person at a Sears kiosk than to make an appointment with a stranger and go into a high-rise in downtown Honolulu for a meeting.

I have clients today that I met at that Sears kiosk in 1984 and 1985. I remember when they could invest $2,000 or $5,000 or $10,000 a year. Today I see them retired with their houses paid off, having no debt, with financial security and millions of dollars in their portfolios. It has been very satisfying to have been a part of their success!

A Note of Sympathy

This is a very special note that one of my father's law partners wrote to my mother at the time of Marshall's death in 2004. Though I am close to Ron Lum, I did not ask his permission to use this note in my book. I didn't want him to say no! It is personal but wise and tender, and I know you'll appreciate his candor as I did.

Dear Ruth,

Two people had the greatest influence on my legal career. Livingston Jenks taught me to fear the law. Never make a mistake!! Marshall taught me to love the law and to enjoy my partners and the firm. The latter is obviously most gratifying. Love conquers fear. I am forever grateful to Marshall for his confidence in me and I will sorely miss him.

Ronald Hung Wai Lum

Adjunct Professor

When Ray Tam gave me his interview, he told me with enthusiasm about teaching at the University of Hawai'i law school. When he later reviewed his transcript, he left this story out. But I think it is indicative of his passion for the law, so I am sneaking it into my book. He is very self-effacing, which is why his final comment is so understated. But you could tell that he was thrilled with his students' gift.

Raymond Tam Around 1977 or 1978 I was asked to teach at the University of Hawai'i law school as an adjunct professor. At the very first class somebody came in with a thermos. I said, "I know that you folks probably are thirsty and hungry. If you are, please step outside." I also said, "You are not going to learn how to try cases by my standing up here, lecturing to you. You are going to do it. Our classes will be held in actual courtrooms. The gentlemen will wear a coat and tie; the ladies will be appropriately dressed. If you don't have a coat, buy one. You are going to graduate in a few months; you are going to apply for a job. You are going to need a coat and tie, so buy them now. In court, it is "Your Honor" or "Sir" or "Judge." Hereafter my name is Mr. Tam and your name is Miss Jones and your name is Mr. Smith.

I had fifteen students and I thought I would probably have about seven students the next week. Instead, I had twenty-one! I would give them a deposition and say, "The witness is going to come to court and he's going to lie. And not only is he going to lie, he's going to lie on page fifty-six." They are looking at page fifty-six. I said, "He says in the deposition, 'The traffic light was red.' He will come to court and testify that the traffic light was green. You will cross-examine."

The following week I came in and said, "I need five volunteers." Everybody raised his or her hand and I sent four of them outside. "Mr. Jones, you were a witness to an accident, and you saw the traffic light?" "Yes." "What was the color of the traffic light?" "It was green" (or whatever the reverse was). And I said, "Are you sure?" "Yes." "Your witness." You talk about panic. Sweat was coming out of them. I called on each of them and then we critiqued their arguments. At the end I demonstrated for them how I would do it.

JG *Did the students enjoy it?*

RT They gave me a plaque at the end of the semester inscribed, "The best law professor" or something like that.

The Search for the Pū Puhi
Who can resist the charm of a research nerd unearthing an invaluable connection to a unique historical event?

Chris Cramer Being a total history and research nerd, my world changed in 2017, the year the *Honolulu Advertiser* was digitized all the way back to the 1800s. In the wee hours one morning, a picture grabbed my attention. It showed a *pū* (conch shell) in the collection of a man named James Washington Lonoikauoaliʻi McGuire.

This pū was the very one blown 200 years ago when the *ʻAi kapu* was broken for the island of Oʻahu. [Queen Kaʻahumanu renounced the ʻAi kapu, which was the political system forbidding men and women to eat together and restricting foods women could eat.] Messengers blew this pū in each district, proclaiming, "The ʻAi kapu is broken!" The sound was said to be like the blast from a steamship.

Afterwards, the pū was hidden in a cave on Lānaʻi for sixty years. When its keeper grew old, he went to Honolulu and marched straight to ʻIolani Palace. There he entrusted this treasure of the kingdom to Mr. McGuire, the caretaker of the palace.

Mr. McGuire's estate went to probate in the 1940s. I thought it was probably scattered to the winds and we'd never see anything in his collection again. I Googled his name and learned that the McGuire collection was in the BYUH (Brigham Young University-Hawaiʻi) museum at Lāʻie. The minute they opened in the morning, I was on the phone asking if they had shells. The student who answered said, "Not really, but you can come and see what we have." I jumped in the car and drove across the island and went through their whole collection. I was looking for a very specific kind of shell, a giant triton. They unlocked the display of the only triton shell. When I turned it over, the animal was still inside; it was not the right one. Before leaving, I visited with the archivist. After scouring the files, he took out a list of everything in the collection. Only one *pū puhi* (blowing shell) was in the McGuire Collection.

Inside a vault with giant doors and rotating handles, we looked inside box by box. In the last box was a great big brain coral. Underneath it was the most amazing giant triton shell. My heart started pounding and the air in the vault grew thick. The *mana* (spiritual power) from this pū was incredible. The last time this was blown, Hawai'i changed forever. Being so close to it in this small vault was almost too much for me. No way was I was going to dare blow that pū!

Can!

Michael "Corky" Bryan and I spoke for almost two hours about ranching, cowboying, and his life experiences. I had turned off the recorder and was thanking him for his time when he said one more thing, a throwaway line, which struck me as deeply profound and has inspired me ever since. Corky is a 76-year-old cowboy who was raised on the 'Ewa Plantation on O'ahu. He has worked in the cattle industry in one capacity or another all his life. If you could hear the recording of his interview, you would hear pauses in his conversation as he becomes overwhelmed with emotion. And you would clearly hear my voice change to a huskier tone in reaction to the tears that come to my eyes as I listen to his story.

In every interview I look for the *moment, the one that most touches my heart. In this case it was when Corky told me he could sum up all his life efforts in one word.*

JG *One word?*

Michael "Corky" Bryan Yes.

JG *What word?*

MB Well, you know how in pidgin English we say, "Can!" or "No can!"? I have discovered that no matter what is asked, I *can*! I can learn it, I can do it, I can be taught, I can teach, I can be boss, I can be bossed."

Nothing I have accomplished could have been done without the people who have taught, corrected, supported, and mentored me from small-kid time. I stand on their shoulders!

Miraculously, no matter what has been asked, whether it be butchering cattle at age twelve, learning to surf as a child from my father on O'ahu's huge North Shore waves, riding a horse, figuring out how to function in a mainland college when pidgin English was my first language, managing a ranch, hiring people, firing people, retraining people from age-old traditions in ranching, converting huge tracts of cane land back to pasture land, adapting to new methods of herd management, interfacing with the high muckety-mucks at the fancy clubs on O'ahu, speaking before the Hawai'i State Legislature, testifying before the United States Congress, or just asking cattle to go where I want them to go—*can*!" (Tears of sentiment, celebration, and joy from both of us.) ✤

Epilogue

Here are answers to a few questions I've been asked about researching and writing Voices of Hawai'i.

It took a lot of energy to interview so many people and compile their stories into a book. Was it worth it?

JG Absolutely. *These have been the most fun three years of my life. I would do it all over again in a minute. I continually met interesting new people who told me fascinating stories. My knowledge of Hawai'i and Hawaiiana was greatly expanded, and the enthusiasm of each person I spoke to was infectious. We'd start an interview with a question about how his or her family got to Hawai'i. Each unique answer vividly explained the diversity that makes up Hawai'i today. I fell in love with each of my speakers and the characters in their families.*

What was your system for managing a project this vast?

JG *I broke the work into sections. One was taking the interviews. I lived in Hawai'i for a month at a time, four different times, and talked to one or more interview subjects per day. I loved this part, though it took a lot of energy to be "up" for every interview.*

Transcribing and editing the transcripts was another part of the project. Then I had to get the transcripts to the interviewee for approval. (I was not going to publish anything that my interviewee wasn't on board with.) Seventy-five transcripts going back and forth via email or USPS—can you imagine? And corrections to each; I could hardly think of anything else. I'm grateful that the participants thought enough of the project to be so wonderfully responsive and timely!

Epilogue

What was the hardest part of this project for you?

JG Not being able to publish every word each person said. The complete interviews capture remarkable intergenerational life journeys. But oral histories, even if they are edited for readability, require a dedicated reader. It seemed wiser to harvest sections of interviews into like-topic chapters. It was fun creating the chapters and figuring out what went into them!

What if there is interest from your audience to read these interviews in full?

JG That would delight me! Since I already have approval from my interviewees, I could amass them all in one place—more likely an online platform rather than a book. This collection of interviews may be of value to future researchers and historians. And many individuals might like to read the full stories of their friends or family members.

And you say you'd do it again? Does that mean we might look forward to *Voices of Hawai'i Volume II*?

JG I would love that. Think of how many stories are still out there to be told. And how many people for me yet to meet! I'm convinced that when people talk heart to heart there is a bond created and we become part of the same tribe. I want more of this in my life and more of this in the world.

INDEX

A

Abercrombie, Neil 114, 181
Adler, Peter 141
Aholo, Lydia 181
Aila, William 196-97
Aiona, James "Duke" 196
Akinaka, Asa 61
Alito, Samuel 165
Allen, Mililani 125
Ames, Kenneth 58
Anderson, Alex 147
Anderson, Frankie 146-48
Anderson, Marty 64
Anderson, Peggy 147
Anderson, Robert 147
Anthony, Garner 27, 70
Ariyoshi, George 59, 109
Awakuni, Catherine 115

B

Bartels, Jim 166, 180
Becker, Loftus 10
Beamer, Helen Desha 123
Beamer, Kapono 112
Beamer, Keola 112
Beamer, Winona 82
Benjamin, Chris 31-35
Bishop, Bernice Pauahi 80, 83
Bishop, Charles Reed 180
Black, Cobey 203
Blair, Marion 146-47
Blangiardi, Rick 210
Bloor, William 153
Bogart, Humphrey 107-08
Boone, Claire 147-48
Boone, Richard 147-48
Boren, Frank 188
Bouguereau, William-Adolphe 183
Bowers, Miki 126
Bowman, Kent 112
Bowman, Pierre 207
Bradbury, Bennett 184
Bradbury, Ray 184
Brand, Manu 127

Brandt, Gladys 82, 84
Breyer, Stephen 165
Brogan, Mary Lou 156
Brokaw, Tom 41-42
Bronster, Margery 156
Brown, Anuhea 111
Brown, Kīhei 111
Brown, Laurence 120
Bryan, Michael "Corky" 24-25, 94-96, 182, 219
Buck, Mike 196
Budge, Carter 115
Bumatai, Andy 112
Burns, John 59
Burrows, Chuck 212
Bush, Barbara 108
Bush, Laura 108

C

Cachola, Fred 82
Cameron, Colin 189, 205
Canlis, Peter 139
Carlson, Carl 23-24, 93-94, 182
Carter, A.W. 68
Case, James 6-7, 42, 78-79, 91, 135-36
Cayetano, Ben 143
Center, George "Dad" 147
Chagall, Marc 184
Champley, Michael 114-15
Chang, Anthony 191
Charlot, Jean 177
Ching, Clarence 62, 69-70
Ching, Gerry 61
Ching, Philip 61
Ching, Stuart 164
Choat, Tamara 91
Choy, Zita Cup 164-66
Clark, Henry 57, 61, 62
Clark, Kauila 95-96
Clark, Sefton "Bee" 57
Clarke, Lois Taylor 53, 203-04
Clinton, Hillary 108
Coble, Linda 71, 206-08

Coble, Robert 206
Coffman, Tom 48-49
Colburn, Lisa 142
Cole, John 115
Conrad, Connie 107
Cook, James 165
Cooke, Charles 11
Cooke, Mary Moragne 101, 168-70, 188
Cooke, Sam 216
Cooke, Samuel Alexander 11, 168-70, 174, 187, 188
Cooper, Nora 205
Cornuelle, Herb 83, 187
Cornuelle, Jean 83
Correa-Pei, Angela 194
Cosell, Howard 203
Costa, Tony 196
Cramer, Chris 193-97, 218-19

D

Daily, Fred 147
Damon, Frank 61
Damon, Sam 69-70
Darvill, Jack 82
Dashefsky, Howard 41
Davick, Bill 192
Davis, Alan 100
Daws, Gavan 213
DeLima, Frank 112
Detor, James 141
Dezzani, David 155-56
Dillingham, Bayard 115
Dillingham, Ben 152
Dillingham, B.F. 106-07, 116, 149
Dillingham, Harold 115
Dillingham, Louise 116
Dillingham, Lowell 59, 106, 149, 152
Dillingham, Margaret 115
Dillingham, Walter 106, 116, 151-52
Dods, Walter 58-59, 148-49
D'Olier, Jordan 161
D'Olier, Mitch 77-78, 148, 160-61

Index

Dominis, John 180
Dominis, Mary 180
Dowsett, Jamie 122
Dowsett, Queenie 122
Driver, James 152
Dudley, Carl 132
Duke, Doris 108

E

Eames, Charles 176
Eames, Ray 176
Edmunds, Sallie 192, 193
Ehrman, Peter 215-16
Ellis, George 173
Erdman, Summer 137
Evans, Dorothy 65

F

Fairbanks, David 112
Fairbanks, Douglas 108
Farden, Carl 109-10, 118, 122-23
Farden, Lucy 109-10, 122-24
Farrington, Elizabeth 203
Fields, Billy 168
Fields, Debbi 205
Fink, Alice 71
Fink, Arthur 41-42, 71-72, 208
Fink, John 41-42, 71-72, 208-210
Fithian, Peter 138
Fitzgerald, Dennis 40-41, 139-140
Flynn, David 148
Ford, Gerald 207
Frear, Mary Dillingham 116
Frear, Walter 116
Freeland, Betty Hay 183
Friedlander, Andy 153
Fukunaga, George 40, 57
Fukunaga, Mark 40, 57
Fukunaga, Peter 57

G

Gill, Gary 197, 198-200
Gill, Lorrin 198
Gill, Tom 198
Goldwater, Barry 206
Goodsill, Curt 14
Goodsill, John 12
Goodsill, Kay 14

Goodsill, Marshall 6-7, 9-17, 82-83, 104-07, 112-13, 170, 174, 216-17
Goodsill, Ruth 6-7, 71, 82, 106-07
Gorak, Thomas 115
Goulet, Robert 205
Grady, Ed 105
Graham, Don 152
Grant, Cary 205
Gray, Maris 204
Greenwell, Frank 92
Greenwell, James "Jimmy" 27, 68, 92-93
Greenwell, James "Kimo" 68
Griffin, James 114-15
Griggs, Mickey 11
Guild, Alice 107, 120-121, 148-50, 166-67, 180
Gutmanis, June 29-30

H

Haia, Moses 26-27, 75-77, 84-85
Haia, Moses Kalei, Jr. 76
Hall, Jack 59
Hannahs, Neil 79-82, 134-35, 197-98
Hannan, Peggy Dillingham 115-17
Hara, John 178
Hara, Tadayoshi 194-96
Haraguchi, Karol 141
Harrison, Guy 152
Hayward, Peter 183
Heen, Walter 84
Heiskell, Andrew 108
Hemmeter, Christopher 205
Henry, Chuck 207
Hibbard, Cooper 96
Hibbard, Henry 13
Hibbard, Jane Goodsill 13, 91
Hibbard, Whit 91
Hiona, Clara 124
Hiona, Tom 124
Hitchcock, D. Howard 183
Ho, Chinn 65, 151-54
Ho, Don 71, 132
Ho, Philip 153
Ho, Stuart 56, 61, 65-66, 151-54

Ho, Tim 138
Ho Tin Hee 132
Hollinger, Vicky 127-28
Holt, Alan 189
Hope, Bob 176
Hoperoft, Tom 63
Horner, Don 162
Horner, Lynne 205
Hussey, Kimo 127-28
Hustace, James 182-84
Hustace, Mollie 182

I

Ige, David 181
Inouye, Dan 109

J

Jenks, Livingston 64-65
Jichako, Jake 72
Johnson, Jeannine 194
Judd, Gerrit 66, 96

K

Kaʻahumanu, Queen 218
Kades, Charles 12
Kahanamoku, Duke 60, 147
Kaiser, Henry 147, 193
Kakesako, Tommy 71-72
Kalākaua, King David 67, 163-66
Kamehameha I 164
Kamehameha II 165
Kamehameha III 66, 96
Kanahele, George 98
Kanakanui, William 183
Kanakaʻole, Luka 29
Kane, Brooke 115
Kawakami, Richard 191
Kekumano, Charles 84
Kelley, Richard 98
Kelly, Marian 86
Kelsey, Thomas 28-29
Kennedy, Joe 195
Kennedy, John 204
Kenney, Ed 110
King, Anne 84
King, Samuel Pailthorpe 84
King, Samuel Wilder 27
Kiraly, Karsh 215

Kirk, Anne Marie 195
Kleissner, Charly 134
Kleissner, Lisa 134
Klimt, Gustav 184
Kobayashi, Bert 58-59
Koda, Harold 178
Korematsu, Fred 46
Kuriyama, Stan 31

L
Lai, Patrick 71
Lake, Maiki Aiu 125
Lam, Daniel 15
Larsen, David 145-46
Lautner, John 176, 177
Lawford, Peter 147
Lawrence, Carol 205
Leahey, Jim 209
Lee, David 170
Lennon, John 205
Liholiho, Alexander 66
Liliʻuokalani, Queen Lydia 30, 164, 180, 181
Liljestrand, Bob 25, 55-56, 175-78
Liljestrand, Howard 174
Liljestrand, Vicky 174
Lincoln, Bill 124
Little, Stephen 173-74
Lobenstein, Mae 127
Long, Betty 204
Loo, Paul 215
Loomis, Robin 44-45
Lorring, John 165
Luahine, ʻIolani 122
Luckman, Charles 154-56
Lum, Ronald 64-65, 216-17
Lum, Willie 151
Lyman, Richard "Papa" 82

M
MacNaughton, Boyd 44, 59, 100, 146
MacNaughton, Duncan 44, 100-01, 145, 148, 151
MacNaughton, Malcolm 44
Maertens, Fred 90

Majors, Lee 148
Makuakāne, Kenneth 21, 29, 55,
Manildi, Lynn 56
Mapplethorpe, Robert 108
Marumoto, Masaji 61
Mason, Carl 84
Mason, Jean 84
Mason, Jeanie 84
Mason, Lynnie 84-85
Mason, Michael 84
Matsuda, Fujio 37-40, 138
Matsunaga. Spark 109
McGuire, James 218
McIntosh, James 160
McKeague, Kimberley 180
McKenney, Luanna Farden 27-28, 109-12, 118
McKenney, Peter 109-11
McKinzie, Edith 29
McLachlin, Beth 209
McLachlin, Chris 209
Medeiros, Art 137
Meiji, Emperor 67
Merrill, Fred 65-66
Michaels, Al 207
Midkiff, Frank 58
Midkiff, Robert 79
Miller, Jessie 113
Miller, Susan 189
Mink, John 170
Mink, Patsy 179, 209
Mitchell, Don 86
Mokuahi, Steamboat 108
Moon, Ronald 16, 17, 54, 68-69, 119
Moore, Joe 208-09
Moore, Randy 136-37
Moore, Sally 62
Moore, Willson 62, 138-39, 154-56, 163-64
Moragne, Jean 101
Moragne, Katie 101
Moragne, Sally 101
Moragne, William 101
Morgan, John 66, 96-100
Morita, Hermina 22, 23, 114-15, 191

Mossman, Sterling 112
Moulton, Kimber 21

N
Nakama, Keo 51, 59-60
Nakamura, Alan 72
Nakamura, Kelli 50
Nakata, Bob 86
Nation, Allan 91
Neutra, Richard 176, 177
Newman, Audrey 187, 188-91, 192
Nishimoto, Brian 140
Nogelmeier, Marvin "Puakea" 29-30, 123-24, 127-28, 133-34, 159-60, 178-80, 182

O
Obama, Michelle 108
Ogawa, Dennis 56
O'Hair, Madalyn Murray 109
Okada, Masaye 46
Okada, Raymond 14-15, 46-48
Okada, Shigeo 46
Olson, Ed 199
O'Malley, Mike 15
Ono, Yoko 205
Ossipoff, Keira 199
Ossipoff, Valerie 193
Ossipoff, Vladimir 8, 173-78
Ossipoff, Xandra 199
Overton, John 128
Owada, Hisashi 165
Owen, John 181

P
Padgett, Frank 27, 37, 58, 70
Pahinui, Gabby 120-21
Palmer, Ed 153
Paton, Diane 43, 107-09, 131-32
Paty, William 97-98, 192
Pauling, Linus 174
Pence, Martin 68-69, 119
Perry, Michael 208
Peterson, Rudy 154
Pezzino, Lisa 195
Phelps, James Barton 9

Philpotts, Kaui 21, 54, 121-22, 204-05
Pietsch, Charlie 147
Pietsch, Diana 183
Pitluck, Wayne 128
Price, Larry 208
Price, Warren 155-56

Q

Quinn, William 60, 163

R

Rabbett, Martin 5
Ragan, Bill 62
Reagan, Nancy 108
Reagan, Ronald 108
Reber, David 113
Reiplinger, Rap 112
Reppun, John 86
Reynolds, Jimmy 148
Rice, Freddy 94
Rice, Oskie 94
Richards, Atherton 58
Richards, Monty 136
Richardson, Philip 176
Richardson, William 119
Rodiek, Anita 59
Rogers, Eddie 93
Rooke, Queen Emma 180
Roosevelt, Franklin 12
Roth, Randy 83
Roth, Susie 83
Ryan, Annie 123

S

Sakamoto, Dean 53-54, 173-78
Sakamoto, Soichi 49-51
Santos, Helena 191
Schindler, Rudolph 177
Scott, James 51
Sevey, Bob 206
Sexton, Lloyd 183
Seymour, Jane 148
Shah of Iran 100
Shearer, Hugh 112
Sheehan, Mike 142
Siegfried, Steve 120

Shingle, A.K. 119
Shingle, Seymour 11
Shingle, Witt 119-21
Silverman, Samuel 153
Smith, Bill 49-51, 59-60
Smith, John "Singin'" 215
Smith, Riley 50, 59-60
Smyser, Bud 83
Smyser, Dee 83
Snyder, Jocelyn 173
Snyder, Sid 173
Soon, Cheryl 141
Sotomayor, Sonia 165
Southworth, Sigrid 169-70, 210-13
Souza, Mihana 127
Spalding, Phil 187
Spielberg, Stephen 98
Sproat, David 127
Steadman, Alva 49
Steadman, Richard 49
Steele, Marti 83
Steele, Dwayne 83, 159-60, 179-80
Stender, Oswald 19, 83, 87
Stevens, Napua 152
Sugai, Masaru 94

T

Tagawa, Alice 40
Takabuki, Matsuo 154
Taketa, Kazuto 45-46
Taketa, Kelvin 45-46, 78, 101-02, 161-63, 187-88
Taylor, Stanley 204
Tam, Raymond 62-64, 69-70, 217-18
Tam, William 87-89, 137
Tavernier, Jules 183
Temple, Shirley 108
Tennent, Madge 182, 183
Theaker, Morley 149
Thompson, Donnis 209
Thompson, Laura 80, 193-94
Thompson, Myron "Pinky" 80, 82
Thropp, James 63
Tongg, Rudy 147

Twigg-Smith, Thurston 57-58
Tyler, Curtis 55
Tyler, Joseph 55
Tyler, Thelma 55

U

Upton, King 154

V

Veary, Nana 5
Volner, Rick 34

W

Watanabe, Jeff 25-26, 48-49, 54, 56, 60-61, 65
Watt, Kevin 96
Webster, Betty 124-25
Weiser, Conrad 113
Weyand, Fred 170
Whitaker, Hal 147
White, Mark 190
White, Mike 98
Wichman, Chipper 174
Wichman, Hauoli 174
Wilcox, Carol 126-29, 140-143, 190-93
Wilcox, Leslie 213
Wilder, Betty 147
Williams, Bud 91
Williams, Janice 212
Williams, Riànna 180-82
Williams, Tom 112-14
Willis, Holtum 152
Wimberly, George 147
Wishard, Harry 183
Woodside, Leinaʻala 127
Wrenn, Heaton 11, 64
Wright, E. Alvey 140
Wright, Frank Lloyd 177

Y

Yap, Mary 124
Yardley, Maili 131
Young, Alexander 147

Z

Zuckerberg, Mark 76

About the Author

Author and historian Jane Marshall Goodsill was born and happily raised on the Hawaiian island of Oʻahu. Over the course of a long career as a Licensed Professional Counselor, she listened to thousands of hours of personal stories and was fascinated by each one. After retirement she served for ten years on her county's historical commission, during which time she refined the art of taking oral histories.

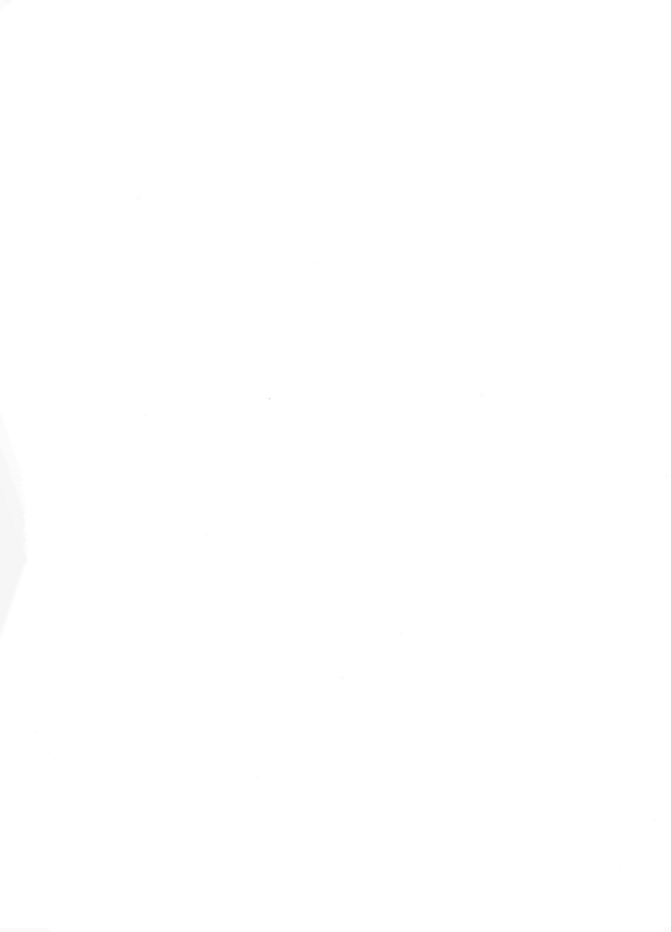